The Foundations of Dual Language Instruction

S0-BBB-105

FIFTH EDITION

The Foundations of Dual Language Instruction

Judith Lessow-Hurley

San José State University

PEARSON

Boston • New York • San Francisco
Mexico City • Montreal • Toronto • London • Madrid • Munich • Paris
Hong Kong • Singapore • Tokyo • Cape Town • Sydney

Executive Editor: Aurora Martínez Ramos
Series Editorial Assistant: Kara Kikel
Executive Marketing Manager: Krista Clark
Production Editor: Mary Beth Finch
Editorial Production Service: Omegatype Typography, Inc.
Composition Buyer: Linda Cox
Manufacturing Buyer: Linda Morris
Electronic Composition: Omegatype Typography, Inc.
Cover Administrator: Linda Knowles

For related titles and support materials, visit our online catalog at www.pearsonhighered.com.

Copyright © 2009, 2005, 2000 Pearson Education, Inc.

All rights reserved. No part of the material protected by this copyright notice may be reproduced or utilized in any form or by any means, electronic or mechanical, including photocopying, recording, or by any information storage and retrieval system, without written permission from the copyright owner.

To obtain permission(s) to use material from this work, please submit a written request to Allyn and Bacon, Permissions Department, 501 Boylston Street, Suite 900, Boston, MA 02116 or fax your request to 617-671-2290.

Between the time website information is gathered and then published, it is not unusual for some sites to have closed. Also, the transcription of URLs can result in typographical errors. The publisher would appreciate notification where these errors occur so that they may be corrected in subsequent editions.

Library of Congress Cataloging-in-Publication Data

Lessow-Hurley, Judith.
　　The foundations of dual language instruction / Judith Lessow-Hurley.—5th ed.
　　　p.　cm.
　　Includes bibliographical references and index.
　　ISBN 13:　978-0-205-59327-9 (pbk.)
　　ISBN 10:　0-205-59327-5 (pbk.)
　　1. Education, Bilingual.　2. Language and languages.　I. Title.

LC3715.L47　2009
370.117—dc22

2007052966

Printed in the United States of America

10　9　8　7　6　5　4　3　2　1　　12　11　10　09　08

Text Credit: p. 44, From *The New York Times*, August 5, 1986. © 1986 *The New York Times*. All rights reserved. Used by permission and protected by the Copyright Laws of the United States. The printing, copying, redistribution, or retransmission of the Material without express written permission is prohibited.

Allyn & Bacon
is an imprint of

www.pearsonhighered.com

ISBN 10:　0-205-59327-5
ISBN 13:　978-0-205-59327-9

To my father, who encouraged me to learn two languages

About the Author

 **Judith Lessow-Hurley** is a professor in the Elementary Education Department at San José State University. Her areas of expertise are bilingual and multicultural education. She works primarily with preservice teachers, most of whom teach significant numbers of second language learners from linguistically and culturally diverse backgrounds. She has worked with professional educators across the country and internationally. Along with her expertise in the education of English language learners, she has studied religious diversity in the context of First Amendment protections for religious freedom in a pluralist democracy. She is the author of "Meeting the Needs of Second Language Learners" (ASCD, 2002).

Contents

• C H A P T E R *3*

ASPECTS OF LANGUAGE   27

• CHAPTER 6

PRIMARY LANGUAGE INSTRUCTION FOR LIMITED ENGLISH PROFICIENT STUDENTS   77

• CHAPTER 7

SECOND LANGUAGE INSTRUCTION   89

• C H A P T E R *8*

*A*SPECTS OF CULTURE   109

• CHAPTER *11*

ℒ ANGUAGE POLICY AND PLANNING   151

• CHAPTER *12*

𝒩 ATIONAL UNITY AND DIVERSITY: THE UNITED STATES IN THE TWENTY-FIRST CENTURY   159

● A P P E N D I X

*O*NLINE RESOURCES   175

$\mathcal{E}$ducation in more than one language has many historical precedents and is necessary and common around the world today. Population changes in the United States are resulting in a virtual flood of public school children whose needs cannot be met without dual language instruction. In addition, our national economic welfare and political security require that we prepare all children with more than one language so they can cope with a shrinking world and an interdependent global economy. Therefore, dual language instruction should be a routine component of schooling for every child. This book is a basic text for teachers in training. It is *not* a book about methodology. The term *bilingual methods* is misleading and often gives rise to confusion and misconstruction. There are, after all, no "bilingual" tangrams, math blocks, or even books or activity sheets.

In the normal course of instructional events, all competent teachers can design objectives, organize materials, structure activities, and devise assessment strategies. Any good teacher doing those things can answer the questions: "What are you doing?" and "Why are you doing that?" A dual language classroom teacher performs the same tasks but must also include language as a variable in all aspects of planning.

What and *why* are basic questions for all teachers, but the dual language teacher must answer an additional and difficult question: "What language are you using to teach each particular child, at any given time, in any particular subject?" While this question is methodological in part, the answer results not only from the nature of the task at hand but also from an interplay of theoretical knowledge about language and culture, state and federal mandates, and administrative decisions about program design.

The foundations of dual language instruction comprise, therefore, a complex mosaic involving theory, research, and discourse from several different areas of scholarship and inquiry. To understand how language works in an educational setting, it must be objectified and identified as a tool to be manipulated for instructional purposes, much as we manipulate books, maps, and other instructional aids. To develop this awareness, we must turn to linguistics for information about the nature of language; to psycholinguistics for information about language and the mind; to sociolinguistics for information about how language works in society; and to psychology, sociology, and anthropology for insights into human interaction and culture.

The purposes of this book are twofold and may at first appear to be contradictory. First, dual language instruction must be removed from its controversial political environment. Misinformation about dual language instruction permeates the public mind and, all too often, the teaching profession itself.

Opposition to bilingual education is the result of several common misconceptions. The first misconception relates to time. Schooling in general, and language learning in particular, are slow processes. In the postmodern era, we have become preoccupied with speed and are often impatient with educational programs that do not yield overnight results. However, human development proceeds at its usual pace, regardless of changes in technology that result in speed and cost savings in other areas of endeavor. It takes time to develop proficiency in a language and particularly to reach a level of competence adequate to the demands of schooling. All too often, programs are judged on results obtained in two or three years—and it's not surprising that such programs fail to demonstrate dramatic success.

Second, many people regard language learning as a difficult and frustrating endeavor. This attitude is usually the result of having experienced traditional, grammar-based approaches to language teaching. It is common to hear people say, "I took three years of French (or Spanish, or German) in high school, and I can't speak a word." Most of the people say they would like to speak another language, but the main thing they learned from language class is that it's hard to do! It's not surprising that they are skeptical about the possibility that an educational program can produce bilingualism without pain.

Finally, and perhaps most dynamically, using languages other than English in public schools empowers minority communities and provides marginalized or excluded groups with a voice in schooling. Despite constant demands for reform in schooling, most of us resist change: alterations in the status quo—in schools and society—albeit for the better, are disquieting. Bilingual education has become a flash point in the current political climate, which targets minorities and attempts to blame them for a host of social and economic woes.

So the first item of business for this book is to take an unemotional look at dual language instruction and examine its component parts in a scholarly fashion. Having done that, however, we must next reinsert it into the social environment and develop an understanding of the politics of dual language instruction and the controversy it inspires.

Many people are surprised to learn that bilingual environments are common around the world and that learning in more than one language is the norm rather than the exception. Dual language instruction in the United States is not new. It enjoyed a significant period of popularity in the nineteenth century. Chapter 1 presents a historical and international overview of bilingualism and dual language education and sets the stage for later discussions of politics and policy. Chapter 2 explains the concept of a program model, details the different models prevalent in the United States today, and describes the competencies required of dual language educators. This chapter also clarifies the distinction between bilingual and multicultural education.

Language is as essential to us as the air we breathe and is equally invisible. On one hand, it is difficult to see; on the other, it is a source of powerful emotion. Because teachers need an objective understanding of language and of bilingualism, Chapters 3 and 4 are devoted to fundamental aspects of language. As a starting point in the process of creating a vision of language as an instructional tool, Chapter 3 offers a definition of language and description of its subsystems. Because discussion of language is so often obscured by attitudes, biases, and emotional attachments, Chapter 3 also analyzes and attempts to defuse people's common language biases. This chapter includes a brief discussion of bilingualism and looks at the debate about Ebonics, or African American Language, which has often been the subject of controversy.

Strategies for teaching languages must be based on what we know about how languages are learned. Chapter 4 reviews current theories of first language development and second language acquisition. Chapter 5 focuses on assessment and includes a discussion of language ability and language proficiency testing.

While no one seems to deny that knowing more than one language is beneficial for children whose first language is English, controversy surrounds the idea of providing first language instruction for limited English proficient children in the United States. Chapter 6 develops a five-point rationale for providing primary language instruction to limited English proficient children which emphasizes the work of Jim Cummins, whose analysis of school-related proficiency has laid much of the groundwork for current thinking in this area. In addition, Chapter 6 describes approaches for providing primary language support in the classroom, depending on program models.

Many program models include some type of direct second language instruction. Chapter 7 discusses the historical development of several approaches to second language instruction and recent innovations in the field. Also included are discussions of specially designed academic instruction in English, which simultaneously addresses content instruction, second language development, and the development of literacy and biliteracy.

Language is a natural focus for the study of dual language instruction, but language is inextricably tied to culture. The increasing heterogeneity of our school population demands increasing attention to cultural diversity. Many school administrators and classroom teachers make a sincere attempt to respond to ethnic diversity through holiday observances, inclusion of ethnic foods in school menus, and selection of materials that reflect different lifestyles. Although positive, these well-intentioned responses to diversity remain essentially superficial.

A culturally responsive classroom must reach beyond surface or artifact culture and attend to the basic differences in the way children from different backgrounds understand, communicate, and learn. Teachers must understand the nature of culture, its relationship to language, and the relationship of specific cultures to the culture of U.S. schools. Chapter 8 outlines a definition of culture, giving examples of its characteristics and manifestations. Chapter 9 describes four analyses of the relationships between culture and school achievement, with emphasis on the contextual interaction model and the work of John Ogbu and Carlos Cortés.

Dual language instruction requires educational planning that is not only based on theoretical considerations but that is also within the framework of federal and state law. The legal foundations for bilingual education are constantly changing. Most recently, California has outlawed the use of primary languages in public school classrooms, and the status of that initiative may impact the entire nation. Chapter 10 provides an updated review of the legislative and judicial foundations of dual language instruction, with special attention to the U.S. Supreme Court's 1974 decision in *Lau v. Nichols*, subsequent legislation and case law, and finally, the No Child Left Behind Act.

Finally, all schooling in the United States takes place in a political context. Dual language instruction manipulates language and culture for instructional purposes. The emotional relationships that people have to language and culture result in a particularly charged reaction to bilingual education. Chapter 11 addresses language policy and planning, offering teachers a perspective on the role of schools in maintaining or suppressing language. Chapter 12, the final chapter, analyzes the politics of bilingualism in the current political context and the relationship of language to the ideas and ideals of U.S. identity.

As a text for teachers in training, this book is intended to be simple; given the scope of the subject, it is necessarily superficial in many areas. With this in mind, annotated suggestions for further reading have been included at the end of each chapter, so that readers may pursue their particular interests in depth. Furthermore, each chapter is followed by questions for thought and suggested hands-on activities to provide students with firsthand insights into and experience in the concepts presented. In addition, while this is not intended as a methods text, suggestions are offered that tie theory to practice and guide teachers toward useful classroom applications of the ideas presented.

This is the fifth edition of this book. Much has changed since I wrote the first edition nearly twenty years ago. There has been a significant move away from publicly supported bilingual education programs in favor of programs that insist on teaching in English to the exclusion of any other languages for instruction or even instructional support. Political tensions about immigration are on the front pages of newspapers, and history is repeating itself as xenophobia is tied, in the public mind, to language restrictionism.

So the objectivity that I try to bring to this discussion of theory, research, and practice in dual language instruction is seriously compromised by my own simple biases. When I started teaching in a bilingual demonstration program in the late 1960s, our program provided Spanish instruction for monolingual English-speaking children of all backgrounds and Spanish maintenance with English as a second language for Hispanic children whose English was limited. Our program had a strong community base and moved effectively toward the goal of making all our children bilingual and biliterate in English and Spanish.

It is ironic that the growing legislative support we hoped for was the undoing of programs such as ours. Faced with mandates for services for large numbers of limited English proficient children, school districts decided that *two-way programs* (as they are now called) were a dispensable luxury. There can be no doubt that the needs of limited English proficient children are an immediate first-order priority. But until we inculcate an understanding of the value of bilingualism in the general population, all programs will always be vulnerable and insecure. As a bilingual person and a bilingual teacher, it is my unshakable conviction that dual language instruction benefits all children.

——Acknowledgments

I would like to extend my gratitude to the following individuals who served as reviewers for the fifth edition of this text:

Donald Hones, *University of Wisconsin, Oshkosh*

Evangelina Jones, *San Diego State University*

Solange Lopes-Murphy, *James Madison University*

Juan Neochea, *California State University, San Marcos*

Luz Mary Rincon, *Texas A&M University*

Basilio Serrano, *SUNY College at Old Westbury*

In addition, I would like to thank my colleagues in the bilingual education community for their support and encouragement, and my husband—for everything.

Historical and International Perspectives

People from the United States are sometimes surprised to find that tourists or immigrants often speak, read, and write several languages. Around the world, bilingualism is more the norm than the exception. This is true now and was also true historically. This chapter will review the history of bilingualism and dual language education around the world and consider examples of the use of two languages at the present time in society and in education.

Societal Bilingualism

THE ANCIENT WORLD

Bilingualism was common in antiquity. Political and territorial consolidation and domination of one or more groups of people by others generally created situations in which conquered groups added the dominant language to their repertoire. Linguistic tolerance on the part of ancient conquerors favored linguistic diversity. Starting in the sixth century B.C.E., ancient Greeks, for example, penetrated and dominated large areas of the Mediterranean. While they preserved and promulgated Greek language and culture through schooling, they had no interest in replacing local languages with their own. With language shifts slow in the making, many individuals maintained the ability to function in more than one language (Lewis, 1976).

To the extent that formal schooling was available, education in more than one language seems to have been the norm in the ancient world. The need for dual language education may have been tied to literacy. The scarcity of written materials meant that a person who wanted to read widely had to read in more than one language (Mackey, 1978).

Education in Europe has always placed value on bilingualism and biliteracy, dating back to the fact that formal schooling was implemented on a large scale by the Romans throughout their empire and that all students were

𝔅ilingualism among Jews

Jewish bilingualism from ancient times to the present has received the special attention of scholars (Lewis, 1976). Hebrew was used for worship by Jews long after it ceased to be a mainstream Jewish language. Dispersed around the world, Jews have learned many languages, while simultaneously maintaining a home or community language. Although no longer widely spoken, Yiddish is perhaps the most familiar Jewish language to English speakers, because it is related to German. As you can see in the following list, many Yiddish words and constructions have entered English.

Bagel: A bread, shaped like a donut, that is boiled and then baked.

Chutzpah: Nerve or audacity.

Glitch: An unexplained malfunction; usually refers to computer programs.

Klutz: A clumsy person (adjective: klutzy).

Maven: An expert; sometimes slightly pejorative—a know-it-all.

Schlock: Cheap or badly made merchandise (adjective: schlocky).

Schmaltz: Over-flowery sentiment (adjective: schmaltzy).

It is interesting to note that there is still a significant population of Sephardic Jews who speak Ladino, a form of Spanish spoken by Jews of Greek, Turkish, and Syrian ancestry and written with the Hebrew alphabet. Spanish was carried to the Middle East by Spanish and Portuguese Jews exiled from Spain in the late fifteenth century.

schooled in Latin regardless of their first language. Latin as the language of schooling has persisted until relatively recently, until the rise of nationalism and the concurrent Protestant Reformation motivated the use of vernaculars for scholarship and education.

THE MODERN WORLD

Bilingualism is common in modern times in almost every corner of the world. In 1982, Grosjean suggested that only Japan and what was then West Germany could be classified as monolingual countries, and even at that time they had significant populations whose first language was not the language of the majority. In general, we live in a multilingual world.

There are many officially monolingual nations that house large linguistic minorities. This is especially characteristic of newly independent developing nations whose political boundaries do not coincide with linguistic boundaries and who have chosen a national language for unification purposes.

A number of countries are officially bilingual or multilingual, including Canada, Belgium, Finland, Cyprus, Israel, and Ireland. Note that official bilingualism does not imply that all inhabitants of a country are bilingual. Often only a small percentage of the population of an officially bilingual country uses both languages regularly. Official bilingualism means that more than one language may be used in transactions with the government or in the schools. Different countries develop different policies with respect to the languages they endorse.

Some countries may have many more languages than their governmental policies recognize. Hindi is the official language of India. It is the most widely used, spoken by nearly half the population (Kinzer, 1998). Yet, in addition to Hindi, 14 languages plus English are officially recognized in the constitution, only a fraction of the 200 different languages spoken on the subcontinent (Khubchandani, 1978). People in India generally speak more than one language, and may well have oral proficiency in five or six. As one author comments, "in spite of mass illiteracy, a societal type of bilingualism/ multilingualism . . . has become the life and blood of India's verbal repertoire" (Sridhar, 1993).

It should be noted that the political dimension of language operates everywhere, and India is no exception. English speakers, generally members of the educated elite, number only about 5 percent of the population, and members of regional parties, in a challenge to the ruling party, have decried English as a colonial language and one which should not be used for public, official purposes (Kinzer, 1998).

China is a nation with enormous territory and diverse cultural groups that has many languages represented within its boundaries. In general, government support for Mandarin Chinese as a unifying national language, combined with tolerance for diversity, has favored bilingualism in mainland China. Following the return of Hong Kong to Chinese rule in 1997, however, the government decided to replace the use of English as the language of instruction in high schools on that island, mandating the use of Cantonese instead. This has caused considerable consternation in Hong Kong, where English is considered an absolute necessity for business success (Gargan, 1997).

In South Africa, dramatic changes in government have led to the recognition of nine African languages as official in addition to English and Afrikaans (National Public Radio, 1995). This is yet another example of the dynamic interaction of politics and language.

A discussion of bilingualism in the world would be incomplete without mention of Paraguay, which is unique. Guarani, the indigenous Indian language of Paraguay, is its national language, and it is also the first language of 90 percent of Paraguay's population. Spanish is Paraguay's official language, used in schools and for other government activities. Over half the population is bilingual, but Guarani, a cherished national treasure, is the language of choice for personal intimacy and poetry (Rubin, 1972).

MULTILINGUALISM IN THE UNITED STATES

When the U.S. Constitution was written, its authors made an affirmative decision not to establish an official national language. Recently, local initiatives have resulted in policies proclaiming the official standing of English. Nevertheless, the United States is a multilingual nation, with many indigenous Native American languages, indigenous Spanish, and the diverse languages of its many immigrant groups, which contribute to the nation's linguistic wealth. (Language policy in the United States is more fully discussed in Chapter 11.)

Education in More Than One Language: An International Perspective

Societal bilingualism is common, and dual language instruction is practiced worldwide. Formats for providing education in two languages are as varied as the world's governments and their constituencies. The following are three cases where governments support more than one language through education.

CHINA

According to Jernudd (1999), China has 56 nationalities, and all but two of those have their own languages. Constitutional policy requires that China take steps to preserve its minority languages. Writing systems have been developed for many indigenous languages that previously did not have them. Media broadcasts are often aired bilingually, and political information is disseminated in a variety of languages (Fincher, 1978). China presently offers home language instruction to many of its ethnic minorities, with gradual introduction to Chinese in the second year of schooling. As you might expect, China's vast size, its uneven levels of development, and the number of ethnicities and languages within its borders hamper full implementation of its language and educational policies (Spolsky, 2004). Where implementation has been successful, however, Chinese authorities have reported an increase in achievement as well as improved attendance on the part of ethnic minority children enrolled in dual language programs (Jernudd, 1999; Wang, 1986).

CANADA

Since the passage of the Official Languages Act in 1967, Canada has been officially bilingual (English and French). The history of bilingual education in Canada is primarily the history of the struggle for equal status for French, which is the minority language. Canada has had notable success with its French–English immersion programs for anglophones (English speakers), which have provided a model for dual language instruction worldwide. (Immersion programs are discussed in detail in Chapter 2.)

Canada continues to struggle with the needs of speakers of so-called heritage languages, languages other than French and English used by indigenous or immigrant minorities. Dual language instructional programs have been established, some with the goal of transitioning children from their primary languages to English, and others with the intention of preserving or restoring proficiency in a heritage language. (For a detailed review of dual language programs for heritage languages in Canada see Cummins, 1984.)

Attempts are being made to preserve the few remaining indigenous languages, deeply endangered by federal policies that Pringle describes as "assimilationist and often brutal, with school-age children removed from their home communities to residential schools in which they were forbidden to speak their mother tongue (even when, on arrival, it was their only language) and were punished and humiliated for doing so" (1999, p. 82).

SWEDEN

Providing dual language instruction in an increasingly diverse world is not without its challenges. Sweden is an example of a country that has attempted to maintain a pluralist position in educating language minority students. In the second half of the twentieth century, Sweden, which had been fairly homogenous, experienced a large influx of immigrants, who currently constitute approximately 12 percent of the population (Boyd, 1999). Bilingual education is provided for immigrant children with the goal of enabling them to function fully in both Swedish and their home languages. Children receive all instruction in the home language, but its use is decreased until, by the fifth or sixth grade, instruction in all subject areas is bilingual ("Bilingual programs in Sweden," 1985). Boyd (1999) points out that as linguistic diversity in Sweden increases, it has become difficult to provide bilingual education for all language groups. Also, there is an increased need for well-trained teachers who have the skills to promote multicultural understanding and positive cross-cultural relations among their students.

The History of Dual Language Instruction in the United States

People are often surprised to discover that dual language instruction has been widely available in the United States since the beginning of its history as a nation. Immigration has been a constant in U.S. history, and languages other than English have been tolerated and even officially recognized from the outset. The Continental Congress, for example, published a number of documents in German to assure accessibility for the large German-speaking minority (Keller & Van Hooft, 1982).

THE NINETEENTH CENTURY

In the nineteenth century, non-English or dual language instruction was offered in more than a dozen states in a variety of languages including German,

Swedish, Norwegian, Danish, Dutch, Polish, Italian, Czech, French, and Spanish (Ovando & Collier, 1985; Tyack, 1974). Both immigrants and Native Americans made instruction in two languages available for their children.

Dual Language Instruction for Native Americans. Formal schooling was locally administered by Native Americans only insofar as the U.S. government allowed. Where locally controlled education was permitted, Native American communities often provided dual language instruction.

The Cherokees established and operated an educational system of 21 schools and 2 academies, which enrolled 1,100 pupils, and produced a population 90 percent literate in its native language. The Cherokee language had a writing system, created by Sequoyah in the early part of the eighteenth century (Foreman, 1938; Kilpatrick, 1965). As a result, bilingual materials were widely available, and by 1852 Oklahoma Cherokees had a higher English literacy level than the white populations of either Texas or Arkansas (Castellanos, 1983, p. 17).

The tribes of the Southeast were particularly successful in dealing with culture contact with Europeans, who called them the "civilized tribes" as a result. The European perception that the southeastern tribes were capable of self-government resulted in some measure of tribal autonomy in education. In addition, several of the southeastern tribes' languages had or developed writing systems, softening the dominance of English and facilitating the availability of dual language education. In general, however, U.S. government tolerance for Native American self-determination, education, and language was tied to political expediency, and those Native American school systems that were permitted to exist and survived the Civil War were eradicated in the latter part of the nineteenth century (Weinberg, 1977).

Dual Language Instruction for Immigrants. Immigrant Germans fared well in maintaining their language through dual language instruction during the nineteenth century. German patriotism in the Revolutionary War was highly regarded, and, therefore, German language and culture were accepted with tolerance. Also, despite the fact that Germans were a minority, they were heavily concentrated in the remote farming areas of the Midwest. As a result of their geographic isolation, they were not viewed as a threat by the rest of the population. Given that education was locally controlled and financed, their concentration enabled them to exert the political strength of their numbers on the schools (Liebowitz, 1978).

In response to political pressure from the German community, German–English dual language programs were instituted in Ohio in 1840, and by the turn of the century 17,584 students were studying German in dual language programs, the great majority of them in the primary grades. Dual language programs were also widespread in Missouri (Tyack, 1974). In 1880 German was taught in 52 of the 57 public schools in Saint Louis, and German–English programs attracted not only German children, but also Anglo-American children who learned German as a second language (Escamilla, 1980).

The Cherokee Writing System

"Sequoyah hit upon the great truth, and what to him was an original discovery, that enlightenment and civilization of a people would progress and develop in proportion as they were able to express themselves and preserve their ideas upon the written and printed page, and exchange these ideas, one with another, by this medium" (Foreman, 1938, p. 74).

Revered and honored by the Cherokee Nation, Sequoyah is known for the creation of the Cherokee alphabet. Its 85 characters, pictured here, represent all the sounds in the Cherokee language. In 1827, the Cherokee Nation published the first edition of the *Cherokee Phoenix,* a bilingual newspaper.

• The Cherokee Alphabet

D *a*	R *e*	T *i*	δ *o*	Oᵘ *u*	i *v*
ſ *ga* Ⓞ *ka*	Ⱶ *ge*	ʎ *gi*	A *go*	J *gu*	E *gv*
ℴʋ *ha*	P *he*	A *hi*	H *ho*	Γ *hu*	ℓ *hv*
W *la*	δ *le*	P *li*	G *lo*	M *lu*	ℐ *lv*
ℴ *ma*	OI *me*	H *mi*	ℐ *mo*	y *mu*	
θ *na*	Λ *ne*	h *ni*	Z *no*	ℐ *nu*	Oʳ *nv*
ʦ *hna*	G *nah*				
I *qwa*	ω *qwe*	P *qwi*	V *qwo*	℘ *qwu*	Ɛ *qwv*
℧ *sa* Ⓞ *s*	4 *se*	℔ *si*	ℐ *so*	℔ *su*	R *sv*
℔ *da*	℥ *de*	ℐ *di*	V *do*	δ *du*	℘ *dv*
W *ta*	℔ *te*	*ti*			
ℴℴ *dla* ℒ *tla*	L *tle*	C *tli*	ℐ *tlo*	℔ *tlu*	P *tlv*
G *tsa*	V *tse*	℔ *tsi*	K *tso*	ℐ *tsu*	Cᵚ *tsv*
ℐ *wa*	℘ *we*	℗ *wi*	℮ *wo*	ℐ *wu*	6 *wv*
℘ *ya*	B *ye*	℔ *yi*	ℏ *yo*	Gᵁ *yu*	B *yv*

Toward the end of the nineteenth century, anti-Catholic bias provoked by an influx of Irish immigrants spilled over onto previously tolerated Germans, many of whom were Catholic. Increasing immigration resulted in a wave of xenophobia that often targeted foreign languages. The large instructional programs in German gave the language a high profile, and the German language became a focus for the antiforeign feelings that flourished in the second half of the eighteenth century.

The onset of World War I brought anti-German feeling to a head, and a rash of legislation aimed at eliminating German language instruction caused the collapse of dual language programs around the country. At the turn of the century, only 14 of the 45 states mandated English as the sole language of instruction in the schools. By 1923, a total of 34 of the 48 states had English-only instructional policies (Castellanos, 1983).

THE TWENTIETH CENTURY

Two by-products of World War I, isolationism and nationalism, took their toll on dual language as well as foreign language instruction. Instruction in foreign languages was virtually eliminated in the period between the first and second world wars. Events in the 1950s, however, revitalized interest in these fields. The successful launching of Sputnik by the Soviet Union caused a reevaluation of education in general and inspired the National Defense Education Act (1958). Knowledge of foreign languages was perceived as essential to our national defense, so the act provided funding for foreign language study.

During the same period, the Cuban revolution (1959) brought a flood of educated Cuban refugees to Florida. In 1963, in response to the needs of the Cuban community, the Coral Way Elementary School in Dade County, Florida, was established. Coral Way offered dual language instruction for both Cuban and non-Hispanic children. The program served a middle-class population, was well funded from both public and private sources, and, unlike many subsequent programs, was neither compensatory nor remedial.

The nation was in the midst of an energetic movement favoring the expansion of civil rights, accompanied by a powerful affirmation of ethnic identity for minority groups. In that political climate, and with the success of Coral Way in the public eye, bilingual programs were quickly established in a number of states, including Texas, California, New Mexico, New Jersey, and Arizona (Ambert & Melendez, 1985).

In 1965 the Elementary and Secondary Education Act (ESEA) was approved and funded by Congress. The act was part of President Lyndon B. Johnson's War on Poverty, and its broad purpose was to equalize educational opportunities. The Bilingual Education Act, or Title VII of the ESEA, was signed into law in 1968. Title VII did not mandate bilingual education, but provided funds for districts to establish programs that used primary language instruction to assist limited English proficient children. In subsequent amendments to the act, funds were allocated for teacher training, research, information dissemination, and program support. (Title VII and other pertinent legislation are discussed in detail in Chapter 10.)

In addition, judicial action provided strong support for services for limited English proficient children. In 1974, the U.S. Supreme Court decision in

Lau v. Nichols held, on the basis of Title VI of the Civil Rights Act (1964), that children must receive equal access to education regardless of their inability to speak English. (*Lau* and other pertinent decisions are discussed in detail in Chapter 10.)

In 1971, Massachusetts was the first state to mandate bilingual education. By 1983, bilingual education was permitted in all 50 states, and 9 states had laws requiring some form of dual language instruction for students with limited English proficiency (Ovando & Collier, 1985).

In the three decades following *Lau*, lack of government support for primary language instruction, combined with strong reactions to the influx of immigrants, has weakened support for dual language instruction. California, for example, with a population of over 1,550,000 limited English proficient children at the present time, eliminated its mandate for bilingual education in 1987, and recently passed a proposition eliminating bilingual education entirely. Arizona and Massachusetts have followed suit.

THE TWENTY-FIRST CENTURY

The number and diversity of immigrants to the United States is on the increase and, amid ongoing and predictable controversies about language policy and immigration reform (see Chapter 11), informed and highly skilled responses are required daily from educators in every area and at every level. Dual language instruction models that emphasize bilingualism as enrichment for all students may broaden the public's understanding of education in more than one language. As we will see in the chapters to follow, that kind of approach is beneficial to individual students and to the nation as a whole.

Summary

Dual language instruction in one form or another has been available all over the world since ancient times. Countries in the world today may espouse one of many potential language policies, but in any case there are bilingual individuals in virtually every nation in the world. Dual language instruction is available in many countries in a variety of formats, depending on the population and the purpose.

Dual language instruction has been available in the United States since before colonial times. Nationalistic feelings that accompanied World War I limited the use of languages other than English in schools, but interest in foreign language instruction was revived after World War II. The success of bilingual programs established in Florida shortly after the Cuban revolution, combined with a political climate that favored ethnic identity and civil rights, inspired the implementation of dual language programs nationwide.

Questions to Think About and Discuss

1. Should the United States have an official language policy? If so, what languages should be recognized as official? What areas of public life should be governed (schools, courts, health care, etc.)?

Activities

1. Interview classmates or acquaintances born or educated outside the United States. Find out how many languages they know and how they learned them. If they attended school outside the United States, find out the following:
   - Was the language of schooling the same as the home language?
   - Were they required to learn more than one language at school?
   - Which languages were used for content instruction?
   - In their view, how common is bilingualism in the country they came from or studied in?

   Compare their language experiences to your own.
2. Dual language instruction was widespread in the nineteenth century. Look into the history of your area and find out if there were educational programs in more than one language prior to 1963.
3. Many languages are spoken in the United States. Make a language map of your area. Depending on where you live, you may want to map your city, town, or county. A rigorous demographic study may be impractical, but school district figures may be a good starting point. Churches that announce services in various languages may help you. Concentration of ethnic businesses is another clue.
4. Inventory the non-English media in your area. Include radio, television, movies, and newspapers. Check the local public library to find out the number and circulation of non-English materials.

Suggestions for Further Reading

Baetens, B. H. (1993). *European models of bilingual education.* Clevedon, UK: Multilingual Matters.

As the introduction to this book points out, there are useful lessons to be learned from European bilingual models. The articles included in this book describe a variety of language circumstances. The interplay of language, culture, politics, and education is more often than not ignored in American conversations about bilingual education. This book calls our attention to subtleties with which we might usefully inform our debate.

Crawford, J. (1989). *Bilingual education: History, politics, theory, and practice.* Trenton, NJ: Crane.

One of the more comprehensive overviews of issues related to bilingual education in the United States, this well-written book provides a detailed analysis of the history and politics of dual language instruction.

Edwards, J. (1998). *Language in Canada.* Cambridge, UK: Cambridge University Press.

Language has been a point of tension in Canadian history. Given the current political climate in the United States, this detailed account of language history and planning in Canada provides useful insights into the complexities of language planning in a multilingual society.

Kaufman, D. (2003, April). Letters for the people. *Language Magazine, 7,* 24–26.

A brief but informative article about Sequoyah, who developed the writing system for Tsalagi, the language of the Cherokees. Tsalagi was the first Native American language known to have a writing system, and this article is worth the attention of anyone interested in language. As an added benefit, the article would be worthwhile reading for middle and high school students as well.

Keller, G. D., & Van Hooft, K. S. (1982). A chronology of bilingualism and bilingual education in the United States. In J. A. Fishman & G. D. Keller (Eds.) (1982), *Bilingual education for Hispanic students in the United States.* New York: Teachers College Press.

A chronology of bilingual education in the United States beginning with the colonial period and ending in 1980 with the creation of the Department of Education Office of Bilingual Languages and Minority Language Affairs. There have been many political changes since this book was published that have had a dynamic effect on bilingual education. Nevertheless, it is an excellent historical record, and reminds us that bilingual education is not a new idea in the United States.

Kloss, H. (1977). *The American bilingual tradition.* Rowley, MA: Newbury House.

An analysis of language policy in the United States and its possessions and protectorates, this book is a classic history of bilingualism and bilingual education and is generally considered a basic source of information in this relatively unexplored area.

chapter 2

Dual Language Program Models

$\mathcal{S}$imply stated, *dual language instruction* is an educational program offered in two languages. This definition is straightforward but lacks specificity. Dual language instruction can be offered in a variety of formats or models, depending on the goals of a program and the population it serves.

Some programs, for example, are designed to promote bilingualism and biliteracy for students. Others use a primary or home language as a bridge to assist students while they learn the dominant mainstream language.

This chapter will explain the concept of a program model and describe various types of programs currently in use in the United States. It will also present an overview of the competencies that teachers must have to provide instruction in dual language classrooms.

What Is a Program Model?

If you were to visit a dual language classroom you might note several features, including the functional use of each language and the methodology for distributing the languages in the curriculum. You would also notice the amount of time each language is used. In a particular classroom, you might observe that Spanish is used for instruction 50 percent of the day. Such an observation, however, takes on meaning only in the context of a program model. A *program model* refers to the span of language use and distribution toward a goal for a specific population, across the grades.

If, for example, the classroom you have visited is a Spanish–English bilingual kindergarten, it would be important to know whether the 50-50 time distribution of languages continues in first grade, or whether the use of Spanish diminishes as children progress, to 40 percent in the first grade and 30 percent in the second, so that children move toward a situation where no Spanish is used at all. Such a program model differs significantly from one where the 50-50 ratio is maintained throughout all grades and both languages are maintained and developed.

Dual language instructional models have been described in a number of ways, some far more complex than others. One theorist cross-referenced the learner, the languages, the community, and the curriculum to arrive at 90 different possible kinds of programs (Mackey, 1972). A simpler typology, based on philosophical rather than linguistic factors, distinguishes between assimilationist and pluralistic program models. Assimilationist programs aim at moving ethnic minority children into the mainstream (dominant) culture. In contrast, pluralistic program models are those that support minority languages and cultures (Kjolseth, 1976).

Transitional Bilingual Programs

WHICH STUDENTS DO TRANSITIONAL PROGRAMS SERVE?

Transitional programs serve students who are limited English proficient (LEP). For general purposes, we can define LEP students as those who have been determined to have insufficient English to function academically in an English language classroom where instruction is designed for native English speakers. Which students are actually designated as LEP may vary from state to state or even from district to district within a state, because tests and testing procedures are not uniform.

It should be noted that the labels we use are significant and shape and reflect how we respond to the world around us. *Limited English proficient* is a deficit-based term—it identifies students by what they can't do, and sets us up to consider serving them in a remedial or compensatory mode. Today, educators generally refer to English language learners, a serviceable and fairly neutral term.

WHAT IS THE GOAL OF A TRANSITIONAL PROGRAM?

The goal of transitional programs is to develop a student's proficiency in English. In a transitional program, the primary language is used for instructional support until students have reached satisfactory levels of English proficiency, usually as defined by a process involving test scores and teacher observations. Students are expected to move out of a transitional program when they are capable of functioning in an English-only classroom. In many programs, the expectation is that children will be ready to make the change after a period of approximately three years.

U.S. government policy tends to favor transitional programs—by far the most common models in use today. There are a number of problems inherent in transitional bilingual programs:

- They foster subtractive, rather than additive, bilingualism. (See Chapter 3 for a discussion of these concepts.)
- They are compensatory and do not involve the monolingual English-speaking community.
- Exit assessments may measure students' face-to-face language skills and fail to consider the specialized language skills needed for academic success. Placement in English-only classrooms on the basis of such programs can lead to academic failure. (See Chapter 6.)
- It is unrealistic to expect all children to master a second language in a three-year period.

TRANSITIONAL PROGRAMS: A LOT BETTER THAN NOTHING

In 1988, the California Association for Bilingual Education published *On Course: Bilingual Education's Success in California* (Krashen & Biber, 1988), a summary and analysis of data from eight programs across the state, including transitional programs. The Eastman Avenue School in Los Angeles reported an increase in the California Assessment Program (CAP) scores for students who participated in a carefully structured transitional program. More recently, a study that looked at the achievement of English learners over eight years and across content areas (CREDE, 2003) concludes that English language learners who attended mainstream programs with no primary language support "showed large decreases in reading and math achievement by Grade 5 when compared to students who participated in language support programs" (p. 3).

Ultimately, we have to think back to the concept of "program." Villarreal points out that effective programs must have enthusiastic leaders who are committed to supporting dedicated, qualified teachers. Effective programs, transitional or otherwise, provide a supportive climate and an instructional program that is both accessible and challenging, built on the linguistic and cultural resources of students, their families, and their communities (Villarreal, 1999). A carefully modeled transitional program that meets those criteria, while not the best of all worlds, offers meaningful support for English language learners and is undoubtedly better than submersion.

Language Maintenance Programs

Language maintenance programs are pluralistic and promote bilingualism and biliteracy for language minority students. Maintenance programs may be the most effective means of promoting English proficiency for limited English proficient students because:

- Concepts and skills learned in a student's first language transfer to the second language.

- A strong base in a first language facilitates second language acquisition.
- Support for home language and culture builds self-esteem and enhances achievement (Hakuta & Gould, 1987).

In other words, maintenance bilingual education, which is additive rather than subtractive, leads to academic success and also facilitates the acquisition of English skills for the language minority student. (For further discussion, see Chapter 6.)

Enrichment Programs

Efforts were made in the late 1960s and early 1970s to provide dual language instructional programs for both language minority children and monolingual English children. The need, however, for language support for limited English proficient children has been overwhelming. In the face of limited resources and staffing, the response has been largely compensatory in nature. The tendency to view dual language instruction as compensatory education has eroded the political base necessary to assure services for language minority students and has denied access to bilingual education for monolingual English-speaking children as well.

Educators have begun to reconsider enrichment or two-way bilingual instruction, which provides dual language instruction for all students. Two-way programs are becoming increasingly popular in areas where magnet schools have been established to facilitate desegregation. Problems in implementing enrichment programs arise from a lack of qualified staff, constant pressure to meet the needs of increasing numbers of non-English speakers, and lack of community understanding and support for dual language instruction.

Immersion Programs

Beginning in 1965 with the now famous Saint-Lambert experiment, success in Canada has inspired a strong interest in immersion programs. In an immersion program all the usual curricular areas are taught in a second language—this language being the medium, rather than the object, of instruction. Immersion instruction should not be confused with submersion or "sink-or-swim" instruction, where non-English-speaking children are mainstreamed in English-only classrooms without assistance and expected to keep the pace. In an immersion classroom:

- Grouping is homogeneous, and second language learners are not competing with native speakers.
- The teacher speaks the child's first language and can respond to student needs.

- Children are not expected to function immediately in their second language and can express themselves in their first.
- First language support is offered in the form of language arts instruction.
- Instruction is delivered in the second language, but is carefully structured so as to maximize comprehension for students.

THE RESULTS OF IMMERSION: THE CANADIAN EXPERIENCE

The implementation of carefully structured additive immersion programs may provide useful educational services to both limited English proficient and monolingual English students in the United States. Results of research and evaluation studies of French early immersion programs in Canada indicate that students:

- Achieve at levels comparable to those of comparison groups who received all instruction in English.
- Fall behind comparison groups initially in English literacy skills, but catch up to and even surpass those groups once English instruction begins.
- Achieve higher levels of proficiency in the second language than students who study it as an isolated subject.
- Attain native-like receptive skills in their second language and, while their productive skills fall short of native proficiency, are quite capable of expressing themselves in the second language.
- Have heightened sensitivity to social and cultural aspects of their second culture (Cummins & Swain, 1986).

The Canadian experience with immersion instruction suggests that the model works best with children from a dominant language group who are not at risk of losing their first language since it is readily available in the environment beyond the school. In other words, immersion programs are most effective when they are linguistically and culturally additive.

IMMERSION PROGRAMS IN THE UNITED STATES

There are several immersion program models currently operating in the United States. Enrichment, two-way, and English immersion programs will be described in the following pages.

Enrichment Immersion Programs. These programs, like the Canadian programs that inspired them, immerse monolingual English speakers in a second language. The Culver City Spanish Immersion Program in California, started in 1971, is the oldest example of a replication of the Canadian model in the United States. Enrichment immersion programs have been used as "magnets" in voluntary desegregation efforts. Such efforts expand participation in enrichment immersion programs beyond middle-class white students to working-class and black students and provide opportunities for research on the effects of immersion on speakers of nonstandard varieties of English (Genesee, 1987).

Two-Way Immersion Programs. In these innovative programs, sometimes called *developmental* or *bilingual immersion programs,* monolingual English-speaking children are immersed in a second language alongside limited English proficient children who are native speakers of the second language. English is introduced gradually until it comprises about 50 percent of the curriculum. The model is actually a combination of maintenance bilingual instruction for LEP students and immersion instruction for monolingual English speakers. The strength of this approach is that it aims at additive bilingualism for all the students involved. The goals of a two-way immersion program are bilingualism and biliteracy for all students.

According to Thomas and Collier (1997), the following factors are present in successful two-way immersion programs:

- Students participate for at least six years.
- The ratio of speakers of each language is balanced.
- Languages are carefully separated.
- The minority language is emphasized in the early grades.
- Instruction is excellent and emphasizes core academics.
- Parents have a strong, positive relationship with the school.

The two-way immersion model was first implemented in San Diego, California, in 1975, and has been replicated nationwide. At River Glen Elementary School in northern California, a linguistically heterogeneous group of kindergarten children starts school each year in a classroom where Spanish is used 90 percent of the time and English 10 percent of the time. By fifth grade, English and Spanish are each used 50 percent of the time in class. The program at River Glen was started as part of a magnet school desegregation program and has been extremely successful in attracting an ethnically diverse student population.

Two-way immersion programs address an issue that has surfaced in research on traditional programs. In traditional programs, the teacher is the only native speaker in the classroom. Native-like language input is therefore somewhat limited, and students in interaction with each other tend to develop what might be characterized as a classroom pidgin of the target language (Higgs, 1991; Swain, 1991). Because two-way immersion classrooms mix students from both language groups, all students have many opportunities to interact with native speakers, which enhances their chances to develop native-like proficiency in their new language.

According to a directory published by the Center for Applied Linguistics (2007), as of November 2006 there were 338 two-way immersion programs in the United States. All programs pair English with another language, most commonly Spanish, which is offered in 316 schools. The other languages offered are scattered among French, Cantonese, Korean, Navajo, Japanese,

Mandarin and German. California has the greatest number of schools offering two-way immersion programs, but programs exist in 29 states and the District of Columbia.

A web search indicates that interest In Mandarin is surfacing in many areas. For example, Iowa, which does not appear in the CAL data as of this writing, is using newly available federal funds to begin two-way immersion programs in both Spanish and Mandarin (Iowa State University, 2006).

Bilingual immersion supports the primary language of language minority students, and offers an enrichment program to English speakers. Results of longitudinal studies indicate that students in these programs achieve high levels of bilingualism as well as high levels of academic competence in their subject areas (Lindholm & Molina, 1998). Another important outcome of two-way immersion programs is that students not only speak each other's languages, they learn to appreciate and respect each other's culture (Guido, 1995; Lindholm, 1994).

ENGLISH IMMERSION

Political pressure in the United States to move away from primary language instruction has resulted in experimentation with English immersion programs, sometimes called *structured immersion,* for minority students (see Table 2.1). One important longitudinal study of English immersion indicates that it is less successful for minority language students than bilingual education with native language support (Ramírez et al., 1991).

——*Models and Realities: What Does Bilingual Education Look Like in Practice?*

Description of program models doesn't always capture the reality of bilingual program implementation. In real schools, educators must deal with the realities of resources, staffing, and the variety of needs that children bring. A report commissioned by the U.S. Department of Education (Fleischman & Staples-Said, 1994) describes ten programs nationwide in districts that range from small to quite large, from rural to urban, serving children from a wide variety of backgrounds and languages.

The smallest of these, a southwestern rural district with a total population of 165, supports 31 LEP migrant farmwork students with an ESL pull-out program. The ESL teacher is Spanish-speaking and uses primary language to assist students in developing primary language literacy skills. The largest district described in the report is urban and located in the Southeast. The district's total enrollment is about 300,000 students, 15 percent of whom are LEP. Of the 45,000 LEP students, most are Spanish speaking, 12 percent speak Haitian

● TABLE *2.1*

Program Models, Goals, and Outcome

Program Model	Goal	Outcome
Transitional	Proficiency in L2 for language minority students (assimilationist)	Subtractive bilingualism
Maintenance	Bilingualism and biliteracy for language minority students (pluralist)	Additive bilingualism
Enrichment/Two-way	Bilingualism and biliteracy for language minority and language majority students (pluralist)	Additive bilingualism
Immersion		
1. Enrichment	Bilingualism and biliteracy for language majority students (pluralist)	Additive bilingualism
2. Two-way	Bilingualism and biliteracy for language minority and language majority students (pluralist)	Additive bilingualism
3. English immersion	Proficiency in English for language minority students (assimilationist)	Subtractive bilingualism

NOTE: L1 = first language; L2 = second language. For language minority students in the United States, L2 = English.

Creole, and a small number speak other languages. Where language concentrations make it practicable, the district offers primary language instruction in core curriculum classes. All LEP students receive English as a second language (ESL) instruction in a pull-out program. A newcomer program serves LEP middle and high school age students who need to develop primary language literacy skills to facilitate their transition to English.

Despite the very different qualities of all the districts described in the report, and the variety of populations they serve, all the teachers interviewed for the report expressed concerns about the need for support and understanding from their colleagues and administrators. Another area of concern was the need for services for parents who themselves do not speak English and are often under-educated as well as overwhelmed by the demands of working several jobs.

Teachers expressed similar concerns in interviews conducted by Lemberger (1997). Her analysis of eight teachers' narratives reinforces the idea that consistent leadership and administrative support are essential to program success.

Newcomer Programs

The challenges of providing appropriate schooling for second language learners are complicated at the secondary level by a number of factors. The structure of secondary schools themselves, with multiple course offerings and tracks, makes it difficult to offer a consistent program for second language learners without restricting choices of electives and limiting their high school experience. Also, even though older students with first language literacy learn English quickly, they may encounter difficulties with advanced high school curricula. For students who aren't literate, the challenge is clear, and materials and methods for meeting their needs are not readily available.

Beyond the demands of classes and assignments, newly arrived students who have had no schooling in their home countries and even those who have are likely to have little knowledge of the way we "do" high school in the United States. Think, for example, about the way bells ring to signal the change of classes. If you grew up and went to school in the United States, that probably seems quite ordinary—so ordinary that you probably barely notice it. If you didn't grow up here, and you were new to this country, daily procedures like the bells in a U.S. school might be perplexing, even overwhelming.

Finally, newly arrived students may have needs associated with the pain of leaving their home countries or adjusting to U.S. society. Some of them may be refugees, some may have left parents and other family behind, and some may have suffered the deprivations and horrors of war.

In an effort to help newly arrived students adjust to the experience and expectations of U.S. schools, some districts have created newcomer programs. Newcomer programs take a number of forms, from an orientation class to a freestanding school, but they generally attempt to assist students to:

- Overcome the trauma of relocation.
- Develop familiarity with the customs and culture of U.S. schooling.
- Develop English proficiency.
- Adapt to U.S. society in general.
- Succeed in their transition to mainstream schools.

Until recently, there was little research on newcomer programs, but the need for such programs and interest in them is growing. Additional information about newcomer programs is available on the web at www.ncela.gwu.edu and www.cal.org.

Also, schools must be responsive to the needs of language minority parents. Traditional forms of parent involvement may not be effective, and schools have to devise innovative, creative approaches to outreach and involvement. All the teachers in Lemberger's study expressed frustration with the limited availability of materials in both native and second languages. This is especially important because LEP students may not have access to many books at home (Krashen, 1997/1998).

It should be noted once again that many "programs" are not programs at all, lacking a consensual set of goals and consistent approaches to reaching them. Lemberger (1997) comments: "A teacher could never be sure that what she taught in one grade would be followed up by another colleague. Native language development might not be supported and built upon from year to year depending on whether the receiving teacher understood the value of maintaining and using the native language" (pp. 147–148).

Critics of bilingual education often overstate the extent of services to LEP students. Many LEP students, however, are not served by any program at all. The Council of Chief State School Officers reports (1990) that in 20 of the 48 states that responded to a survey on services to LEP students at least 25 percent receive no services. Four states responded that they fail to serve 60 percent of their LEP student populations. The report characterizes the current state of service to LEP students as "an abdication of legal responsibility as well as social responsibility" (p. 22).

Dual Language Instruction in Private Schools

Professional attention generally focuses on dual language instruction in public school settings. Despite current interest in two-way and enrichment programs, most address the needs of limited English proficient children. Bilingualism, however, is widely considered the hallmark of an educated person, and dual language instruction has found outlets in the private school arena as well.

Dual language instruction for privileged sectors of society has been available in the United States for quite some time. For example, Bryn Mawr School in Baltimore, Maryland, established in 1885, offers French, Latin, Greek, German, and Spanish as enrichment for students in kindergarten through fifth grade (Tomlinson & Eastwick, 1980).

According to one comprehensive report, there are approximately 6,500 private schools in the United States that provide some form of education in a language other than English. At the time the study was completed, the Jewish community accounted for nearly half that number, providing schooling in both Hebrew and Yiddish, but at least 108 languages were represented in private schools (Fishman, 1985).

It would be difficult to estimate the number of such schools at the present time, but there are revealing examples. For instance, the Association of Northern California Chinese Schools lists 84 member schools (ANCCS, 2003). Some of them enroll upwards of a thousand students. These are generally "Saturday" schools, offering Chinese instruction on weekends only. Note that children who attend these schools develop language and literacy in two languages. In other words, they actually receive a bilingual education—it just happens under more than one roof.

As part of a federal project on bilingual education, researchers made site visits to 24 private schools that had dual language instructional programs. They found that private schools use many of the same methods as public schools for providing dual language instruction. Despite the lack of innovation, private dual language programs are distinguished by their emphasis on the value of knowing two languages (Elford & Woodford, 1982). This emphasis appears to persist, even in the current political climate. For example, the International School of the Peninsula in Palo Alto, California, offers a full curriculum in both Mandarin Chinese and French to approximately 500 students, many of whom are American-born English speakers. In its mission, the school states: "We are committed to developing well-rounded individuals with a broad international awareness and the ability to communicate in at least two languages" (International School of the Peninsula, 2003).

Reports in the popular press indicate that demand for second language instruction has spread to include private preschools (Wells, 1986). The value placed on bilingualism by those who can afford to pay for private schooling raises an important issue: Why is dual language instruction desirable for a socioeconomic elite but undesirable for minority language groups? Despite the current lack of government support for bilingual programs and public misconceptions about their value, perhaps two-way enrichment programs will change attitudes about bilingualism and dual language instruction.

Bilingual Teachers

All too often lay people, and even some professionals, assume that bilingual teachers are teachers whose only qualification is that they speak two languages. That would be the same as assuming that an English teacher is any person who speaks, reads, and writes English! A good bilingual teacher, like all good teachers, has attitudes, knowledge, and skills that are particular to the students and the subject matter. What good teachers do, and what they need to know to do it, is the subject of ongoing conversation among professionals at every level.

Clearly, bilingual teachers need to be bilingual and biliterate in English and in the language of their students. But they need other competencies as well. They need to understand the nature of language and how languages are learned so they can create appropriate learning environments for second language learners.

In addition, they must understand their students' culture in ways that transcend surface culture and address the values and beliefs underlying the ways their students act in and out of classrooms. Understanding of culture, combined with awareness of the social contexts of their students, allows effective bilingual teachers to reach out and connect with the families and communities of the students they serve. Understanding the historical and political contexts of bilingual education and of their students supports teachers' abilities to advocate for their students' needs in a climate increasingly characterized by hostility toward newcomers and diversity.

Finally, like all teachers, bilingual teachers must be skilled at assessing students' needs, as well as planning appropriate goals, objectives, and activities to meet those needs and gathering evaluative data on an ongoing basis as students grow and change. Bilingual teachers plan and prepare in more than one language, and strive to meet multiple content and language objectives as students learn two languages through bilingual instruction. Currently, 44 states and the District of Columbia offer certification for teachers of English as a second language, and 28 certify bilingual teachers. Seventeen states require that teachers placed in bilingual classrooms have the appropriate certification (NCELA, 2007).

Summary

Dual language instruction may be transitional or maintenance-oriented. Immersion models have received attention recently because they have proven effective in Canada for teaching minority languages to majority children. A variety of immersion designs are currently being tried in the United States. Enrichment programs that provide second language instruction for monolingual English speakers are increasing in popularity. Dual language programs are available in private schools as well. Teachers who work in dual language instructional settings need specialized training in both bilingual and multicultural education.

Questions to Think About and Discuss

1. If you were going to build a program that served English language learners from the ground up, what would it look like? What outcomes would you try to achieve? To meet those goals, what kind of program model would you implement? What competencies would you expect teachers to have?

2. Consider your own teacher preparation program: Does it adequately prepare you to meet the needs of second language learners? If so, how, and if not, what experiences and expectations would you choose to add or improve?

Activities

1. Visit a public dual language instructional program. Interview a program administrator, a teacher, a parent, and a student enrolled in the

program. Find out what they perceive the goals of the program to be. Analyze the program design. Does the program model fit the goals that the participants envision?

2. Visit a private school that offers dual language instruction. What program model is in use? What are the goals of administrators, teachers, parents, and students in this school? Describe the student population of the school.

Suggestions for Further Reading

Cummins, J. (1989). *Empowering minority students.* Sacramento: California Association for Bilingual Education.

This book examines the relationship between minority students' experience of schooling and the sociopolitical context of education. Language and bilingual education are explored from the perspective of critical pedagogy, and programs that have been successful for language minority students are described.

Cummins, J. (1996). *Negotiating identities: Education for empowerment in a diverse society.* Ontario, CA: California Association for Bilingual Education.

Negotiating Identities is more a simple update of Empowering Minority Students. Cummins expands on the notion that bilingual education cannot be thought of simply in terms of language, and this book guides the reader to think about language and schooling in terms of power relations and the impact of social and political contexts on the relationships of students and their teachers.

Cummins, J., & Swain, M. (1986). *Bilingualism in education.* London: Longman.

This book explores the nature of bilingual proficiency and suggests that positive linguistic, cognitive, and academic consequences result from high levels of proficiency in two languages. Results of research and evaluation studies related to Canadian French immersion programs are described in detail.

Frederickson, J. (1995). *Reclaiming our voices: Bilingual education, critical pedagogy & praxis.* Los Angeles: California Association for Bilingual Education.

Critical pedagogy creates a classroom world wherein students can find their own voices, engage in creative dialogue, and transform their lives and their worlds. This collection of articles brings the reader into the conversation about critical theory and pedagogy tied directly to considerations of language, culture, bilingualism, and biculturalism.

Genesee, F. (1987). *Learning through two languages: Studies of immersion and bilingual education.* Rowley, MA: Newbury House.

An examination of immersion programs for majority students in Canada and bilingual programs for minority language students in the United States. A chapter on immersion in the United States details programs in California, Maryland, and Ohio.

Genesee, F. (Ed.). (1994). *Educating second language children: The whole child, the whole curriculum, the whole community.* Cambridge, UK: The Cambridge University Press.

This collection of articles links schools, families, and communities, and addresses the second language learner's experience in all those contexts, reaching beyond language to incorporate social and cultural dimensions as well.

Krashen, S., & Biber, D. (1988). *On course: Bilingual education's success in California.* Sacramento: California Association for Bilingual Education.

Following a summary of a rationale for primary language instruction, this book provides descriptions of bilingual programs in California that have been successful in improving student achievement.

Lemberger, N. (1997). *Bilingual education: Teachers' narratives.* Mahwah, NJ: Lawrence Erlbaum Associates.

The author interviewed eight bilingual teachers from a variety of backgrounds who teach in a variety of settings. The book includes the teachers' own stories, as well as an analysis of the issues and themes that emerge. No book to date better captures the on-the-ground experience of teachers in bilingual classrooms.

Office of Bilingual Bicultural Education, California State Department of Education. (1984). *Studies on immersion education: A collection for United States educators.* Sacramento: California State Department of Education.

The first section of this book presents an overview of major issues related to immersion programs. The second section includes descriptions of programs in Canada. Section three looks at immersion education in the United States.

Olsen, L. et al. (1994). *The unfinished journey: Restructuring schools in a diverse society.* San Francisco: California Tomorrow.

Using descriptions of a number of programs currently in place, this report shows how schools can effectively restructure to meet the needs of diverse student populations.

Skutnabb-Kangas, T. (1981). *Bilingualism or not: The education of minorities.* Clevedon, UK: Multilingual Matters.

Far more than a simple discussion of program models, this book provides an insightful analysis of bilingualism and the education of minorities from a broad political perspective. Included are discussions of bilingualism of children from a variety of language backgrounds, the neurolinguistic and cognitive aspects of bilingualism, the impact of social and educational policy on immigrant children, and a typology of dual language programs accounting for differences between majority and minority students.

chapter 3

Aspects of Language

$\mathcal{T}$his chapter will ask you to think critically about the nature of language. This may be difficult because language is almost invisible to us. We acquire language when we are very young and use it for a multitude of purposes every day. But, unless we have a scholarly interest, we rarely stop to look at it.

Textbooks on linguistics or communication disorders provide detailed introductions to the concept of language. This chapter will not investigate language in depth but is intended as an overview of various technical and academic ways of looking at language.

From a teacher's point of view, it is important to know what language is and how it works because language should be used in a planned way, much as we use other instructional materials and media. This chapter has two purposes, which will allow us to objectify language so that we can use it effectively for dual language instruction. First, we will define language and look at its component parts. By defining language, we will render it more visible and acquire the basic vocabulary necessary to discuss numerous aspects of dual language instruction.

Second, we will consider some of the common preconceived notions about language. We have strong emotional bonds to our language because it is the vehicle through which we convey our experience and culture. Therefore we need to separate basic concepts about language from attitudes that may interfere with our ability to use language as a classroom tool or to deal equitably with children whose language backgrounds differ from our own.

The Study of Language

The study of dual language instruction requires us to consider language from at least four different perspectives. *Linguistics* describes the structural aspects of language. Much of the basic vocabulary needed to discuss language acquisition and language proficiency comes from the field of linguistics.

Psycholinguistics deals with the relationship of language and the mind. Psycholinguists consider how language is acquired and how language is processed in the human mind.

Neurolinguistics is the study of language and the brain. Neurolinguists try to figure out how brain development and function and language ability are linked. For example, neurolinguistic researchers have sought evidence that will prove or disprove the so-called critical period theory that the brain changes during puberty in ways that make language learning harder after early adolescence than before.

Sociolinguistics is the relatively new and exciting field of inquiry that investigates how language works in society. Sociolinguists study the language dynamics of everyday interactions between people. If you have ever considered dialect differences or the manner in which people alter their speech when addressing a superior or a member of the opposite sex, you have made sociolinguistic observations.

Planning and delivery of effective dual language instruction are based on theory, research, and practical applications from all these areas of language inquiry.

What Is Language?

The American Speech-Language-Hearing Association defines *language* as a complex and dynamic system of conventional symbols used in various modes for communication and thought (American Speech-Language-Hearing Association, 1983). Let us take a closer look at this definition.

A system is organized, governed by rules, and works toward a purpose. Automobile engines and the digestive tract are examples of systems. Language is a system—it is ordered and purposeful. The essential purpose of language is communication. A careful focus on the purpose of language dispels many unfortunate attitudes people have about languages and, concomitantly, about each other. Also, as we shall see, understanding the basic purpose of language is useful for understanding how languages are acquired and provides important insights as to how languages should be taught.

Language is an orderly combination of conventional symbols. The symbols are the words we use to label the objects, actions, and ideas that we perceive in our reality. These symbols are conventional—that is, we assign a socially agreed-on symbol to objects and ideas so we can talk about them. We all agree on a name for a particular object or idea for purposes of communication.

In English, for example, we use *chair* to identify a common object used for supporting us in a sitting posture. A Spanish speaker refers to the same object as *silla*. It's altogether arbitrary: no matter what you call it, you can still sit on it. The concept of the arbitrary nature of symbols used in language becomes important when we start to investigate bilingualism. As we shall see, bilingual people have a strong understanding of the arbitrary nature of the symbols of language, which enhances their problem-solving skills.

Subsystems of Language

Breaking language down into its subsystems facilitates understanding of how it works and provides us with some of the vocabulary necessary for discussing language acquisition, language proficiency, and second language instruction. Language is generally considered to have five fundamental subsystems.

THE PHONOLOGICAL SYSTEM

The phonological system is the sound system of a language. When we hear speech, we perceive phonemes, the smallest distinguishable units of sound that carry meaning for us in our language.

It might seem as though we ought to be able to hear the distinctions between all the sounds that humans produce, but that is not the case. Each language makes use of only a small number of the wide range of possible sounds that human beings are capable of uttering and discerning.

For example, in English it makes a significant difference to you if someone *pats* you on the head or *bats* you on the head. But in some languages, the sounds that we write as *p* and *b* are heard as identical, a phenomenon easier to understand if you consider that both sounds are produced using the same parts of the mouth in the same fashion. The only difference is that the initial sound in *bat* includes the use of voicing, while the initial sound in *pat* does not. Not all languages distinguish between voiced and voiceless sounds, which sound distinctive to native English speakers. For speakers of languages that do not distinguish between these sounds, English words such as *ban* and *pan* or *bay* and *pay* sound alike.

Sign languages, not having sound systems, have an equivalent system known as *cherology*. Cheremes are the smallest units of gesture that are distinguishable and carry meaning to a speaker of sign (Wilbur, 1980).

THE MORPHOLOGICAL SYSTEM

The morphological system is the system of how words are built. Morphemes are meaningful units, which can sometimes stand alone as words, but often appear in combination with other morphemes. For example, the word *girl* has one morpheme, which carries the meaning of a young female human. *Girls* has two morphemes. The second morpheme, *-s*, indicates the concept of plural. *Girls* is a single example, which sidesteps more complicated morphological issues, such as the relationship between *man* and *men*. A complex analysis of the theory of morphology is out of place here. However, it is important to know that words are built systematically, much as sentences are.

SYNTAX

Syntax refers to the structure or architecture of sentences. It is common but inaccurate to think of syntax as grammar. Syntax, however, is descriptive rather than prescriptive. For example, "I don't have a pencil" is recognizable to a native speaker of English as an acceptable sentence. On the other hand, "A pencil don't have I" sounds awkward. It does not conform to the generally accepted patterns or rules of English.

On the other hand, look at the sentence "I ain't got no pencil." A native speaker of American English knows that it is an English sentence and conforms to English syntax. Nevertheless, we have a tendency to judge "I ain't got no pencil" as incorrect English. It is not standard usage, and its use would be ill-advised for a formal situation such as an employment interview. From a purely descriptive standpoint, however, it fits into basic English sentence patterns. Despite the fact that it may make schoolteachers shudder, it is used in classrooms countless times every day, and, from a syntactical point of view, it works in English.

In sum, *syntax* refers to the rules that govern a language. *Grammar,* on the other hand, has a prescriptive connotation—it looks at whether or not a particular construction conforms to a language standard. We shall analyze the meaning of standard language later in this chapter.

SEMANTICS

Semantics is the study of meaning. Semantics was considered the purview of philosophers until fairly recently. Modern analyses have led linguists to conclude that while meaning and structure are inextricably connected, syntactical analysis of language is insufficient to explain meaning (Hayes, Ornstein, & Gage, 1977). One area of inquiry in semantics is the study of words. Words can be analyzed with reference to their denotations. Earlier in this chapter, we talked about conventional symbols, and we agreed that *chair* refers to a piece of furniture used for sitting. *Chair,* however, can denote several things, depending on the context. In a committee meeting, for example, *chair* may well denote the person who organizes the meeting, or the action of leading the group.

Words also have connotations that supplement their denotations. While the words *Asian* and *rice-eater* may refer to the same individual, they have very different connotations. *Asian* refers to a person's geographical or cultural origins; *rice-eater* has pejorative connotations far beyond an observation on dietary habits.

The subtleties of denotations and connotations are a minefield for second language learners. Good dictionaries provide information about semantic distinctions, but there's still room for error. David Sedaris (1997), in a humorous essay about learning French, tells how he decided to learn ten daily words and practice them while doing errands in a small town in Normandy. "Out of the five translations for a given English word, I would manage to write down and memorize the most bizarre and obsolete. This was the case with the word 'glove.'" In an attempt to converse with the butcher about the weather, Sedaris remarked "It is brisk this evening.... Perhaps I should wear the heavy steel mitts worn by medieval knights as they rode into battle" (p. 71). In other words, Sedaris selected the word *gauntlet* from the options offered in his French dictionary. The difference between *glove* and *gauntlet* is semantic.

In addition to analyzing the dimensions of particular words, semantics studies phrases and sentences and analyzes different kinds of ambiguities. For example, the sentence "They were hunting dogs" has structural ambiguities. Thus, two differing meanings are represented with the same surface structure of language. Advertisers often take advantage of ambiguities. An advertisement for Toyota comments, "People drive us" (*New York Times Magazine*, 1997, p. 31). Two advertising messages are cleverly packaged in one short phrase. One tells us that people drive these cars (they're popular, people like them), and the other suggests that the company is motivated to serve people and meet their needs. That's semantics!

As language users, we daily sort out many different and ambiguous meanings. Our intuitive understanding of semantics enables us to tune into correct meanings by relying on linguistic context.

PRAGMATICS

Pragmatics is not an internal linguistic subsystem, such as phonology, morphology, syntax, and semantics. Rather it is the system of the use of language in social contexts. Language use is determined by the function of an interaction and by the relationship of the people involved (Bloom & Lahey, 1978). For example, "I now pronounce you man and wife" has no meaning if uttered by a child in play, but significant consequences when stated by an appropriate official during a wedding ceremony.

In language, one form may serve several functions. "It's ten after five" may be a response to a direct question. It may also be a way of suggesting to people that they have arrived behind schedule. Uttered in a particular context, it may mean "We're going to get stuck in rush hour traffic!" Conversely, one function may take many forms. The question "Can we begin?" and the hint "We're running short on time" both serve the same function.

Native speakers intuitively understand pragmatic systems. If someone asks, "Can you tell me the time?" a native English speaker, acting on knowledge about language and social context, knows that it is inappropriate to answer yes.

IMPLICATIONS FOR TEACHERS

Understanding the subsystems of language provides teachers with insights into the challenges that face second language learners who are learning English. For example, an analysis of the phonological system of English shows that there are actually about fifteen vowel sounds in American English, represented by various combinations of letters. No wonder it's a challenge for speakers of other languages to learn to read and write English!

On the other hand, morphological analysis can be helpful for some students learning to read. Spanish speakers, for example, can benefit from thinking about cognates. Spanish uses lots of Latin-based words for ordinary conversation, whereas English uses the German-based variety for day-to-day conversation, saving the Latin-based words for "best." Think about this: In casual English, it's likelier that I "met" you on the way to the store than that I "encountered" you. Students whose first language is Spanish may have less trouble understanding the word *encounter,* because the everyday Spanish word is *encontrar.*

There are many published programs for teaching reading and second language. Teachers need to select from among them and also tailor them to the needs of specific groups and individual students. A good understanding of the way language works is an important tool for evaluating different approaches as well as for using them effectively.

*W*ritten Language in a Computerized World

Email, bulletin boards, and chat rooms have added a new dimension to written communication. Acronyms are often used as a kind of shorthand. Emoticons, symbols made of letters and other keyboard symbols, express feelings that might not come across otherwise. Below are some common acronyms and emoticons that you may come across when you communicate in cyberspace. The list is hardly exhaustive, and like all language forms, is constantly evolving and changing. For an in-depth look at how language is evolving in the computer age, read *Language and the Internet,* by David Crystal (Cambridge University Press, 2001).

ACRONYMS

BTW	By the way	LOL	Laugh out loud (also lots of love)
CUL8R	See you later	LTNS	Long time no see
FOAF	Friend of a friend	OTOH	On the other hand
FTASB	Faster than a speeding bullet	ROFL	Rolling on the floor laughing
GGN	Gotta go now	SOP	Standard Operating Procedure
HHOK	Ha ha, only kidding	TIA	Thanks in advance
IMHO	In my humble opinion	YWSYLS	You win some, you lose some

EMOTICONS

: -)	A smile, happy, funny	: - I	Disgusted
: - (	A frown, sad, unhappy, bad news	(:-&	Angry
; -)	A wink	: - o	Shocked, amazed

The conventions of emoticons are different in Japanese. Here are some examples:

(^^) (^0^)	Smile or laugh	(#^^#)	Turn red
(^_-)	Wink	(^_^;)	Cold sweat, nervousness
(^.^)	Kiss		

Other Aspects of Communication

Apart from language, communication is enhanced by paralinguistic ("beyond language") and nonlinguistic messages, which can be transmitted in conjunction with language or without the aid of language. Paralinguistic mechanisms include intonation, stress, rate of speech, and pauses or hesitations. Nonlinguistic behaviors include gestures, facial expressions, and body language, among others.

Paralinguistic and nonlinguistic behaviors differ from culture to culture and language to language. Such differences are often the cause of misunderstandings in cross-cultural situations. Students who wish to become proficient in a second language should pay careful attention to the nonverbal behaviors that pertain to the languages they are studying.

Language Attitudes

In the foregoing section we have treated language almost clinically. Remember, however, that in the introduction to this chapter we said that it is necessary to identify the attitudes or biases we have and separate them from basic concepts about language. Language exists in political and social contexts that must be understood so we can use language as an instructional tool and also respond equitably to students with a language background different from our own.

It is difficult to pinpoint attitudes we hold about language because the emotional bond we have to our native language is extremely strong. Søren Kierkegaard, the nineteenth-century Danish philosopher and writer, referring to the porridge his mother prepared for him when he was a child, reflected that no other porridge could ever be as flavorful. We can draw an analogy between language and Kierkegaard's porridge—no language ever seems quite as rich or evocative as our own.

In this section we will investigate a few of the commonly held attitudes about language.

ARE SOME LANGUAGES BETTER THAN OTHERS?

One prevalent attitude is that some languages or varieties of a language are more correct or better than others. For example, Spanish speakers are often asked if they speak Castilian. The Spanish word for Castilian is *castellano*. In Spain *castellano* refers to the regional dialect of the province of Castile. In parts of Latin American, *castellano* is used to refer to Spanish in general. The uninformed English speaker, however, who refers to Castilian generally means something along the lines of "the King's English"—a proper, high-class form of the language.

This attitude and many others can be dispelled by focusing on the fact that the primary purpose of language is communication. A Spanish speaker answering the phone in Argentina says *allo* (hello). Other Latin Americans pick up the receiver and say *diga* (speak). Mexicans say *bueno* (good or well). Mexicans joke about the expression, claiming that their phone system is so bad that any time they can get a call through is *bueno!* None of these responses is better than any other. Depending on where you are, there are many appropriate ways to answer a phone in Spanish. It makes sense to facilitate communication by responding according to local custom.

ARE SOME LANGUAGES MORE EXPRESSIVE THAN OTHERS?

One common attitude that people hold about language is that there are ideas or feelings that can be expressed in one language that can't be expressed in another. An expression of this bias is that some languages are less logical than others. In particular, people sometimes suggest that some languages are not useful for communicating about technology.

As Muriel Saville-Troike remarks (1982, p. 82), "While all languages may be inherently capable of serving all purposes humans may ask of them, specific languages evolve differentially through processes of variation, adaptation, and selection." In other words, as people in a society have a need to communicate in a particular way or about a particular subject, their language expands and adapts to meet their need.

For example, there are several cultures in the South Pacific that commonly use a large squash-like vegetable we call breadfruit for a variety of purposes. Breadfruit is used as a basic food, but also serves several ritual and ceremonial purposes. People in those cultures have many words for breadfruit that indicate its color, ripeness, size, and particular use. In the United States we rarely encounter a breadfruit, and the one name we have for it may not be familiar to you at all. Nevertheless, with some circumlocution and explanation, English can produce all the nuances necessary to talk about breadfruit.

Some languages borrow to meet expanding technological needs. There is a bias against borrowing, and some governments have even passed laws to limit loan words. According to an article in *Newsweek* (Doerner, 1987), the French government has established a secretary of state for francophone affairs, and judgments have been levied against companies that use English words in advertising in lieu of French equivalents.

Hebrew, however, is an example of a language that has borrowed extensively to meet the needs of modernization and yet has maintained its linguistic integrity. Preserved for centuries almost exclusively as a liturgical language, Hebrew came into everyday use with the creation of the state of Israel in 1948. Biblical Hebrew was, of course, incompatible with the demands of the modern world. It might be possible, for example, to create a circumlocution for *telephone* by saying "a way to talk to people at a distance through wires." But that would be cumbersome in real-life situations when you want to say, "Answer

Neologisms

Languages are constantly changing. At the lexical level, words become obsolete, and new words come into use. New words, or neologisms, are formed in several different ways. We make new words from old ones by adding prefixes and suffixes. For example, from *structure* we get *superstructure* and *infrastructure*. Our media-driven society acquired a suffix from Watergate and we've used it to describe any number of political scandals, thus "Monicagate." We also borrow words from other languages, which you know if you like a croissant with your latte. Back-formation, making verbs from nouns, is a common process that gives us verbs like "to impact," "to parent," "to incentivize." Back-formation seems to excite controversy among grammarians (Andrews, 2001), but it happens all the time.

Technology is evolving at an unprecedented rate, giving rise to a lot of new words, many of which derive from acronyms. So, for example, *laser* comes from light amplification by stimulated emission of radiation. *Modem,* from modulator-demodulator, isn't quite an acronym. It's more of a compound word, which is another way neologisms are made. *Cyberspace* and *infomercial* are new compound words that have quickly become familiar to us all. Sometimes we blend words (*motel* or *brunch*) or we shorten or clip words to make new ones. *Blog* is short for weblog, much as *ad* is short for advertisement.

Jeremy Bentham, a nineteenth-century British philosopher and social reformer, coined many words in his time that are in common use today. For example, Bentham gave us *international* and *maximize*. Bentham may be best known, however, for his auto-icon. On display in a cabinet at University College London as requested in his will, the auto-icon is Bentham's skeleton, dressed in his own clothes and topped with a wax head. Readers who want to know more about the auto-icon (and what happened to Bentham's actual head) can log on to www.ucl.ac.uk. To take a look at the very newest words in English go to www.logophilia.com.

the telephone!" So Hebrew borrowed the word *telephone,* and in Hebrew it sounds much like the English word.

At the same time, the Academy of the Hebrew Language attempts to coin Hebrew neologisms (new words) to keep up with modern needs and demands, without incorporating too many loan words or English derivatives. After some deliberation, the Academy settled on *tanuron* or "little oven" for toaster oven in an attempt to avoid the use of the English word *toaster* (Schmemann, 1996).

We have looked at only a few of the many possible attitudes about language. Linguists agree that all languages are linguistically equal and that every language is equally capable of expressing whatever its speakers need to communicate.

Attitudes about language persist because people feel close personal and emotional ties to the languages they speak. Mandy Patinkin, the vocalist, recorded an album of Yiddish songs. While doing so, he invited several

Yiddish-speaking friends to discuss translations and pronunciations. Describing the ensuing "friendly battle," he comments, "It became clear to me they were battling to preserve their ancestors' neighborhoods, the way the word was spoken on their parents' streets, their homes, their corners" (Patinkin, 1998). Such attitudes and emotions are understandable. A teacher who works with language minority students, however, must be aware of language attitudes as potential misinterpretations of the nature and purpose of language as a human endeavor.

Language Varieties

STANDARD

The term *standard* has been used in the foregoing section, but it has not been defined. It is commonly assumed that there is a standard, fixed, and correct form of a language against which we can measure a given sample of that language. But the concept of an immutable and proper language form contradicts the very nature of language itself. As we have seen, language is flexible, responsive, changing constantly.

Students of language sometimes suggest that a language is a dialect with an army. That somewhat humorous assertion gets close to the truth about language variation. The term *standard* is elusive precisely because it has its roots in politics rather than in any basic truth about language.

Standard language is the language of the group in power. Formal attempts are made to standardize language. For example, Spanish is regulated by 22 language academies, the oldest of which is the *Real Academia Española* (The Royal Spanish Academy), created in Spain in 1713 by King Philip V.

The most recent academy was established in New York in 1987 in an attempt to protect Spanish from becoming anglicized (Chavez, 1987). The United States has the fifth largest Spanish-speaking population in the world, and Spanish is in constant contact with English. One result is words like *carpeta* (rug), *roofo* (roof), and *lonche* (lunch). Another outcome is the addition of words like *taco* and *burrito* to the American English lexicon.

Spanish, along with the other Romance languages, is itself the product of languages in contact. When the Romans conquered Iberia, speakers of indigenous Iberian languages learned Latin. They spoke it with an accent, overlaid grammatical structures from their native tongues, and sprinkled it with local words for familiar concepts and objects. That natural process formed the basis for what we know as modern Spanish.

Languages are dynamic; they change to meet the communication needs of their speakers. It is possible for a "language government" such as an academy to set a standard. However, the standard set is not as crucial as *who* is doing the setting.

DIALECT

Dialects are variations of a language used by particular groups of people. Regional dialects often have distinct vocabularies. A water pistol on the East Coast of the United States is a squirt gun on the West Coast. In Spanish, a peach is *melocotón* in Puerto Rico and a *durazno* in Mexico. Dialects may also differ phonologically or syntactically from place to place.

Regional differences in languages may reflect differences in language history. American English includes usages that sound archaic to the British ear and may well be remnants from colonial times. American English also includes a large lexicon of words borrowed from Spanish (McCrum, Cran, & MacNeil, 1986).

People often relate regional dialects to stereotypes. For example, in the United States, speakers of Bostonian dialects are sometimes considered "stuffy." Southerners are said to drawl and are considered lazy and slow moving. Such biases have nothing to do with the real nature of dialects or the people who speak them. Despite our biases, regional differences present few problems for native speakers. Humans are quite responsive to language and quite flexible in their ability to communicate.

Just as language varies from place to place, it also varies among different social groups. Social variations of language are sometimes called *sociolects*. Professor Higgins, in *My Fair Lady,* was well aware of the different responses people have to different sociolects when he undertook his project of turning a flower seller into a member of high society.

Any individual's particular speech, or *idiolect,* is influenced by both regional and social class factors. From a teacher's viewpoint, it is important to remember that language can vary for many reasons and stay conscious to the biases that may come into play when we are exposed to different varieties of language. This awareness will help us avoid prejudging a student's abilities based on our own perceptions of language.

PIDGINS AND CREOLES

Sometimes languages in contact produce pidgins. This happens when speakers of two different languages, compelled to talk to each other, develop a bare-bones code for communication. Pidgins can emerge in a variety of contexts for a number of reasons. According to Stockwell, "[Pidgins] have arisen typically in time of imperialism, slavery, plantation labour migration, war and refugee situations, and around trading ports" (2002, p. 18). Born of necessity, pidgins are limited and simplified languages, but they are systematic and rule-governed.

A pidgin is nobody's first language, but as soon as a new generation learns a pidgin, it becomes a creole. Creoles are generally far more complex and elaborated than the pidgins from which they evolve, since they have to serve the full range of their speakers' needs. According to Todd (2001), over

100 million people speak some kind of creole, including 5 million speakers of Haitian Creole and 5 million speakers of Afrikaans.

Gullah, also known as Geechee, is an American creole. Gullah developed in the nineteenth century from contact between English and languages of West Africa spoken by enslaved people. Today it is still spoken on the Sea Islands off the coast of South Carolina and Georgia. Many people in the United States are familiar with Gullah through the speech of Uncle Remus in Joel Chandler Harris's tales of Bre'r Rabbit. In 1995, the American Bible Society published a Gullah translation of the Gospel according to Luke, called De Good Nyews Bout Jedus Christ Wa Luke Write. You may be familiar with the following verse:

> 2:10. Bot de angel tell um say, "Mus don't feah! A habe good nyews. Cause ob dis nyews, oona gwine rejaice. All de people gwine rejaice tommuch." (American Bible Society, 1995, p. 10) (*2:10. And the angel said unto them, Fear not: for, behold, I bring you good tidings of great joy, which shall be to all people.*)

REGISTER

People use different varieties of language, depending on the setting, relationship between speakers, and the function of the interaction. A *register* is a situationally appropriate form of a language.

Sociolinguistic concepts such as register are important to consider when assessing language proficiency and providing second language instruction. A person learning a second language may have a good accent or control of syntax and still lack the ability to function in a variety of life situations. For example, you may have experienced difficulty if you learned a second language in a classroom setting and then attempted to enter into the quick give-and-take of an informal gathering among friends.

BUT IS IT SLANG?

The word *slang* is commonly used to refer, somewhat pejoratively, to nonstandard speech. Speakers of one variety of English, for example, may comment that speakers of another variety "speak slang." From a professional perspective, *slang* has a more precise meaning. According to one linguist, "One of the main defining features of 'slang' appears to be its ephemeral nature" (Wardhaugh, 1993, p. 165). In other words, slang is usage that is popular for a while and then fades away. In some cases, however, slang may become acceptable and enter common usage. In that case, it is no longer slang.

More Than One Language

Information about the number of languages in the world and the number of speakers of those languages is readily available. There is little data, however,

In Your Classroom
Teaching Students about Language

The study of language and its history is beneficial at every level. Entertain young students, build their vocabularies, and expand on social science lessons by engaging them in activities that consider the origins of words.

Many English words have their origins in other languages, and some even come to English several languages removed. Words travel as the baggage of trade and also of conquest. *Apricot,* for example, is a Greek word with "al" or "the" added as a prefix from Arabic. The word traveled to Europe with the Moorish conquest of the Iberian peninsula and found its way into English when the Gauls conquered the Anglo-Saxons in the eleventh century! The words below are a tiny sample of words in English from other languages. Use your own knowledge of languages and the dictionary to discover the languages of origin for these words. (Hint: They're organized in language groups.)

- Algebra, almanac, nadir, zenith, zero
- Dungaree, khaki
- Aria, piano, soprano
- Avocado, chocolate, guacamole
- Adobe, brocade, canyon, guerrilla

You may want to do this activity with your own students using words that have come into English from their primary languages. It's one way that monolingual teachers can value the languages their students bring to the classroom.

regarding the number of people in the world who are bilingual or multilingual. It would be difficult for a researcher to collect that information, since theorists have defined *bilingualism* in many different ways.

WHAT IS BILINGUALISM?

A strict definition of *bilingualism* suggests that a bilingual person has native-like control of two languages (Bloomfield, 1933). Yet while many of the readers of this book undoubtedly function in more than one language, probably few would claim native-like capability in each language in every situation. Discussions with multilingual people reveal that they make choices about language use that are affected by the setting and function of the particular interaction (Miller, 1983). People who function in two or more languages know that those who have equal and highly developed capacity in two or more languages are relatively rare and generally much admired.

Grosjean, in *Life with Two Languages* (1982), surveyed monolingual and bilingual college students to find out how they interpreted the term *bilingual*. He asked them, "If someone told you that X was bilingual in English and

French, what would you understand by that?" (p. 231). In this survey, both monolingual and bilingual students indicated that *bilingual* means speaking two languages, and high ratings were given by both groups for the description "fluent in two languages." Unlike monolingual students in the study, however, bilingual students gave a high rating to "regular use of two languages." In that regard, bilingual students agree with many modern theorists who tend to favor the idea that use of two languages, rather than fluency, is the hallmark of bilingualism.

CODE-SWITCHING

Bilinguals sometimes alternate the use of two languages from sentence to sentence, or even within one sentence. *Code-switching*, as this is called, may be misinterpreted by monolinguals as an inability on the part of a bilingual individual to speak either language properly.

Analysis by linguists and sociolinguists, however, has demonstrated that code-switching is a systematic and rule-governed language behavior. Within certain linguistic constraints, bilinguals may code-switch to:

- Fill a lexical need: "*Le puse al niño en el* daycare."
- Emphasize a point: "Get up now. *Levántate!*"
- Express ethnic solidarity: "*Andale pues;* let's get together soon."

Other reasons for code-switching may include the desire to convey emotional or personal involvement, to include or exclude someone from a conversation, and to assert the status of the speaker (Grosjean, 1982).

In general, a person who code-switches demonstrates linguistic creativity and sophistication. However, a second type of code-switching, called *regressive code-switching* (Gonzalez & Maez, 1980), occurs in children who are losing their first language and leaning on their second language to supply missing elements. This kind of situation raises à pedagogical issue: Should teachers code-switch in dual language classrooms, or keep the languages entirely separate?

Experts generally agree that teachers should restrict code-switching to the intersentential type. That is, teachers should switch languages only from sentence to sentence and not intrasententially, or within a sentence. They should, however, accept intrasentential code-switching

> ### The Poetry of Code-Switching
>
> Soy un ajiaco de contradicciones.
> I have mixed feelings about everything.
> Name your tema, I'll hedge;
> name your cerca, I'll straddle it
> like a cubano
>
> (ajiaco: stew; tema: theme; cerca: fence)
>
> SOURCE: Gustavo Pérez-Firmat, in *Bilingual Blues.* Arizona State University, Tempe, AZ: Bilingual Press/ Editorial Bilingüe, 1995.

by their students (Ovando & Collier, 1985). There is some evidence, however, that complete separation of the two languages of instruction is beneficial to the development of both (Cummins & Swain, 1986). Concurrent use of language in the classroom and other instructional approaches are discussed in Chapter 6.

BILINGUALISM: A HANDICAP OR A TALENT?

Research prior to the 1960s tended to support the notion that bilingual children did poorly in school, and bilingualism was generally regarded as an academic handicap. Later analysis of those early findings reveals that the studies were biased against ethnic minority students. Sampling techniques and statistical analyses were flawed, and investigators failed to take into account other variables such as social and economic factors. Also, tests were usually administered only in English.

The assumption that bilingualism was a handicap led to unfortunate practices such as punishing children for using languages other than English in school, even at play. Rejection of a child's language and, by implication, culture adversely affects that child's self-concept and chances for academic success. In retrospect, the bilingualism-as-handicap position can be seen as a self-fulfilling prophecy.

Despite suggestions that early research on bilingualism may have been methodologically flawed, there have been recent studies that support the conclusions of earlier work and show that bilingual children score lower on verbal tests of intelligence or academic achievement than their monolingual counterparts. Other studies, however, indicate that bilingual children perform better than monolinguals on tests of linguistic skills, divergent thinking, sensitivity to communication, and general intelligence. (See Baker, 2006, for a review.) How can we explain this apparent contradiction?

Quite simply, children can be enriched by knowing more than one language as long as they are *additive* rather than *subtractive* bilinguals. An *additive bilingual* has learned a second language in addition to the first, whereas a *subtractive bilingual* has gradually lost one language while acquiring a second. The distinction is significant from a pedagogical viewpoint because research indicates that children with high levels of proficiency in two languages show "positive cognitive effects" (Cummins, 1981, p. 39). In effect, children who come to school speaking more than one language, or who learn a second language in school, will benefit academically as long as both languages are nurtured and developed to the fullest extent.

────⬤ *The Ebonics Debate*

In 1996 the Oakland Unified School District in northern California passed a resolution that identified Ebonics, sometimes called Black English or Black Vernacular, as a distinct language and proposed teaching students in Ebonics as a bridge to standard English. The debate that ensued about the resolution was startling both in terms of its ferocity and the inaccuracy of understandings on which it was based. It quickly became clear that the controversy about Ebonics and its use in schooling was fueled by deep and often unexplored feelings about race, ethnicity, culture, and language.

Ebonics, a term derived from the words *ebony* and *phonics*, refers to a variety of English sometimes also called Black English, Black English Vernacular, or African American Language. Ebonics has been a stigmatized variety of English, moreso perhaps than other varieties because it is associated with black people who have historically borne the brunt of racism and discrimination in American society. White America is often uncomfortable when Black America asserts its power, whether in the streets, the voting booth, or the public schools. Assertions about the validity of a particular language or dialect are often politically informed, as we shall see in Chapter 11, and it should not have come as a surprise to the authors of the Oakland resolution that the policy they promulgated was likely to provoke ardent responses across the political spectrum.

Dialects spoken by African Americans have historically been seen as deficient rather than simply different. In an article that is now a classic discussion of dialect and language bias, Labov (1995/1979) demonstrated that attitudes about what he called *Black English Vernacular* notwithstanding, it was clearly a communicative, and in fact, highly expressive variety of English. More recently, Williams (1991) has asserted that various features of what he calls *African American Language* can be traced back to languages brought to this continent by enslaved Africans. This ought not to be a radical notion, given what we generally know about languages, but is often received with skepticism by those who would deny African Americans any claim to a heritage that precedes their enslavement.

It should be noted that there are many forms of Black English. Many African Americans speak standard English, and many are bidialectal, using standard English in their schools and places of employment, and some form of Ebonics in their personal and community interactions. This should not seem unusual or startling, since we are all multidialectal.

Lawrence Block, in his mystery novel *A Walk Among the Tombstones* (1992), describes how TJ, a detective's street kid sidekick, tries to extract the number of an unlabeled pay phone from an operator. She refuses his request when he asks in Black English, so he calls another operator, and speaking standard English, successfully obtains the number. When Matt, the detective, expresses amazement at TJ's ability to switch back and forth, TJ muses "They two different languages man, and you talkin' to a cat's bilingual" (p. 116). TJ is dated, but he understands that for African Americans, like everyone else, the ability to use more than one dialect is an asset, not a liability.

Zora Neale Hurston was one of the first African American writers to capture the richness of black dialect on paper. In an essay describing Hurston's work, Claudia Roth Pierpont makes an eloquent observation about Black

English: "This is dialect not as a broken attempt at higher correctness but as an extravagant game of image and sound. It is a record of the unique explosion that occurred when African people with an intensely musical and oral culture came up hard against the King James Bible and the sweet-talking American South, under conditions that denied them all outlet for their visions and gifts except the transformation of the English language into song" (Roth Pierpont, 1997, p. 80).

Summary

Language is a system of arbitrary symbols used for communication. The field of linguistics describes the structure of language. Psycholinguistics investigates the relationship of language to the human mind, while sociolinguistics investigates how language varies as it is used in social situations. People have unfounded and emotional biases about language, but, in fact, all languages are responsive to the communication needs of their speakers and are equally suited for communication. Standards are arbitrary and determined by the dominant group in any society.

People who speak two languages may not use both of them with the same degree of facility in every situation. Sometimes bilingual people code-switch. This is not an indication of imperfect mastery of language. Code-switching can be seen as a sophisticated and expressive language strategy. Early research on school achievement suggested that bilingual students were at a disadvantage compared with monolinguals, but recent studies indicate the contrary. Understanding the nature of language and objectifying it as a tool are essential for teachers who work with second language learners.

Questions to Think About and Discuss

1. Read and analyze the following verse from the poem "Jabberwocky" by Lewis Carroll: What language is it written in? How do you know? What information does each subsystem of language give you for making that determination?

   'Twas brillig, and the slithy toves
   Did gyre and gimble in the wabe:
   All mimsy were the borogoves,
   And the mome raths outgrabe.

2. Identify the ambiguity in each of the following sentences and add words, a phrase, or a sentence to eliminate it.
   - John married Isabel.
   - The American history teacher is good looking.
   - Martha thinks she is a genius.

3. Read the following letter, which appeared in the *New York Times*. Analyze the author's language attitudes. Do the author's beliefs about language match up with the understandings you have about the nature of language?

> To the Editor:
> As a native of Japan, I am well aware of the importance of the Confucian ethic as an explanation for the academic success of Asian students. However, there may exist another reason why Japanese children, say at Sendai, can do better in mathematics. When I was tutoring my wife's granddaughter, who is a Caucasian, I was struck by the awkwardness of the English language for reciting the multiplication table.
>
> As an example, you must pronounce 4 × 4 = 16 as "4 times 4 is 16" in a rather unrhythmical way. We can say the same in Japanese, "shi-shi-ju-roku" with a singsong musical rhythm. We learn the multiplication table up to 10 × 10 in this fashion. Even after 39 years in this country, I revert to the Japanese method because of its ease.
>
> I can well imagine that the relative difficulty of memorizing the multiplication table in English may cause boredom and loss of interest in math for many youngsters in this country. Of course, math does not consist solely of such routine. However, this example demonstrates the subtle influence of language structure.
>
> Another possibility is the effect of the tone of the language. Japanese is rather imprecise but psychologically warmer than the more precise but perhaps drier character of the English language. This subtle difference may also cause different psychological attitudes in the learning process of youngsters.

4. A letter appeared in an advice column in a magazine aimed at young women. The letter writer commented that she would prefer to be called a *girl* or a *lady* than a *woman*, concluding "Women must battle patriarchy, but we must choose our battles." The response from the columnist suggested, "Ponder the following headlines:
   • Women battle patriarchy.
   • Ladies battle patriarchy.
   • Girls battle patriarchy." (Goldhor Lerner, 1993, p. 40).
   Do these three headlines sound different to you? Why? What subsystem are you working with when you try to answer these questions?

5. Working with your classmates, try to translate the following British sentences into American English:
   • My car needs work on the buffer, the windscreen, the bonnet, and the wings.
   • On the way home, could you stop at the chemist's and the news agent?
   • Take the lift. It's just past the pillar box.
   • I called the booking office, and they were out of stalls.
   • Run those through the franking machine and post them.

6. Which of the following assertions are true? Why or why not?
   • Italian is more romantic than English.

- Physics and mathematics cannot be discussed in Navajo.
- English is the most logical language in the world.
- Languages that have writing systems are more creative than languages that do not.
- The languages of primitive societies do not have complex syntactical systems.
- "He gots a hat" is not English.

7. According to an article in the *New York Times* (Speech Therapist, 1993), there is a speech therapist in New York who specializes in transforming people's accents. According to the article, "He teaches senators how to drop their regional accents when they are in Washington, and how to pick them up again on the campaign trail" (p. A10). Why would a public figure want to be able to change language varieties at will?

8. Slang is a form of language that is popular for a short period of time. In some cases, slang enters the language mainstream, and may become standard usage. The word *dis,* derived from disrespect, originated among African American young people, gained popularity among young people in general, and now appears in newspapers and magazines. Can you think of any other examples of slang that have moved toward the linguistic mainstream?

9. *Jargon* is specialized occupationally-related language. Think about your own employment. What kinds of specialized language do you use?

10. It is now possible to access translations on the World Wide Web. Computer translations, however, are far from perfect. An attempt to translate "She is having a bad hair day" into Italian, for example, resulted in "It is for you a defective day of hats, no?" (Kelley, 1998). What are the factors that make translation from one language to another difficult? Do you suppose it will ever be possible to render poetry from one language into another by computer? Why or why not?

Activities

1. Tape record a non-native speaker of English in an informal conversation. Analyze the language sample from a structural perspective: Does the speaker have a noticeable foreign accent? Is the speaker's syntax close to native standards? Apart from your observations about structure, how would you rate the speaker's overall communicative competence? Share your samples with your classmates. Discuss your conclusions.

2. Talk to people who speak more than one language about their experience and understanding of bilingualism. What do they think *bilingual* means? How did they learn their languages? Which languages do they use for different situations? What attitudes do they have about their languages? About bilingualism in general?

Suggestions for Further Reading

Bryson, B. (1994). *Made in America: An informal history of the English language in the United States.* New York: William Morrow.

> You might be surprised to know that President Benjamin Harrison established a Board on Geographic Names in an attempt to standardize place naming in the United States. According to this entertaining book, Greasy Corner, Arkansas, Bugtussle, Texas, and others equally picturesque escaped this standard and are still on the map. Made in America *is a treat for language students.*

Crystal, D. (1997). *The Cambridge encyclopedia of language* (2nd ed.). Cambridge, UK: Cambridge University Press.

> This book touches on everything you ever wanted to know about language in an entertaining format that includes maps, illustrations, and lists of every description.

Freeman, D. E., & Freeman, Y. S. (2004). *Essential linguistics: What you need to know to teach reading, ESL, spelling, phonics, grammar.* Portsmouth, NH: Heinemann.

> All teachers are concerned about teaching reading and language arts to all their students. A solid background in the nature and dynamics of language is in many respects the most useful tool for effectively developing students' literacy. Essential Linguistics *provides that background at an appropriate level of depth for beginning teachers.*

Morris, D. (1977). *Manwatching: A field guide to human behavior.* New York: Harry N. Abrams.

> An entertaining analysis of nonlinguistic communication, this colorfully illustrated book discusses gestures, eye contact, clothing, cosmetics, use of objects, and other human behaviors that transmit messages.

Nunberg, G. (2001). *The way we talk now: Commentaries on language and culture.* Boston: Houghton Mifflin.

> A collection of essays on language most of which were aired over the last ten years on National Public Radio. Thoughtful and informative, these essays make the reader stop and take a new look at the language we use every day.

Tannen, D. (1990). *You just don't understand: Women and men in conversation.* New York: Morrow.

> Gender differences are fascinating, and it's not surprising that this discussion of the ways that men and women use language was a long-standing best seller.

Wardhaugh, R. (1993). *Investigating language: Central problems in linguistics.* Oxford, UK: Blackwell.

> An excellent overview of language and the theories about how humans learn it. Includes a glossary of basic terms.

Wolfram, W., & Ward, B. (Eds.). (2006). *American voices: How dialects differ from coast to coast.* Oxford, UK: Blackwell.

> Written by well-known experts for a broad-based audience, this engaging book describes a multitude of American regional and social dialects. Short chapters describe the features of the many ways we speak English in the United States, and the occasional insertion of a regional glossary is both informative and entertaining.

chapter 4

Language Development

In the period between birth and age four or five, children learn to express themselves with language. How they accomplish this impressive feat is not completely understood, although great strides have been made in the study of language development in the last 25 years.

A survey of the research in language development is an enormous undertaking. An understanding, however, of how children acquire language is essential for dual language curriculum development and instruction. This chapter will present a brief overview of first language development and second language acquisition theories.

First Language Development: Memorizing or Hypothesizing?

People often assume that children develop a first language by simply imitating what they hear around them; in fact, that was once the traditional view of first language development. According to the behaviorist view, for example, children reproduce language, or approximate imitations of what they hear, and are reinforced by rewards, such as attention or response.

Although such views were widely held well into the twentieth century, the notion that imitation and habit formation are the primary bases for language development is flawed. Imitation theory does not account for the creative capacity of language—the child's ability to produce original utterances.

The well-known linguist Noam Chomsky revolutionized thinking about language development in the early 1950s when he suggested that children are born with an innate capacity to develop language. Chomsky suggested that children have a built-in mechanism, which he called the *Language Acquisition Device,* or LAD, that preprograms them to develop grammar based on the linguistic input they receive. Today it's easy to create an analogy for Chomsky's model based on computers: think of the LAD as the operating system, and a particular language as software, installed incrementally as input is received.

Chomsky's view dramatically altered thinking about language development. Psycholinguists moved away from the traditional behaviorist idea that language is developed through habit formation and began to consider the idea that children discover the organizing principles of the language they are exposed to. Recent theory has expanded Chomsky's original focus on syntax, suggesting that children make sense of semantic and pragmatic systems of language as well. Overall, however, modern theories agree that children develop language by hypothesis testing, or rule finding.

RULE FINDING

As we saw in the first chapter, language is a system, governed by rules at the phonological, morphological, syntactical, semantic, and pragmatic levels. The rule-finding approach to language development suggests that children develop hypotheses about the rules of their language based on the input they receive and then test those hypotheses by trying them out.

The evidence we have for children's rule finding comes from the "errors" they make when they apply the rules they have formulated. *Error* has a special meaning in this context. It does not mean *mistake,* but refers instead to the forms generated by applying rules that do not take irregularities or exceptions into account. Errors of this kind are called *overgeneralizations.* These systematic errors reveal the strategies the child is using to create language. The rules of the child's system can be inferred from the error patterns.

Some syntactical overgeneralizations may be familiar to you. English-speaking children quickly find the general rule for plurals: *Cat* becomes *cats,* *dog* becomes *dogs,* and so on. Having arrived at a way to construct plurals, a child will then say "I have two foots." *Foots* is an error resulting from a systematic attempt to apply the rule for plurals to all situations, without taking exceptions into account.

On the phonological level, English-speaking children notice that a word may have more than one syllable. They express that fact by repeating the first syllable or syllables (Ervin-Tripp, 1976). A small child, daunted by the word *refrigerator,* converts it to *freda-freda.* The child is saying "I can't quite manage it yet, but I know this word has more than one syllable."

In Spanish, the first-person form of a verb in the present tense results from dropping the infinitive ending and adding "-o" to the root. For example, *tomar* (to take) becomes *tomo* (I take); *comer* (to eat) becomes *como* (I eat). When you ask small children in Spanish if they know something, they often reply *sabo,* from the verb *saber* (to know). *Sabo* seems logically correct, but it is an "error" resulting from overgeneralization of a rule. The syntactically correct form is an exception to the rule. As children mature, they learn to use *sé.*

Children even overgeneralize at the semantic level of language. For instance, a young child may use the word *doggie* to refer to other animals, like cats and horses. In that case, *doggie* is an overgeneralization that refers to four-footed furry animals.

When children grasp the organizational principles underlying language, they can produce and understand novel utterances—things they have never heard or said before. Rules children generate sometimes produce language that differs from adult language. Child language, however, is neither haphazard nor an inept imitation of adult language. Child language is a system in itself—in fact, a series of systems, that gradually evolves into the adult form of the language.

First Language Development and Comprehensible Input

Chomsky originally proposed that LAD allowed children to make sense of the linguistic input they were receiving, even though that input was fragmented and confused.

Contrary to Chomsky's assertion, subsequent research indicates that linguistic input directed at children is in fact carefully organized (Macaulay, 1980). This reversal of thinking about linguistic input is important. It moves the focus for the study of language acquisition from the biological component to the social component, which features the child and the provider of linguistic input as active participants in language development.

CHILD-DIRECTED SPEECH

Child-directed speech is a phenomenon that has intrigued linguists and psycholinguists. Recent research has analyzed the special register used with children, sometimes called *child-directed speech, caretaker speech,* or *motherese.* In certain settings, it seems that mothers engage in a special kind of "conversation" with their babies while nursing them (Snow, 1977). Such a conversation might seem one-sided, with the mother doing most of the talking, except that mothers are exceptionally forgiving about what they will accept as a response. Initially, burping, yawning, sneezing, and other incidental sounds are acceptable to a mother as responses. Long before the emergence of the child's speech, these interactions between mother and infant apparently teach turn-taking, a basic skill in human communication.

One recent study compared the way Russian, Swedish, and American mothers talked to their children with the way women generally speak to other adults. The researchers noticed that mothers exaggerated vowels, slowed their rate of speech, and raised their pitch when they talked to their infant children. One possible explanation is that this kind of speech provides a model that is easy for babies to imitate. Mothers' linguistic modifications were similar across three languages, which suggests that these strategies may be universal (Barinaga, 1997).

Apparently, adults and even other children naturally modify their speech to encourage children's language development. Comprehensible input for children is provided through a variety of strategies such as:

- Speaking slowly.
- Using simple vocabulary—in short, simple sentences.
- Avoiding pausing before the end of a sentence.
- Exaggerating intonation and raising voice pitch.
- Repetition.

An instruction for an adult, for example, might be: "The cereal is on the second shelf to the left of the coffee." On the other hand, for a child the same instruction might take this form: "See the red coffee can? Up on the shelf over the blue dishes? Yes, that one. The cereal is next to it. Good, you got it."

THE SOCIAL AND CULTURAL CONTEXTS OF LANGUAGE ACQUISITION

Research on caretaker speech, or motherese, as characterized above, has generally focused on middle-class English speakers (Peters, 1985). This focus is shifting as we begin to recognize that language learning is inseparable from culture learning. In an analysis of language acquisition among the Kaluli of Papua New Guinea, Schiefflin (1985) remarked, "Every society has its own ideology about language, including when it begins and how children acquire it" (p. 531).

Kaluli people (Schiefflin, 1985) assume that infants are incapable of understanding, and they rarely address them directly except to use their names. It is assumed that children begin to speak when they use the single-syllable words for *mother* and *breast*. From that time on, children are instructed directly by their caretakers in how to respond to a third party. For example, if two children are playing, a Kaluli mother may instruct one to respond to the other, "Give me that," followed by the instruction, "Say like that."

Givón (1985) reports that the Utes, who are Northern Plains Indians living in the United States, discourage interaction between adults and children. In general, people are not encouraged to speak out in council until they have reached the age of 40 or 50. It is not surprising, therefore, that Ute children are expected to listen and not talk to adults. These children receive most of their linguistic input from other children.

In other words, language acquisition is a subset of the larger socialization process. It is a particularly important subset because nearly everything we do involves language. The primary knowledge a child learns through language is how to become a competent member of a particular society. The Kaluli and the Ute cultures illustrate that concepts about the nature of children, the nature of language, and therefore the nature of linguistic interaction vary from one culture to another, depending on values and beliefs.

INPUT MODIFICATION

It is interesting to note that as the child's language develops, the strategies and modifications of adult language providers change (Garnica, 1977). As children mature, adults reduce the number of special cues and hints they provide to facilitate communication. Adults are remarkably patient with tiny infants, accepting even the sounds of body functions as responses in conversation. We are more demanding of toddlers, but still tolerant of the limits of their language ability. The older a child gets, the more we expect a child's language to approximate the norms of adult language.

Awareness of the modification of input for new language learners helps us develop strategies for second language instruction and content instruction in the second language. Linguistic modifications made consciously as part of an instructional program can assist students to gain competence in a second language.

STAGES OF FIRST LANGUAGE DEVELOPMENT

Crying. Children all over the world move through the same stages of language development. At first, children cry to express dissatisfaction. Crying is not speech, but it does have elements of speech, such as intonation, pattern, and pitch. Recent experimentation suggests that infants use the fussy transitional period between quietude and crying to explore their speech organs and discover new sound possibilities (Campbell-Jones, 1985). Between the ages of two and four months, babies add cooing, an expression of pleasure or satisfaction, to their repertoire.

Babbling. At about the age of five months, babies begin to babble. Babbling children are exploring the potential range of speech production, practicing using their speech organs, and controlling them via the brain. The sounds made by a babbling child are not particularly related to the sound of the language that child hears. All normal children are born with the same organs for speech production, and all babbling babies sound much the same.

The quality of babbling changes, however, at about the age of six months, when children begin echolalic babbling. At that stage, a child seems to produce with greater frequency the sounds that are prevalent in the language the child is hearing. There are conflicting views about the function of echolalic babbling, but it seems to be a ruling-out process, where the child eliminates those sounds that are not meaningful in the native language and attempts to imitate those sounds that are (Sachs, 1985).

Telegraphic Speech. Around the age of one year, children can produce a one-word utterance, and, sometime in the second year, speech expands to two-word utterances. These early utterances generally refer initially to the appearance or disappearance of something: "All-gone milk" is a concept that has significance for very young children. Psycholinguists have attempted to identify the relationship between cognitive and linguistic development. In general, they have concluded that children have to grasp a concept, or at least a rudimentary version of it, before they can produce the language for it (Gleason, 1985).

The Origins of Human Language

Nobody is really certain how or when humans began to talk, but people have always speculated about the origins of human language. According to Crystal (1987), in the seventh century B.C.E., an Egyptian king sent two newborns to live with a shepherd who had strict orders not to speak to them. From the sounds they made, the king concluded that Phrygian was the first human language. Experiments of that sort have been reported throughout history, but the puzzle has not been solved.

Otto Jespersen, a Danish linguist who lived in the first half of the twentieth century offers an idyllic theory of how humans developed language:

> [T]he genesis of language is not to be sought in the prosaic, but in the poetic side of life: the source of speech is not gloomy seriousness, but merry play and youthful hilarity. And among the emotions which were most powerful in eliciting outbursts of music and of song, love must be placed in the front rank. . . . In primitive speech I hear the laughing cries of exultation when lads and lasses vied with one another to attract the attention of the other sex, when everybody sang his merriest and danced his bravest to lure a pair of eyes to throw admiring glances in his direction. Language was born in the courting days of mankind. (pp. 433–434)

Recently theorists have proposed the less romantic idea that human language evolved from primate calls (Pinker, 1994), from grooming behaviors (Dunbar, 1996), or from gestures (Corballis, 2002).

Experts also debate when human language emerged. McWhorter (2001) suggests that human speech began about 150,000 years ago. Whatever its origins and whenever it developed, our complex communication code sets us apart from all other species. Lieberman (1998) eloquently concludes his book on the origins of language suggesting that "surely we must use the gift of speech, language, and thought to enhance life and love, to vanquish needless suffering and murderous violence—to achieve yet a higher morality. For if we do not, Eve's descendants will reach their end. . . . And no other creature will be here to sing a dirge or tell the story of our passing, for we alone can talk" (p. 151).

Meanings expand during the two-word stage, and children develop telegraphic speech. Telegraphic speech is abbreviated, or elliptical in nature, like the language used in telegrams. Children in this stage rely on gestures to elaborate what they mean. For example, "Daddy up" may mean "Daddy, wake up," "Daddy, pick me up," "Daddy, stand up," or any number of things, depending on the situation. After the two-word stage children move to a three-word utterance stage. As the child's utterances grow longer, reliance on gestures diminishes, and complex grammatical forms develop. Figure 4.1 illustrates the stages of language development.

ORDER OF ACQUISITION

The stages of language development are universal and progress from the simple to the complex. Remember, however, that what may be simple in one

● FIGURE 4.1   The Stages of First Language Development

Age	Language Accomplishment	Examples
0–2 months	Crying (expresses discomfort)	
2–4 months	Cooing (expresses satisfaction or pleasure)	aaa, ooo
4–9 months	Babbling, changing to echolalic babbling	gagaga, mamamama
9–18 months	One-word utterances	milk
18 months– 2½ years	Two-word utterances; the beginning of syntax, expanding to three-word utterances	more milk, baby up now
2½–4 years	Expanded syntax and vocabulary	I eated the cookie

(Note that every child develops at a different rate. Ages are always approximate.)

language can be relatively complex in another. For example, in English, we can indicate that the book belongs to Mommy by saying "Mommy's book." In Yiddish, a highly inflected language, the construction changes to "the book of the Mommy," and the word for *Mommy* is altered to indicate that it has become an indirect object in the phrase. English-speaking children will learn to express possessive forms earlier than their Yiddish-speaking peers.

A normal child enters kindergarten with a vocabulary of approximately 8,000 words and an excellent grasp of syntax, which provide the foundation for the language and literacy development that will follow in school. This accomplishment provides a strong rationale for providing primary language instruction in the early grades. As we will see, it is logical to begin early skill instruction in that language, building on the conceptual and linguistic framework the child brings to school.

CHILDREN AS SOCIOLINGUISTS

Like adults, children alter their language to respond to the setting, the function of the interaction, and the relative status of the individuals involved. For example, children differentiate between formal and informal speech, possibly as the result of the emphasis adults place on politeness.

Children also assign different language characteristics to males and females. While most evidence of gender-related speech differences is anecdotal rather than empirical, we do know that there are societal stereotypes regarding language and gender. It has been demonstrated that as early as preschool, children participate in common stereotypical expectations about how males and females use language. For example, using puppets and role playing, researchers found that young children consider tag questions and indirect requests appropriate for females, and associate direct and competitive speech with males (for a review, see Warren-Leubecker & Bohannon, 1985).

Bilingual children develop a keen sense of the relative prestige of their two languages (Saville-Troike, 1976). Teachers must be aware of the relative status of each language they use in a dual language setting, so as to counteract the negative biases children may bring to the classroom (Legarreta-Marcaida, 1981).

Second Language Acquisition

How do people learn a second language? Do they rely mainly on transferring knowledge from their first language to their second? Or do they recapitulate first language development, sorting out the organizing principles of their new language as they are exposed to it?

Proponents of the transfer approach have analyzed the errors people make in their second language to see if they are the result of interference from the old habits of their first. Proponents of the developmental position look for evidence that learners engage in a rule-finding process as they acquire their second language. Understanding the process of second language acquisition is useful to dual language teachers because it can provide insights into ways to structure effective second language instruction.

Researchers in the area of second language acquisition have discovered that the process is quite complex because language learning is a multifaceted problem-solving activity. Much as they would approach any problem, people approach language learning using the information and abilities they already have. Using first language knowledge and skills may produce errors that resemble interference, but which are in fact evidence of a creative cognitive strategy for solving the new language puzzle. In other words, transfer of language information may be part of the process. In addition, evidence suggests that second language learners may also recapitulate the first language developmental process. The surface manifestations of that process, or the language they produce, may not resemble first language development at every stage because the learners come to the process with useful prior knowledge and cognitive maturity.

Given the many variables that might affect the process of second language acquisition, it is not surprising that researchers have launched their investigations from a variety of viewpoints. The following sections briefly discuss the possible effects of age, personality, and social setting on learning a second language. Remember, however, that these factors are artificially distinguished for study purposes. Our best understanding of second language acquisition indicates that the process involves an integration of psychological, social, and linguistic factors.

THE EFFECT OF AGE

It is generally assumed that children learn second languages better than adults do. Lenneberg (1967) lent credence to that notion when he proposed that a second language is best learned in the "critical period" between the age of two years and the onset of puberty. He suggested that the ability to learn languages is debilitated by the completion of a process of lateralization in the brain, when each side of the brain develops its own specialized functions. A recent study using a form of brain scanning has produced evidence that young language learners learning two languages use the same part of the brain for both, whereas older learners use a different part of the brain for their second language than they used for their first (Kim, Relkin, Lee, & Hirsch, 1997).

The critical period idea is intuitively appealing, but it should be noted that much empirical research has focused primarily on pronunciation. Some analysis suggests that children who learn their second language before puberty do in fact acquire native-like pronunciation, unlike adults, who usually speak a second language with an accent. Larsen-Freeman and Long (1991) summarize the research on the effect of age on second language acquisition, commenting "younger is better in the most crucial area, ultimate attainment, with only quite young (child starters) being able to achieve accent-free, native-like performance" (p. 155).

According to Bialystok and Hakuta (1994), younger is indeed better, but with an interesting twist that aligns nicely with the new neurolinguistic findings described above. They suggest that if in fact there is a critical period, it is less likely to be related to brain lateralization and the onset of puberty at adolescence, and more likely to be the period before the age of five. They qualify that notion, commenting that "one reason why children younger than five years old behave like native speakers is that they *are* native speakers" (p. 79). In other words, before the age of five or so, children are acquiring a language as a native speaker might, and are not really second language learners at all.

The comparison of adults and children and the focus on pronunciation obscure the real issue for educators. What is of interest to us is whether

---

ℒearning a New Language

To tell you the truth, the hardest thing about coming to this country wasn't the winter everyone warned me about—it was the language. If you had to choose the most tongue-twisting way of saying you love somebody or how much a pound for the ground round, then say it in English.

SOURCE: The mother, in ¡*Yo!* by Julia Alvarez. Chapel Hill: Algonquin Books, 1997.

younger or older children are better at developing the kind of second language proficiency they need for school. And the answer to that question is complex. Collier (1987) points out, "It depends. It depends on the learner's cognitive style, socioeconomic background, formal schooling in first language, and many other factors" (p. 1). Collier goes on to conclude, however, that it is safe to say that children between the ages of eight and twelve acquire a second language faster than children between the ages of four and seven, which may be related to cognitive maturity and first language competence. Children past the age of twelve seem to slow down, and that may be because the demands made of them in school are out of keeping with the level of language that they bring to bear. (See Chapter 5 for a discussion of Cognitive Academic Language Proficiency, the kind of language children need for school.)

THE EFFECT OF PERSONALITY

If you have been a second language learner you may have found on occasion that your ability to use the language is enhanced after you've had a glass of wine in a relaxed, informal setting. It may surprise you to know that researchers have also noticed this phenomenon and have actually studied the effect of alcohol on second language performance. This is not as silly as it may appear at first glance, because it would be useful for us to understand the role of personality factors like inhibitions in second language learning.

If you are a person who can easily shed your inhibitions, you may be willing to take some of the risks involved in trying out a new language. Other personality characteristics may also affect your ability to learn a second language. For example, if you are a person with strong self-esteem, you may be well equipped to withstand some of the embarrassment that naturally occurs when you make language errors. If you are naturally outgoing, you may be likely to become involved in situations where you can use and practice your new language and facilitate its development (Brown, 1987).

Some caution is called for here: In the first place, it is difficult to define personality traits. Even with operational definitions, personality traits are difficult to measure. Nevertheless, it seems clear that individual psychological traits have an effect on the ability to learn a second language.

THE SOCIAL FACTORS

Communication is at the heart of language, and the need to establish communication is a powerful motivation for language development. Therefore, it is essential to consider the nature of interaction between people in social contexts and the effects of that interaction on second language acquisition.

In first language development, for example, it has been noted that motherese, or caretaker speech, is often ungrammatical. In one well-known study (Brown, Cazden, & Bellugi, 1973), it was found that parents do not correct statements made by their children if they are grammatically deficient, but do correct them if they are untrue. In other words, parents are more concerned with the content of communication than with form.

Richard-Amato (1988) points out: "When the child says 'Daddy home' for the first time, no one labels this a mistake. . . . Instead it is thought of as being ingenious and cute and the child is hugged or rewarded verbally" (p. 36). Caretakers are delighted by a child's verbalizations and are anxious to promote interaction that may facilitate language development. Likewise, in situations with second language learners or speakers, native speakers may alter or modify their speech to facilitate understanding and response. This has been called *foreigner-talk*. In general, second language learners may do well in settings that emphasize communication.

One observer (Seliger, 1977) has noted that small children will participate in and appear to enjoy interactions that may be difficult or impossible for them to comprehend, which may function as a way of generating input. It is possible that the inclination to initiate and maintain interaction may be a strategy that distinguishes successful second language learners. In other words, some people may be better than others at creating situations that generate input, which brings us back to the question of the effect of personality on language ability and demonstrates the links between the social and psychological aspects of second language learning.

Integrative Models of Second Language Acquisition

Sufficient information on second language acquisition exists to enable us to formulate hypothetical models of the process. Models can then provide frameworks for additional research and coherent instructional programs. The sections that follow discuss two theoretical approaches to second language acquisition. These are but a small sample of the ways this process has been analyzed, but the two theories described here are useful because they integrate psychological and social considerations.

THE ACQUISITION–LEARNING DISTINCTION

Stephen Krashen (1981) has proposed a distinction between *language acquisition* and *language learning*. Language acquisition, in informal terms, is picking up a language—learning it unconsciously from the social environment. Language learning, on the other hand, is learning a language or learning about a language in a formal sense, for example, in a classroom setting. According to Krashen's theory, children develop language through acquisition, by understanding language that is a little beyond their capabilities, presented by language providers who communicate with the child in a modified form.

These small increments of language, available to the learner when they are embedded in comprehensible input, are particularly accessible in nonthreatening, low anxiety situations. Krashen refers to the affective component of language learning as an *affective filter,* a kind of emotional barrier to language learning that must be lowered if acquisition is to take place.

Krashen suggests that language learning is different from language acquisition in the following way: Learning provides a *monitor,* which allows the learner to correct language output. This monitor, however, is useful only when the learner knows the appropriate language rule, has time to use it, and is focused on form, as in writing. In this framework, acquired language is viewed as more important and more useful than learned language in the quick give-and-take of ordinary communication. According to Krashen, in real communication situations, second language learners most often use the language they have acquired, rather than the language they have learned.

The distinction between learning and acquisition, the concept of the monitor, and the role of affective considerations may shed light on some of the issues currently debated in second language theory. The theoretical distinction between learning and acquisition and the monitor construct provide keys to the process in general. Krashen's theory suggests that transfer errors, or errors that reflect first language structures, appear when an individual is relying on the monitor. To the extent that an individual functions in an acquired-language mode, "errors" will replicate developmental errors.

The model also suggests answers to questions about specific variables. For example, it addresses the concern about the relationship between age and the ability to gain a second language. In the short run, older learners seem to gain competence in a second language more rapidly than young children. The model suggests that they may be better monitor users. On the other hand, children outperform adults in second language in the long run. Krashen's theory suggests that children are less likely to rely too heavily on the monitor and are less prone to the anxiety that often accompanies second language learning. Similarly, individual variation in second language ability can be explained in terms of both individual ability to use a monitor appropriately and quickly and individual willingness to take risks and rely on acquired language.

Krashen's theory has gained tremendous popularity among classroom teachers and has led to the development of innovative methodology that moves significantly away from grammar-translation and other traditional approaches. (The natural language approach, based on Krashen's theory, is discussed in Chapter 7.) At the same time, Krashen has drawn fire from critics of the model (Ellis, 1988; Larsen-Freeman & Long, 1991) who suggest that it is flawed because:

- The concept of an unbreachable distinction between acquisition and learning doesn't fit with what we already know about subconscious and conscious learning, which seem to exist on a continuum.
- Krashen doesn't really tell us what goes on cognitively during acquisition and learning.

- We cannot empirically test either the acquisition–learning distinction or the monitor construct.

Finally, Krashen's model places more emphasis on the importance of input than output. In Krashen's view, hypothesis testing is an internal process whereby learners match up input with the knowledge they already have about the language. From his perspective, output is mainly useful insofar as it generates input. Swain (1985), however, has suggested that output is essential to language acquisition. Talking to someone in a new language requires the speakers to use all the language resources they have to come up with language the listener can understand—something that might be called "comprehensible output" (Swain, 1985, p. 249).

If we assume that both input and output are essential to language acquisition, we are led to consider the dynamic interaction between the language learner and the social environment. The next section describes a theory that places interaction in a central role.

LANGUAGE LEARNERS AND LANGUAGE SPEAKERS INTERACT

In 1979, Lily Wong Fillmore completed a study of ten early primary school children, in which five Spanish speakers were paired with five English speakers for an hour of daily play time. The Spanish-speaking children in the study used similar strategies to acquire English in varying degrees, but no one was more successful than Nora. Wong Fillmore remarks, "The secret of Nora's spectacular success as a language learner can be found in the special combination of interests, inclinations, skills, temperament, needs, and motivations that comprised her personality" (p. 221). "Nora put herself in a position to receive maximum exposure to the new language" (p. 222).

Wong Fillmore (1985) suggests that three components are necessary for an effective language learning situation:

- The learners.
- The speakers of the language the learner wants to learn.
- The social setting that brings learners and speakers together.

Once the learners and the speakers have been brought together, three types of interactive processes take place. First, there are social processes. In social processes, learners assume that the language used is relevant to the immediate situation, and speakers cooperate with that assumption. Second, there are linguistic processes. Learners use what they already know about language to try to make sense out of the linguistic input they receive. And third, there are cognitive strategies that learners use to figure out the relationships between what is happening and the language being used. Nora made maximum use of the strategies Wong Fillmore describes. It's important to notice that Nora, like other young children, did not have a language learning agenda. Rather, she wanted to make friends and play with other children, and learned English as a concomitant to social involvement.

Wong Fillmore also suggests (1991) that the ability of language learners to utilize strategies is affected by the social context. She emphasizes that all the factors are interrelated and proposes that situations involving contact with speakers of the target language and consequently the amount and type of input a learner receives may be related to the age of the learner.

For example, in the United States, young newcomers attend school, where they are likely to meet English speakers and to have classroom experiences that provide them with comprehensible input in English. Older immigrants, however, often find jobs where coworkers share their primary language, which limits their exposure to English. Also, older learners may find it harder than younger ones to get the kind of interaction they need to develop a new language. Young children can manage their social interactions with language that is not very complex. In fact, very young children often play happily together even though they may not understand each other's language. Adults, on the other hand, cannot participate fully in social interaction without the use of language, so beginning speakers are at a social disadvantage.

Wong Fillmore's model proposes that variations in language learning may result from a complex relationship of differences in individual personalities, cognitive abilities, and social skills, as well as from the social context itself. Wong Fillmore's analysis emphasizes the dynamic role of social interaction in second language learning.

Summary

Traditionally it was assumed that children developed language through imitation and habit formation. Chomsky revolutionized thinking about language development by theorizing that we can explain original utterances only by assuming that children have an innate language learning device that enables them to deduce the rules of syntax. Subsequent theorists have suggested that children apply this rule-finding approach to the semantic and pragmatic systems of language as well.

Theorists in second language acquisition ask whether second languages are acquired by transfer of first language knowledge or through a developmental process that parallels first language acquisition. Krashen distinguishes between language learning and language acquisition in an attempt to explain why some research produces evidence of transfer and other research substantiates the developmental process in second language development. Wong Fillmore suggests that learners make use of cognitive, linguistic, and social strategies during social interactions to acquire a new language.

First language development and second language acquisition theories will enable teachers in dual language settings to make decisions about methodologies for first language development and second language instruction.

Questions to Think About and Discuss

1. Think about the pedagogical implications of Krashen's and Wong Fillmore's theories of second language acquisition. In other words, based on their theoretical frameworks, how would you best organize your classroom to maximize second language learning?

Activities

1. Record an audio or video of an interaction between a child age one to three and the child's parent. Identify the strategies the parent uses to facilitate the communication. For example, how does the parent acknowledge the child's role in the conversation? Does the parent repeat what the child says? Paraphrase or elaborate on the child's contribution. Identify any strategies the child uses to maintain or prolong the interaction. What stage of language development has the child reached? Give examples that support your choice.
2. Visit a classroom and observe an English as a second language lesson. Note the materials and the methods. What assumptions are being made in this setting about how people learn language? For example, does instruction mainly consist of oral pattern drills? Completion of grammar exercises?
3. Interview an immigrant who is learning English as a second language. How does this person view the process of second language learning: Is this person taking classes or learning the language informally? Is the process easy or difficult? What is the most difficult part of the process? In this person's view, what factors have facilitated the process; that is, what helped the most?

Suggestions for Further Reading

Bialystok, E. (Ed.). (1991). *Language processing in bilingual children*. Cambridge, UK: The Cambridge University Press.

The articles in this book contain descriptions of original research on bilingual children's acquisition of language. The chapter by Wong Fillmore, "Second-language learning in children: A model of language learning in social context," is an excellent summary of her longitudinal research and the conclusions she has drawn from it.

Bialystok, E., & Hakuta, K. (1994). *In other words: The science and psychology of second language acquisition*. New York: Basic Books.

An update on second language acquisition theory that brings together a variety of perspectives, organized around language, the brain, the mind, the self, and culture as the "channels that jointly comprise the ecosystem of language learning" (p. viii). Discussions of research offer insights into the complexity of second language learning. This is an extremely readable book, enhanced by anecdotes and reflections gleaned from the authors' own experiences that allow the reader to connect research and theory to everyday experiences.

Brown, H. D. (1987). *Principles of language learning and teaching* (2nd ed.). Englewood Cliffs, NJ: Prentice-Hall.

An update of a well-known book on second language learning, this edition provides clear, concise explanations of theories of second language acquisition. The book is enhanced by the addition of an "in the classroom" section at the end of each chapter that highlights second language teaching methodologies.

de Villiers, P. A., & de Villiers, J. G. (1979). *Early language.* Cambridge, MA: Harvard University Press.

An easy to read, straightforward discussion of the course of language development, this book is enlivened by samples of children's language.

Gass, S. M., & Selinker, L. (1994). *Second language acquisition: An introductory course.* Hillsdale, NJ: Lawrence Erlbaum.

A detailed, comprehensive, multidisciplinary analysis of adult second language acquisition.

Gleason, J. B. (Ed.). (1985). *The development of language.* Columbus, OH: Merrill.

Ten articles that provide an overview of theory and research of first language development across the entire life span. The chapter on language in society (Warren-Leubecker and Bohannon) is an excellent summary of research regarding acquisition of the social rules of language.

Krashen, S. D. (2003). *Explorations in language acquisition and use: The Taipei lectures.* Portsmouth, NH: Heinemann.

Based largely on a series of lectures that the author presented in 2001 at National Taipei University in Taiwan, this book provides an excellent review of Krashen's theories, along with a discussion of comprehensible output and its role in second language acquisition.

Larsen-Freeman, D., & Long, M. H. (1991). *An introduction to second language research.* New York: Longman.

Just about everything you wanted to know about second language acquisition is included in this well-organized book, which explains second language acquisition research methods, describes and critiques prevailing theories, and discusses implications for instruction.

Lightbown, P., & Spada, N. (1993). *How languages are learned.* Oxford, UK: Oxford University Press.

Contains an overview of theories of first language development and second language acquisition, followed by a discussion of approaches to teaching second language that emphasizes the relevance of research to practice.

Miller, T. (2007). *How I learned English.* Washington, DC: National Geographic.

A fascinating collection of very short essays by Latino writers, scholars, and professionals describing their encounters and struggles with English. In the foreword, the well-known journalist Ray Suarez comments that if you have ever tried to learn a new language, "you will recognize yourself somewhere in these pages" (p. xiv).

Ventriglia, L. (1982). *Conversations of Miguel and Maria: How children learn English as a second language: Implications for classroom teaching.* Reading, MA: Addison-Wesley.

Based on analysis of children's conversations, this book analyzes second language acquisition strategies and presents classroom methods based on those strategies. Emphasis is on the importance of social context in second language acquisition.

chapter 5

Student Assessment

$\mathcal{A}$ccountability is at the top of the educational agenda in the United States at the present time. Educators as well as the public are increasingly interested in setting standards for students, measuring student performance with reference to those standards, and ascertaining the effectiveness of educational programs in supporting student achievement. The federal legislation called the No Child Left Behind Act (a reauthorization and revamping of the Elementary and Secondary Education Act) has accountability as its centerpiece.

Assessment involves making determinations about appropriate standards, identifying where students start, figuring out what constitutes adequate performance, and deciding when students have achieved it. But schooling is multidimensional, classrooms are complex, and what success looks like is hard to define in our large and diverse society. Therefore, assessing student performance is difficult and often controversial. In addition, the complexities inherent in student assessment are significantly multiplied when students are second language learners who may be capable of the academic work demanded of them but may not have the language skills to demonstrate or express their abilities.

This chapter will begin with issues that educators who test second language learners must address in order to make sound judgments about learners' needs and capabilities. It will also include an overview of three kinds of assessments related to second language learners: language proficiency testing, high stakes testing, and diagnostic testing for placement in special programs.

Testing Second Language Learners: General Issues

RELIABILITY

Reliability asks the question, "Does this instrument produce the same results each time it is used?" Obviously, no two testing situations are identical. Some rooms are more comfortable than others. Students who are tested in the afternoon may be more tired than students who are tested in the morning. But a test is reliable when, over a meaningful sample, small situational variations do not produce large variations in scores. Interrater reliability is one important measure of reliability: If two people score the same test, will they come up with comparable scores? Obviously, interrater reliability is not an issue with multiple-choice tests. But reliability of this kind may be a concern in language-proficiency testing, which often includes oral interviews and writing samples. Test scorers need careful training to ensure interrater reliability on those kinds of measures.

VALIDITY

Validity asks the question, "Does this instrument actually test what it says it is testing?" It's hard to know whether an instrument is testing a student's ability with reference to content when that student is working in a new language. Imagine yourself, after several years of Spanish or French, trying to take a university-level final examination administered in your new language in a history or chemistry class. Even if you had mastered the content, you might not be able to completely understand the questions, and you might not be able to express yourself as fully as you would in English.

CONTENT BIAS

The language used in a standardized achievement test may interfere with test validity. For example, as we saw in Chapter 3, vocabulary may differ among regions or social classes. A monkey is a *mono* to a Puerto Rican Spanish-speaking child and a *chango* in the southwestern United States. As we saw earlier, languages not only have different lexicons, they have different grammatical structures as well. For example, Spanish incorporates the subject into the verb. When you say "I have," you can say "yo tengo," but you don't have to. You can simply say "tengo." It's standard, and you will be understood. A translated test that doesn't take structural differences into account will not produce an accurate assessment of a student's ability (Kester & Pena, 2002). Test items that use standard language forms may be perplexing to children who speak regional or social variants of a language.

CAN YOU ELIMINATE CONTENT BIAS WITH TRANSLATION?

Test translation is attractive, since it appears simple and inexpensive and does not require the development of new tests. There are, however, significant disadvantages to translated tests. Translations do not eliminate and may even aggravate content bias. Consider, for example, the word *bat*, a one-syllable English word, easily decoded by a beginning reader. The word *bat* (referring to the animal) translates in Spanish to *murciélago*, a polysyllabic word with an irregular accent, far beyond the skills of an early reader. Such examples are numerous; they serve to illustrate the difficulties inherent in translating tests.

CONSTRUCT BIAS

Most standardized tests are constructed around the values and experiences of mainstream middle-class culture. That is to say, the "correct" answers reflect the values and experiences of a particular normative group, generally the white middle class. So to some extent, standardized tests measure a child's degree of assimilation or "Americanization." Recently, for example, a writing test that is part of the Massachusetts Comprehensive Assessment System asked fourth-grade students to write about a memorable snow day. Several teachers claimed that the item was culturally biased on the grounds that many of their students from the Caribbean and Southeast Asia had no experience of snow or recollection of snow days ("When a Snow Day," 2003).

Cheng (1987) notes that children from various Asian language backgrounds may be unfamiliar with items such as utensils commonly used in the United States for baking, fitted sheets, pumpkin pie, and a whole host of objects, events, people, and ideas that are part of American culture. They may be unable to answer questions that would appear quite simple to a child raised in a highly assimilated mainstream environment.

PROCEDURE

In addition to content, test procedures may also be culturally biased. Expectations, for example, that children will speak up when addressed, or offer elaborate information in response to a question, are not appropriate in every culture. Language proficiency testing situations may be threatening for particular children or cultural groups. Even a very verbal child may refuse to speak freely to a stranger or a person with authority. As Solano-Flores and Trumbull note, "Tests are cultural products, and taking a test is an event for which each student has a 'conceptual frame.' Students' varying cultural and linguistic backgrounds may prepare them with different 'scripts' (schemes) or principles for approaching such an event" (2003, p. 3).

NORMING

Finally, standardized tests are "normed." In other words, the test is given to a group of people and from the outcomes, test developers determine what constitutes "normal" performance. What is normal to one group of people, however, may not be normal to another. To the extent that a norming group excludes people from a particular race, culture, or ethnicity, that test may be considered invalid for making determinations about the excluded group.

Language Proficiency

WHAT IS LANGUAGE PROFICIENCY?

Over the years, many of my students have expressed discomfort about their accents in a second language. However, after listening to and discussing several taped samples of people who speak English as a second language, they generally agree that accent, and even syntax, are not the keys to a person's ability to speak a language. Even this brief and rather superficial exercise leads us to thinking about communicative competence. What are the factors that enable a person to actually use a language in a way that fulfills its main purpose—communication?

MODELS OF LANGUAGE PROFICIENCY

Some theorists employ complex concepts to define and describe the ability to use language. One model cross-references linguistic and sociolinguistic components with comprehension, production, reading, and writing to produce a grid with 64 measurable intersections of proficiency (Hernandez-Chavez, Burt, & Dulay, 1978).

A more succinct framework identifies four components of communicative competence (Canale & Swain, 1980):

- Grammatical competence, which includes the mastery of the sound system of a language, its syntax, and its semantics, as well as knowledge of vocabulary.
- Sociolinguistic competence, which includes the mastery of the use of appropriate forms, registers, and styles of language for different social contexts.
- Discourse competence, which includes the ability to connect utterances in a meaningful way and relate them appropriately to a topic.
- Strategic competence, which includes the ability to compensate for breakdowns in communication.

ACADEMIC LANGUAGE PROFICIENCY

Because such theories fail to account for the developmental relationship between a student's first and second languages, these and similar models of communicative competence have been criticized as inapplicable to minority students' acquisition of English. Native speakers acquire language skills in a predictable order, but the same order of acquisition may not apply to the acquisition of a second language. Second language acquisition may depend on a number of variables, including age and previous schooling. For example, a person may master literacy skills in a second language without ever completely mastering its pronunciation, or vice versa.

Apart from developmental considerations, these general theories of communicative competence fail to take into account the particularities of the school setting, where both the required tasks and the style of communication differ significantly from other daily experiences and communication. Jim Cummins (1994) has formulated a model of language proficiency that accounts for the demands of the classroom.

Cognitively Demanding Tasks. In school, many tasks required of children are new. New tasks tend to be cognitively demanding; that is, they require more thinking. As a task becomes more familiar, it becomes cognitively less demanding and requires less thinking. Reflect for a moment on your own experience of learning to drive. At the outset, driving was probably a demanding task that required a great deal of your attention. If you have been driving for some time, however, you probably do so quite automatically. Practice has made this a cognitively undemanding task. Similarly, reading is generally an automatic skill for most adults. Children who are learning to read, however, are engaged in a cognitively demanding activity.

Communication and Context. Communication can be described on a continuum from context-embedded to context-reduced (Cummins, 1994). Context-embedded communication takes place in the presence of environmental clues. For example, you may have traveled and shopped in a place where you knew little or none of the local language. You were probably able to make your purchases by communicating with gestures and intonation, especially since you and the shopkeeper shared certain assumptions about the nature and purpose of your interaction. In other words, your transaction was supported by context clues.

Context-reduced communication, on the other hand, takes place in the absence of context clues. Most classroom communication is context-reduced. Much as we may try to mediate our lessons with hands-on activities, objects, and illustrations, we are often several steps removed from real-life experience. It is possible, of course, for a class to discuss the weather using context clues such as the students' clothing or an illustrative chart, because weather is concrete and visible. It is far more difficult, however, to provide context clues for abstract concepts such as democracy or photosynthesis.

Language Proficiency in School Settings. The outcome of cross-referencing the intensity of context with the level of cognitive demand can be illustrated with the simple diagram shown in Figure 5.1. Much of what takes place in classrooms falls in quadrant D of the diagram. In other words, what happens in classrooms is often context-reduced and relies heavily on written and verbal explanations in the absence of concrete clues. In addition, classroom tasks are generally cognitively demanding, requiring students to focus on tasks that are new and challenging. According to Cummins, in order to properly assess

● FIGURE *5.1*   Context and Cognitive Load

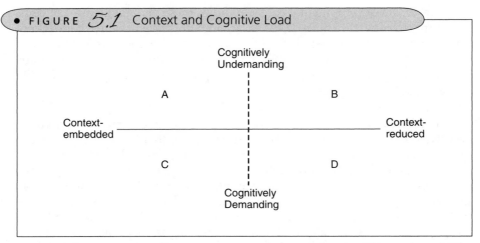

SOURCE: J. Cummins, "The Role of Primary Language Development in Promoting Educational Success for Language Minority Students." In California State Department of Education (Ed.), *Schooling and Language Minority Students: A Theoretical Framework* (Los Angeles: Evaluation, Dissemination, and Assessment Center, California State University, Los Angeles, 2nd ed., 1994, p. 12.)

students' language ability, it is useful to distinguish between two types of language proficiency:

- *Basic Interpersonal Communicative Skills (BICS):* the language skills required for face-to-face communication, where interactions are context-embedded.
- *Cognitive/Academic Language Proficiency (CALP):* the language skills required for academic achievement in a context-reduced environment.

Limited English proficient children quickly acquire BICS in English from their playmates, the media, and their day-to-day experiences, but in assessing their language proficiency we must recognize the distinction between those skills and CALP. The language skills required in any classroom are context-specific and quite different from the basic skills necessary for everyday communication. If we fail to recognize this difference, we may erroneously assume that children have acquired sufficient proficiency in English to succeed in a classroom where only English is used, when in fact they have not.

The distinction between BICS and CALP is not the only theoretical approach to describing language proficiency. The terminology, however, has become popular among practitioners. Cummins's theory has nurtured an awareness that the dynamics of school-related language proficiency are important for an understanding of the rationale for providing academic support in a student's first language as part of the instructional program (see Chapter 6).

HOW IS LANGUAGE PROFICIENCY ASSESSED?

Language assessment is a critical aspect of dual language instruction. Knowledge about a student's language abilities is essential for placement in an appropriate program. Furthermore, the No Child Left Behind Act requires states to assess language proficiency. Generally, language proficiency is assessed using standardized tests. Language proficiency tests may be categorized according to the nature of the tasks they involve and the way they are scored.

- *Discrete point tests:* Based on the assumption that language is the sum of discrete structural units such as phonemes and morphemes, these tests assess mastery of each of the units (Day, McCollum, Cieslak, & Erickson, 1981). For example, a discrete point test might assess phonological ability by asking a student to distinguish between minimal pairs such as *ten* and *den.*
- *Integrative tests:* These tests attempt to assess an individual's ability to use a language for communication. This requires an assessment of a student's understanding of both linguistic and social contexts of a language.

It is possible for a test to require tasks that involve natural and spontaneous language production, which is then scored in a discrete point fashion. For a test to be truly integrative, it should be scored globally, with emphasis on the ability to communicate.

Discrete Point Tests.　Discrete point tests are the least favored in current thinking about communicative competence. Discrete point testing has its roots in the structural linguistic approaches of the 1950s, which emphasized language acquisition as the development of habits across language structures such as phonemes, morphemes, and syntax. Discrete point tests are not generally measures of communicative competence. Second language instructors are often frustrated when students who score well on a language assessment test are not capable of using the language in real-life situations (Day, McCollum, Cieslak, & Erickson, 1981).

Why Are Discrete Point Tests Used?　Despite the inadequacies of discrete point tests, they are often used in schools. Reasons for this may be:

- *Theoretical:* Selection of assessment instruments in some districts may have been made at a time when research in the areas of language acquisition and bilingualism was relatively new.
- *Political:* Legislative mandates for assessment of large numbers of non-English-speaking children required hasty responses on the part of school districts.
- *Practical:* The need to service large numbers of children may have led districts to select assessment instruments that were simple to administer. Also, large-scale testing is expensive. Once a district has made a commitment to a test, a change may be economically unfeasible.

Integrative Tests: Assessing Communication.　Most of the tasks that generally comprise discrete point tests never come up in ordinary discourse. It is unlikely, for example, that anyone would ever ask you to convert a list of nouns into their plural forms in the course of an everyday conversation. But what kinds of tasks can actually demonstrate an individual's understanding of a language and its social context?

Surprisingly, research indicates that dictation is a useful measure of a person's overall language ability. Apparently, the ability to divide up and write down what you hear when you take dictation requires an understanding of meaning. Dictation selections used to assess language ability must approximate normal discourse and should be presented in sequences that are long enough to challenge a student's short-term memory. Dictation tests obviously assume that students are already able to read and write.

Another integrative technique for assessing language ability is cloze testing. A cloze task requires the test taker to fill in the blanks in a passage where words have been left out. It is possible to adapt cloze techniques for children by presenting passages orally.

There are a variety of oral production tasks that can be effective for eliciting language samples from young students to provide material for an assessment. Apart from structured interviews, students can be asked to retell a story or to describe a craft project they have completed using materials supplied by the examiner. In whatever manner an oral production task is structured, it should, as much as possible, motivate spontaneous conversation.

Despite its usefulness, integrative testing is not as common as discrete point testing. Integrative testing is often time-consuming and may require extensive training for test administrators. Also, the concept of global scoring is perceived by many educators as subjective and therefore risky.

The Need for a Multidimensional Approach to Assessment. Formal language proficiency assessment for elementary school children is often limited to assessment of their proficiency in English. Such assessments are incomplete and fail to identify potential strengths and weaknesses. A child who is proficient in English may be proficient in another language as well. A child who is deficient in English may be proficient in another language. A child who is deficient in more than one language may have special needs.

In addition, any given language test is but one sample of an individual's language performance. We know that performance differs from competence and that we can only infer competence from performance. Furthermore, as we have seen, there are many factors that might affect any particular performance. Therefore, language proficiency assessments should include multiple measures. Both discrete point and integrative tests can be useful. In addition, informal teacher observations over time may be far more accurate than any particular test. Multidimensional assessments are needed in order to profile a child's full linguistic repertoire.

Standardized Achievement Testing

The No Child Left Behind Act requires that all states measure student performance in reading and mathematics on an annual basis. The law requires the

In Your Classroom
English Language Proficiency Assessments at a Glance

No Child Left Behind requires that all states develop standards and assessments for English language learners. The first step in the process is identification and assessment of English learners' language proficiency. A variety of approaches has emerged. The following is intended to provide a sample of the kinds of materials currently in use. Readers will want to check their own state requirements and seek information regarding the tests used in their schools.

COMMERCIALLY PREPARED TESTS

Many commercially prepared tests have been revised to specifically address No Child Left Behind requirements. Your district may use one of these so-called off-the-shelf tests. The following is a short list of widely used tests, but the list is far from exhaustive, and your district may use one not included here. Note that web addresses are those of publishers. Links to information about specific tests are readily available on publishers' sites.

- Woodcock-Muñoz Language Survey (WMLS): www.assess.nelson.com
- Language Assessment System (LAS): www.ctb.com
- IDEA Proficiency Test (IPT): www.ballard-tighe,com
- Stanford English Language Proficiency Test (SELP): harcourtassessment.com

STATE-DEVELOPED TESTS

Your state may have developed its own test. California for example, uses the California English Language Development Test (CELDT) and Colorado uses the Colorado English Language Assessment (CELA). Both were developed by CTB McGraw-Hill, www.ctb.com.

CONSORTIUM-DEVELOPED TESTS

To support states in meeting NCLB requirements, the federal Department of Education funded consortia that developed assessments for participating states. For example, the World-Class Instructional Design and Assessment Consortium (WIDA) developed tests that are now in use in Alabama, Delaware, the District of Columbia, Georgia, Illinois, Kentucky, Maine, New Hampshire, New Jersey, North Dakota, Oklahoma, Pennsylvania, Rhode Island, Vermont, and Wisconsin. Your district may be part of a consortium.

---

inclusion of limited English proficient students in accountability programs and testing. States cannot opt out of testing second language learners and must also ensure that those students make progress toward achievement goals over specified time periods. Many states are using standardized tests as the cornerstone of their accountability programs.

Standardized tests are often high stakes tests with outcomes that may have a significant impact on any individual student's educational future. Therefore, educators should be cautious to avoid the obvious pitfalls in standardized testing. Ideally, student assessment should be based in multiple measures. (NCLB is discussed further in Chapter 10, Legal Foundations of Dual Language Instruction; performance assessment for English language learners is discussed in Chapter 7).

Diagnostic Testing for Placement in Special Programs

Minority and language minority students have been historically overrepresented in special education settings and underrepresented in gifted settings. These disproportionalities were the subject of several court cases in the mid-twentieth century. One important federal court decision, *Diana v. State Board of Education in California* (1970), established the right of minority students to nonbiased assessments. *Diana* and other significant cases about discriminatory assessment laid the groundwork for the Education for All Handicapped Children Act of 1975 (PL 94-142), a federal law that sought to ensure due process rights for exceptional children and their parents as well as addressing the need for nondiscriminatory assessment procedures.

More than a quarter of a century after the passage of PL 94-142, disproportionate representation is still an issue. According to research by Artiles et al. (2002), data from California indicate that while Latino students are not overrepresented to the same extent as African American students in special education, English learners are overrepresented, and particularly so in the secondary grades.

The reauthorization of PL 94-142 called the Individuals with Disabilities Education Act (IDEA) of 2004 (42 USC. Section 1400 et seq) mandates that public schools provide a free, appropriate education to all eligible children and youth with disabilities from birth to age 21. IDEA mandates services for children and youth with a wide range of disabilities, including autism; various forms of hearing, visual, and physical disabilities; learning disabilities; emotional disturbances; and speech and language impairment.

IDEA requires that service providers consider cultural and linguistic issues when they identify and evaluate children for disabilities. Tests used must be racially and culturally nondiscriminatory. To the extent possible, tests must be administered in a child's native language. Efforts must be made to assure that parents understand and participate in decisions about their child's educational placement. Furthermore, state data about enrollment in special education programs must be disaggregated by race and ethnicity.

IDEA may be one of the most far-reaching and forward-thinking mandates in educational history, but legislation does not always equal implementation. Implementation of IDEA requires trained staff and adequate resources and tools. Underfunded school districts, already stretched to meet the needs of second language learners, have difficulty meeting the mandates of the law.

Summary

New accountability measures focus on student assessment. Three kinds of testing that have a direct impact on second language learners are language proficiency testing, standardized achievement testing, and diagnostic testing for placement in special programs. Assessing second language learners is complex, and each of those assessment modalities requires attention to language, culture, and the nature of testing.

Questions to Think About and Discuss

1. If you are or have recently been a student, think about the examinations or projects required in your classes or program of study. If you are currently teaching, think about the examinations you use and the assignments or projects you require in the grade or classes you teach. Reflect on the following questions: Do you think they are good measures of skills and understandings? If so, why? If not, how would you measure whether students meet the objectives of the course or program? What accommodations, if any, would make it more possible for students to display knowledge and abilities?

2. Think about a person you know who speaks English as a second language. This person could be a family member, friend, colleague, student, even someone you have met casually in the course of going about your daily business. If you were going to describe this person's proficiency in English, what would you say? What features or characteristics come to mind as you formulate your description or evaluation? If you speak more than one language, how would you characterize or evaluate your own proficiency in your non-native language? What features or characteristics come to mind as you formulate your description or evaluation?

Activities

1. Record a speaker of English as a second language in an informal conversation. Analyze the language sample from a structural perspective. Does the speaker have a noticeable foreign accent? Is the speaker's syntax close to native standards? Apart from your observations about structure, how would you rate this speaker's overall communicative

competence? Share your samples with your classmates. Discuss your conclusions.

2. Obtain a copy of a language assessment instrument used in an educational setting in your area. Consider the following:
   - What are the steps for administering the test? Who may administer it? Is special training required to administer it? How long does it take to administer?
   - What is the theoretical rationale for the test? Are the tasks discrete point or integrative? Is the scoring discrete point or global?
   - Is this test used alone or in combination with other measures?
   - Do you consider this test appropriate for assessing the language ability of children in a dual language program? Why or why not?
   - What kinds of decisions are made based on the results of this test?

3. Many states have developed content standards for students in K–12 schools and have initiated accountability programs that include standardized testing. Find out what your state is doing in this regard. How are English language learners incorporated into your state's accountability program? Critique this approach based on what you know about testing.

Suggestions for Further Reading

Baca, L. M., & Cervantes, H. T. (1998). *The bilingual special education interface* (3rd ed.). Upper Saddle River, NJ: Merrill.
A basic and comprehensive overview of the needs of the exceptional second language learner, this book incorporates an excellent summary of issues related to language acquisition and bilingual education in general.

Cheng, L. L. (1987). *Assessing Asian language performance: Guidelines for evaluating limited-English-proficient students.* Rockville, MD: Aspen Publishers.
In addition to an overview of issues related to language proficiency testing in general, this book focuses on Asian language background children and discusses the needs of speakers of Chinese, Vietnamese, Laotian, Hmong, Cambodian, Filipino, Korean, Japanese, Hawaiian, and Chamorro.

Cohen, A. D. (1980). *Testing language ability in the classroom.* Rowley, MA: Newbury House.
Attempts to meet the needs of the second language teacher on a daily basis. Contains practical information about test construction and discusses approaches to testing functional language ability.

Erickson, J. G., & Omark, D. R. (Eds.). (1981). *Communication assessment of the bilingual bicultural child: Issues and guidelines.* Baltimore, MD: University Park Press.
A discussion of issues and procedures in language assessment. Analyzes differences between discrete point, quasi-integrative, and integrative tests. Appendix C contains an annotated bibliography on the communication assessment of the bilingual child.

Gonzalez, V., Brusca-Vega, R., and Yawkey, T. (1997). *Assessment and instruction of culturally and linguistically diverse students with or at-risk of learning problems: From research to practice.* Boston: Allyn & Bacon.

Providing appropriate services for culturally and linguistically diverse services is a special challenge. This book addresses the challenge from a variety of perspectives. The book includes an analysis of bilingualism, considers assessment issues, and discusses instructional strategies. The discussion of the legal aspects of bilingual and special education is detailed and comprehensive, and educators will find the chapter on working with families particularly worthwhile.

Hamayan, E., & Damico, J. (Eds.). (1991). *Limiting bias in the assessment of bilingual students.* Austin, TX: Pro-ed.

Flawed assessment instruments and procedures result in the erroneous placement of bilingual students in special education classes, or the failure to consider them for classes for the gifted. The articles in this book provide an overview of the historical and legislative context for bilingual special education, delineate practical considerations related to assessment, and describe alternative approaches that may limit the bias in assessment. Appendices include annotated lists of language proficiency tests and academic ability tests appropriate for language minority students.

Losen, D. J., & Orfeld, G. (Eds.). (2002). *Racial inequity in special education.* Cambridge, MA: Harvard University Press.

Commissioned by the Harvard Civil Rights Project, this book explores inequities in special education, both in terms of placement and qualities of services.

Menken, K. (2008). *English learners left behind: Standardized testing as language policy.* Clevedon, UK: Multilingual Matters.

This book analyzes the impact of No Child Left Behind on English language learners and looks at how high stakes tests have affected curriculum and instruction.

Miller, J. (1983). *Many voices: Bilingualism culture and education.* London: Routledge & Kegan Paul.

A fascinating recounting of the bilingual experience, explicated through interviews with a variety of multilingual subjects who express their perceptions about their languages, how they learned them, and the ways they use them.

Spolsky, B. (1995). *Measured words: The development of objective language testing.* Oxford, UK: Oxford University Press.

Spolsky reminds us that "Blood cholesterol levels, or weight, or heartbeat can, with all their complexities and variations from time to time and situation to situation, be measured with some reasonable degree of confidence. Love, or pain, or . . . language proficiency, are so inseparable from the possessor and his or her sociopsychological context that any simple measure is necessarily flawed" (p. 352). This is the story of language proficiency testing, carefully studied in its historical and political contexts, told with insight and humor.

Valdés, G., & Figueroa, R. A. (1994). *Bilingualism and testing: A special case of bias.* Norwood, NJ: Ablex Publishing.

According to the authors' introduction, "This book is directly concerned with the reasons underlying bilingual children's poor performance on standardized tests" (p. 2). The book addresses the concern with an analysis of the dimensions of bilingualism and an examination of testing and concludes with a discussion of implications and recommendations for further research.

6

Primary Language Instruction for Limited English Proficient Students

Amanda is a second-grade student in a private school in an affluent suburban area. Her father is a computer software engineer and her mother is an attorney. In school, Amanda receives instruction in her subject areas in English; she studies French as a second language. In second grade, French is also used for art and social studies as well as related cultural activities and events. As Amanda progresses toward sixth grade her French instruction will increase, and she will develop speaking, reading, and writing skills.

Lilia was born in the United States of parents who were born in Mexico and speak no English. Lilia attends second grade in a public school in an economically disadvantaged urban area. When she entered kindergarten, Lilia was assessed as limited English proficient. She is enrolled in a program that offers her subject area instruction in Spanish, accompanied by daily classes in English as a second language. In addition, Lilia receives social studies and physical education instruction in English and participates in schoolwide activities and assemblies where English is used. As soon as Lilia can score above the 37th percentile on a standardized achievement test administered in English, she will be placed in a classroom where no Spanish is used.

Few people question the value of additive bilingualism for English-speaking children. Amanda's friends and family are impressed by her ability to speak French, and many have expressed the wish that they had received a comparable education. But controversy surrounds the idea of providing public school instruction for limited English proficient students in their native language while they learn English as a second language. Lilia is expected, appropriately, to learn English. While she may maintain her ability to speak Spanish, it is unlikely that she will ever become fully bilingual and biliterate.

This subtractive bilingual scenario will not only limit her abilities in Spanish, but may have a negative impact on her abilities in English as well.

This chapter will present a five-point rationale for providing primary language instruction for limited English proficient children and will outline instructional approaches for implementing primary language support in the classroom.

A Rationale for Primary Language Instruction

TRANSFER OF CONCEPTS AND SKILLS

The construction of a rationale for primary language instruction can be approached from several directions. We will begin by responding to the often expressed criticism that classroom time spent in the primary language is wasteful. That idea is based on the assumption that languages are learned and maintained separately in the human brain. There is no evidence to support that model of language learning, which has been called the *Separate Underlying Proficiency model* (Cummins, 1994). In fact, research supports the opposite notion, or *Common Underlying Proficiency model* of language learning, which assumes that skills and concepts learned in one language transfer to another.

How Does Transfer Work? Reading illustrates a process where there is significant transfer of behaviors, skills, knowledge, and attitudes from one language to another. A detailed analysis of the skills and subskills that comprise literacy would be out of place here, but consider a few of the concepts that provide the foundation for reading. You may find it difficult at first to identify them, because reading is highly automatic for literate adults!

Look at Figure 6.1, and try to read the Hebrew word. You are given some hints about direction and about sound–symbol correspondence. As you worked out the word, were you engaged in learning to read? This exercise, using a language with an unfamiliar alphabet, has demonstrated that when you read in a new language, you apply literacy skills you already have to language-specific information.

Now consider some of the components of reading. Reading requires the understanding that print carries meaning. We develop this awareness in children through reading readiness instruction. Adults read to children, point out signs and other sources of information in print, label objects in the classroom, and teach them to read and write their names.

Other prereading skills include directionality, sequencing, and the ability to distinguish among shapes and sounds. Those skills are not language bound; they transfer, as does the knowledge that written symbols correspond to sounds and can be decoded in a particular direction and order.

> • FIGURE *6.1*   Reading a New Language

Hebrew may seem baffling to many of you because it uses an unfamiliar alphabet. Using the language-specific information provided, try to read the Hebrew word. After you have read it, think about the literacy skills you already have that helped you.

Language-specific information:

- *Direction*—Read Hebrew from right to left.
- *Sequence*—Some vowels are placed under consonants.
Read the consonant first, and then the vowel.
- *Sounds and symbols*—Here are some correspondences that you will need to know:

שׁ = *sh*, as in *shoe*

ל = *l*, as in *lamp*

מ = *m*, as in *mouse*

ָ = *o*, as in *tonic* or *cot*

וֹ = *o*, as in *home* or *bone*

Try to read this word (turn the page upside down for the answer):

שָׁלוֹם

"The word you read is *shalom*, which means "greetings," or "peace.""

In addition to basic skills, reading habits and attitudes have a significant impact on an individual's ability to read. A sense of being a literate, capable person who can listen, concentrate, and complete a task transfers from one language to another (Thonis, 1983).

Reading is only one of the many areas where transfer from one language to another is significant. Content areas can be studied in any language, and the concepts are added to the common underlying cognitive store. From a pedagogical viewpoint, the message is clear. Instructional time spent in a child's primary language is not wasted. Skills, concepts, and knowledge acquired in one's first language will be readily available in one's second.

PRIMARY LANGUAGE DEVELOPMENT AND SECOND LANGUAGE ACQUISITION

Providing instruction in a child's primary language enhances acquisition of a second language. Unlike the notion of transfer, this idea seems counterintuitive, and yet it is a related concept, grounded in the Common Underlying Proficiency model.

Research has demonstrated (see Cummins, 1981, for a review) that older immigrant children, with substantial educational preparation in their own language, fare better in achieving second language proficiency than younger immigrant children. Evidently, the older children have a well-developed conceptual base in their primary language as a result of their previous schooling and literacy. Learning a second language, for them, is a matter of translating concepts and ideas that are already firmly established. They need only learn new labels, unlike younger children who face the more difficult task of having to learn basic concepts in a new and unfamiliar language.

For example, basic concepts involving spatial relationships are often reinforced in preschool or kindergarten as part of prereading and early mathematics. For small children concepts like *over, under, behind,* and *around* may be unfamiliar. Learning them in a new language is difficult. For adults, who have internalized spatial relationships, they are relatively simple. Learning them in a new language requires only learning new words for relationships that have long become conceptually automatic.

The apparent contradiction that instructional time spent in a first language facilitates acquisition of a second is resolved by the Common Underlying Proficiency model. If we think in terms of a bank or reserve of language, with all deposits adding to the balance, we see quickly that a child who is poor in one language will be poor in another. Primary language instruction is the easiest way to increase a child's language wealth.

STUDENTS NEED TO DEVELOP CALP

In Chapter 5 we discussed the distinction between Basic Interpersonal Communicative Skills (BICS) and Cognitive Academic Language Proficiency (CALP), theoretical constructs developed by Cummins. BICS refers to the basic language skills necessary for communication in context-embedded settings, whereas CALP is the type of language proficiency needed to function in a classroom environment, where required tasks are context-reduced.

Students need to develop CALP in order to function adequately in academic situations. Relying on the ideas that concepts and skills transfer from one language to another and that students with a strong cognitive base will easily make the transition to a second language, the thesis that CALP should be developed in a student's first language follows.

Critics often suggest that language minority students should spend no more than three years in primary language programs. Cummins has suggested (1981) that it takes an average of five to seven years for children to develop

CALP in any language. Recent longitudinal research by Thomas and Collier (1997) reinforces that assertion. They analyzed approximately 700,000 school records from five school districts across the United States with large populations of language minority students. They conclude that in the absence of any primary language instruction it takes seven to ten years for a non-native speaker of English to reach native-like age and grade-level performance. Students who arrive in the United States with two to three years of schooling in their country of origin, in other words, with two to three years of primary language instruction, reach age and grade-level performance after five to six years.

Finally, the data indicate that students in high-quality bilingual programs need four to seven years to reach the performance level of native speakers. Clearly primary language instruction should be seen as more than a temporary vehicle for content coverage. For language minority children, primary language instruction is a tool for conceptual development that will enrich their ability to function in both first and second languages.

EFFECTS OF BILINGUALISM ON ACHIEVEMENT

It was suggested previously that early research in the field of bilingualism led to the conclusion that knowing more than one language was an educational handicap. Some recent studies, however, have indicated that bilingual children have greater cognitive flexibility and better language skills than monolingual children. This is logical, since bilingual children have more opportunities to play and work with language than do their monolingual counterparts.

Inconsistencies in studies on bilingualism have perplexed researchers for some time. The "threshold hypothesis" (Cummins, 1994) suggests that positive effects of bilingualism are associated with high levels of proficiency in more than one language. In other words, children who have acquired a high degree of proficiency in a second language while maintaining their abilities in a first show positive effects compared to those with partial or limited bilingualism. Once again, we are led to the conclusions that additive bilingualism has positive effects and that language minority children should be provided with instruction in their primary languages.

PRIMARY LANGUAGE INSTRUCTION AND SELF-CONCEPT

The notion of self-concept is intangible and complex. A person's self-concept is made up of an intricate network of factors, including:

- *Comparisons*—"How do I compare with other people?"
- *Perceptions of others*—"How do I think other people see me?"
- *Ideals*—"How would I be if I could be any way I choose?"

People develop their self-concept through the experiences they have with others. Some individuals have a particularly powerful impact on the self-concept of children. Parents play an important role in self-concept development, as do teachers (Amoriggi & Gefteas, 1981).

Children are natural sociologists and sociolinguists, well aware of attitudes in their environment regarding their culture and language. Children who perceive negative attitudes in the school setting toward their first language will become involved in subtractive bilingualism. Bilingualism is correlated to positive academic effects in situations where both languages have perceived value in the home and community (Cummins & Swain, 1986).

According to Thomas and Collier, the sociocultural context of schooling is an important factor in the schooling of language minority students. Two-way programs that encourage integration of native speakers of English with language minority students enhance the status of the minority language (Thomas & Collier, 1997). In order for bilingual programs to succeed, schools must promote the idea that the language children bring to school is prestigious and appropriate for use by educated people.

—Overall, What Does the Research Indicate?

There have been several attempts to evaluate the effects of bilingual programs on a large scale. Two well-known and often cited studies are a national evaluation of Title VII funded projects completed by the American Institute for Research (Danoff, Coles, McLaughlin, & Reynolds, 1977a, 1977b, 1978) and a study commissioned by the Office of Planning, Budget and Evaluation of the United States Department of Education (Baker & de Kanter, 1981).

Neither of those studies produced evidence favoring bilingual education, but both engendered heated controversy. Criticism has generally centered around research design and methodology. Two important factors call the results of the studies into question:

1. Many programs are labeled *bilingual,* but there may be a low degree of comparability among them. Immersion programs, as well as English as a second language pull-out programs, may be labeled *bilingual* by administrators seeking compliance with state and federal regulations, or researchers who fail to understand the distinctions. In some areas, shortages of adequately trained staff result in assignment of monolingual teachers to "bilingual" classrooms where primary language support may be limited or nonexistent.

2. An effective research design requires that programs be randomly assigned to sites and then evaluated. There are no studies where this condition, called *random assignment to condition,* has been met. Consequently, program evaluation results are difficult to interpret.

The Baker and de Kanter analysis, which was actually a synthesis of 28 smaller studies, has been reanalyzed and compared using statistical processes that control for differences in the nature of the data (Willig, 1985). The reinterpretation provides evidence that supports bilingual education and the use of the primary language in the classroom.

In a later article, Rossell and Baker (1996) analyzed 72 studies in an attempt to compare transitional bilingual education, defined as a program that develops literacy skills and teaches content areas in the students' primary language along with graduated ESL instruction, to three other types of the programs: *submersion* (or *sink-or-swim*), *structured immersion,* which offers instruction in English with primary language support "in the rare instances when the student cannot complete a task without it" (p. 10), and ESL pull-out. They concluded that transitional bilingual education was rarely better than regular classroom instruction, and never better than structured immersion.

Krashen (1996) reexamined all the studies analyzed by Rossell and Baker that could be found in the published literature, concluding that their overall study is seriously flawed. He points out that Rossell and Baker were willing to include studies about programs that were not spelled out in any detail, but merely called *bilingual.* Crawford also notes (1997) that Rossell and Baker ignore the use of primary language where it suits their purpose, lauding one successful program for its English-only approach, when in fact the use of English was supported with nearly a half day of primary language instruction. In other words, if a program worked, they chose to not call it a *bilingual program.*

Furthermore, Rossell and Baker started out with 300 studies and ruled out those they found methodologically unacceptable. Krashen suggests that several studies ruled out showed results that would support the use of primary language in a bilingual program model. Finally, Crawford (1997) points out that "Rossell and Baker relied heavily on program evaluations from the 1970s, when bilingual pedagogies were considerably less developed than they are today" (1997, p. 36).

Clearly program research on the benefits of primary language instruction for language minority students is inconclusive. The issues are further clouded by politics. The U.S. Department of Education has repeatedly questioned the value of dual language instruction and has taken steps to expand funding for English-only programs. On the other hand, a report published by the U.S. General Accounting Office (1987a) supports dual language instruction.

Basic research on bilingualism, however, leaves little room for doubt as to the value of primary language instruction for language minority students (Hakuta, 1985). In communities that show a high regard for two languages and in educational programs that encourage additive bilingualism, knowing two languages is positively associated with intellectual and academic achievement (Cummins & Swain, 1986).

 If Primary Language Instruction, Then How?

Some experts have suggested that for limited English proficient students, primary language instruction should be carried out for as much as 70 percent of the school day in early grades (Legarreta-Marcaida, 1981) with English taught as a second language. As children master English, content instruction in English can be increased. A ratio of 50-50 English and other language through sixth grade sets the stage for additive bilingualism, which opens the door to academic achievement.

Given the obvious constraints of a school day, how is it possible to deliver instruction in two languages across the curriculum? Several methods have been proposed.

SEPARATION OF LANGUAGES

Languages may be separated by time, in alternate-day or half-day formats. In a team teaching situation, or when a teacher works with an aide, languages may be separated by person, with each person using one language exclusively. Languages may be separated by place, with rooms or classroom areas designated for particular languages.

Two-way immersion programs require that languages be separated by person, and often by place as well. Two-way immersion teachers are bilingual but early primary children often assume that their teachers speak only one language, even though teachers respond to students' questions and comments in both. It's possible that young children don't yet conceptualize receptive ability, that is, understanding a language, as part of "speaking" a language.

Languages may also be separated by subject. When languages are separated by subject, the ethnic or minority language is often used for areas such as social studies and art, with science and mathematics reserved for English. This is language stereotyping and should be avoided, because it damages the prestige of the minority language. Likewise, when languages are assigned by person, it is often the teacher's aide who speaks the minority language. Although skilled aides play a necessary and important role in dual language classrooms, a scenario where authority figures in a school speak only English, and only subordinates use the minority language, damages minority language prestige.

CONCURRENT TRANSLATION

Commonly used but not well understood, concurrent translation involves using two languages interchangeably during instruction. There have been several criticisms of this approach:

- Teachers often code-switch, assuming that they are engaged in concurrent translation. While code-switching is linguistically coherent, it is pedagogically random—that is, the switches a bilingual speaker may make in ordinary conversation do not necessarily meet instructional objectives for language development or delivery of content.
- In practice, concurrent translation often approximates direct translation; students quickly learn to tune out the language they don't understand, waiting for the information in the language they do.

- Concurrent translation can be strenuous and tiring for a teacher to implement. Two teachers, or a teacher and an aide, can implement the method, assuming the availability of sufficient staffing.
- Teachers often overestimate the amount of time spent using the children's primary language and, in fact, spend a disproportionate amount of time speaking English.

The New Concurrent Approach (NCA), developed by Rodolfo Jacobson (1987), suggests using a structured form of code-switching for delivery of content instruction. In Jacobson's method, language switches are carefully planned. There are no intrasentential switches, and all switches are made at the completion of a thought group. Planned switches are justifiable for:

- Conceptual reinforcement and review, to assure that all children have mastered the lesson material.
- Lexical enrichment, to give children the vocabulary necessary to discuss a particular subject in both languages.
- Appropriateness for curriculum—that is, ethnically related events or subjects may be treated in the appropriate language.

PREVIEW-REVIEW

The preview-review approach incorporates elements of NCA. In preview-review, content areas are previewed in one language, presented in the other, and reviewed in the first. This method may be particularly useful at the upper primary and secondary levels, where content materials such as science or social studies textbooks may not be readily available in minority languages.

Note that concurrent and preview-review approaches are appropriate for content instruction. Language development in either language and second language instruction should be delivered in the target language.

Cooperative Learning

Cooperative learning is a classroom management strategy that departs from traditional whole-class instructional formats and opens up opportunities for first and second language development. In cooperative learning, the class is divided into teams, whose members work together and rely on one another to learn concepts, solve problems, and complete projects (Kagan, 1986).

A cooperative strategy may be as simple as peer tutoring, where students assist each other with drills and practice for material such as spelling words or math facts. Or cooperative learning can involve teamwork to complete complex projects that require planning, research, and implementation.

There are more chances for students to communicate in a cooperative format than in traditional settings. In addition, the quality of communication is higher as students try to negotiate content-related meaning (Kagan, 1986; Long & Porter, 1985), because cooperative learning creates two-way tasks where each participant has information that the others need.

Cooperative learning models provide rich communication opportunities for limited English proficient students. For example, *Finding Out/ Descubrimiento* (Cohen, 1986) uses science and math content to teach critical thinking skills. Students are assigned to task groups with rotating roles such as facilitator, safety officer, and reporter. Groups work on problems in learning centers in areas such as optics, electricity, and water. Materials are provided in English and Spanish, and bilingual students serve as translators. Students can complete their activities working in either language.

Cooperative learning strategies do not involve explicit manipulation of language. Primary language use is permitted in cooperative grouping, but the strategy seems to promote acquisition of the dominant language—English. In that sense, cooperative learning strategies might be classified as a second language teaching approach. It is clear, however, that cooperative strategies produce more opportunities for content-related communication among students than a traditional, teacher-centered classroom environment. Thus they enhance academic learning. In addition, cooperative strategies motivate students and promote a positive affective climate. These qualities make cooperative learning particularly appropriate for a dual language classroom.

Summary

Program research provides evidence of the value of primary language instruction for language minority students, but is inconclusive. Basic research on bilingualism, however, provides strong support for the value of additive bilingualism. Primary language instruction is justifiable because:

- Concepts and skills learned in one language transfer to another.
- Primary language development facilitates second language acquisition.
- Students need time to develop cognitive academic language proficiency.
- Proficiency in two languages has positive effects on achievement.
- Primary language instruction enhances self-concept.

Primary language instruction can be offered in a variety of formats including:

- Separation of languages by person, place, time, or subject.
- Concurrent translation.
- Preview-review.
- Cooperative learning strategies.

Questions to Think About and Discuss

1. Imagine that you are going to create a primary (K–6) school from the ground up. Among its intended outcomes, this school has as a goal that all its students will be bilingual and biliterate by the time they finish sixth grade. Under ideal circumstances, what kind of program would you recommend? What is your rationale?
2. Following up on the first question, what kinds of programs would you recommend in middle and high school for students who graduate from your ideal school? Why?

Activities

1. Visit a classroom within a dual language instructional program. What language strategy does the teacher use in content areas? How does that fit the program model?
2. Monitor language use in the classroom during the observation period:
   - What percentage of time is each language in use?
   - What are the purposes for which each language is used? Which language is used for instruction in each area? What language is used for reinforcement and praise? For discipline? For instructions?
   - Are language switches purposeful? What purposes can you discern?
   - Are bulletin boards and other classroom displays bilingual?
   - Are materials available in both languages? Are the materials comparable in quantity and quality?
   - Which personnel use which language? How proficient are instructors and assistants in the classroom languages?
   - Overall, are languages assigned equal value in this classroom?
3. Develop an instructional unit in social studies, science, or mathematics that utilizes cooperative learning strategies.
4. Many parents, concerned that their children learn English as quickly as possible, are uneasy about the use of primary language in school. Prepare a PowerPoint presentation for a parent group that explains the benefits of primary language instruction.

Suggestions for Further Reading

Cummins, J. (1994). Primary language instruction and the education of language minority students. In California State Department of Education (Ed.), *Schooling and language minority students: A theoretical framework* (2nd ed.) (pp. 3–46). Los Angeles: Evaluation, Dissemination, and Assessment Center, California State University, Los Angeles.

Cummins's article sets forth a theoretical framework with an analysis of supporting research that provides a rationale for providing primary language instruction for limited English proficient students. This article, along with others in this new edition, also explores the social, political, and cultural dynamics of schooling for language minority students.

Gonzalez, A., & Guerrero, M. (1983). *A cooperative/interdependent approach to bilingual education.* Hollister, CA: Hollister School District.

This handbook provides detailed practical information about the jigsaw method of cooperative learning. Sample lessons, time lines, and record-keeping forms assist teachers in implementing the jigsaw process in their classrooms.

Kagan, S. (1986). Cooperative learning and sociocultural factors in schooling. In California State Department of Education (Ed.), *Beyond language: Social and cultural factors in schooling language minority students* (pp. 231–298). Los Angeles: Evaluation, Dissemination, and Assessment Center, California State University, Los Angeles.

A comprehensive introduction to cooperative learning strategies, this article overviews research results of cooperative learning with special attention to the outcomes of cooperative learning strategies for minority students. The article is particularly useful because it contains an overview of training models and resources available for teachers and schools.

Krashen, S. D. (1996). *Under attack: The case against bilingual education.* Culver City, CA: Language Education Associates.

This succinct book is a collection of articles previously published by the author that address commonplace criticisms of bilingual education. Krashen provides data to demonstrate that the students who appear to succeed without bilingual education often have what he calls "de facto bilingual education." Chapter 4, "Does Literacy Transfer?" supports the importance of teaching children to read in their first language.

chapter 7

Second Language Instruction

$\mathcal{T}$he term *English as a second language* (ESL) often evokes images on a continuum—ranging from a program separate from a dual language instructional model, involving high-intensity English training, to minimal "pull-out" instruction where limited English proficient children are taken out of their classroom to receive ESL instruction for a small portion of the school day.

Some people erroneously assume that there is a distinct difference between second language instruction and bilingual instruction. Second language instruction, however, is an integrated part of any dual language instructional model. Most dual language instructional programs target limited English proficient students and have an ESL component. However, programs that include monolingual English speakers now exist, and they provide an opportunity for them to learn a second language as well.

Language development is basic to schooling, and, as we have already seen, first and second language development can take place in the context of many models. Apart from language development through content instruction, approaches have been developed that focus on second language instruction *per se*. Specific second language methodologies will not be addressed in detail in this chapter, since that is more appropriate to a methods text. This chapter will briefly review traditional and innovative language teaching approaches.

A NOTE ABOUT TERMINOLOGY

Literature about language instruction sometimes refers to *foreign language instruction,* such as English as a foreign language (EFL), and also to *second language instruction,* as in English as a second language (ESL). Instructors generally use the term *second language* when it is a language widely used in the immediate social environment. A *foreign* language is one that the student is not likely to encounter in the social environment outside the classroom.

For purposes of dual language instruction it is convenient and logical to refer to *second language instruction*. Programs in the United States are generally geared to teach English to students with limited proficiency in that language. English is clearly a dominant language in the United States and is available in the general social environment. Many programs have two-way goals as well, intending either to restore ethnic languages to children whose families have lost them or to give children in general the opportunity to acquire a new language. Usually the languages offered are present to some extent in the United States, which is a multilingual environment. These languages can therefore be referred to as second languages.

Literature that refers to teaching EFL has information that is relevant and applicable to second language instruction. Regardless of the source of information, we will use *second language instruction* as an inclusive term.

Early Viewpoints on Second Language Instruction

GRAMMAR-TRANSLATION

It is common to hear someone say, "I studied French (or Spanish, or German) for years in school, but I can't speak a word." Many of those people were probably instructed with the grammar-translation method, which focuses on learning language rules and working with written texts. Seldom successful, the grammar-translation method is a remnant of the study of Latin grammar, which was highly valued in the Middle Ages. Medieval scholars, however, pursued the intricacies of Latin grammar for its own sake, not necessarily to gain proficiency in the use of Latin. It is likely that the skills they had in day-to-day Latin were gained through direct contact with the language in communicative situations.

As the use of Latin as a vehicle for everyday conversation declined, Latin texts were increasingly translated into vernaculars. The prestige, however, attached to the study of Latin and Greek persisted, as did the idea that the development of grammar skills transferred to other areas of thinking. Resistance to formal study of modern foreign languages continued until well into the eighteenth century, and the grammar-translation approach prevailed despite attempts to devise alternatives (Grittner, 1969).

THE SEARCH FOR ALTERNATIVE APPROACHES

Diller (1978) tells the fascinating story of Francois Gouin, a nineteenth-century Latin teacher from France, who decided to teach himself German. Gouin began by memorizing a German grammar book and 248 irregular verbs, an effort that took him ten days. Despite these efforts, he was unable to understand a word of spoken German. Convinced, however, that he was on the right track and only needed to broaden his knowledge, he set about memorizing 800 German roots. At that point, unable to engage in even simple conversation or to translate written German, he purchased a dictionary and proceeded to memorize 30,000 words in 30 days, an effort that all but destroyed his eyesight, but failed to make him proficient in German.

Imagine his surprise to find that his three-year-old nephew had learned to speak French during a three-month vacation in France! Focusing his attention on his nephew's accomplishments, Gouin developed the *Series Method*, which involves learning a new language through an ordered series of concepts that introduce new vocabulary and grammatical patterns.

Gouin's method was devised on the basis of limited information about language learning, since he focused exclusively on his nephew and never investigated children's language development strategies further. However, his insights about the need to provide real context for language teaching were brilliant, and his early efforts certainly demonstrate the lengths to which people have gone to master a new language.

Another nineteenth-century language instructor, Maximilian Berlitz, literally stumbled on his approach. Berlitz ran a small language school in Providence, Rhode Island. Incapacitated by illness, he hired a French instructor through the mail to teach his students. It was only when the instructor arrived in Providence that Berlitz discovered that his new employee spoke only French. With no alternative, he sent the Frenchman off to do the best he could. When he was sufficiently recovered to visit his school, Berlitz was astonished to discover his students happily conversing in French with far more skill than they had ever acquired before. Based on that revelation, Berlitz developed the *Direct Method*, an approach that immerses students in the second language (Simon, 1980). In the Direct Method, the student's first language is not allowed in the classroom. Materials are presented through a variety of media in an orderly progression, and grammar rules are taught inductively. Although Berlitz gets surprisingly little mention in scholarly discussions of second language instruction, he is a pioneer in immersion methods, and large numbers of students are enrolled in Berlitz schools around the world today.

Late nineteenth- and early twentieth-century attempts to replace grammar-translation with more effective means of second language instruction generally failed to gain popularity. The grammar-translation approach held sway until the onset of World War II.

Modern Approaches to Second Language Instruction

THE AUDIOLINGUAL APPROACH

World War II raised public awareness about the inadequacies of language teaching in the United States. Faced with a pressing need for personnel with skills in many languages, some of which had never been studied or codi-fied, the U.S. Army developed a revolutionary approach to second language instruction that was called the *audiolingual method.*

The audiolingual approach is based on the assumption that language development requires habit formation and reinforcement. It involves students in language activities that include three components:

- Practice and memorization of situation-based dialogues.
- Drills to reinforce the major patterns in the dialogues.
- Conversation with a native speaker about the topic of the dialogue.

The audiolingual approach was successful and caught on rapidly with some modifications. Some deviations from the original format enhanced the methodology. For example, the original program focused exclusively on the development of oral skills. Teachers quickly found that written materials were useful—especially for adult learners who had often invented their own writing systems as an aid to memorization.

On the other hand, audiolingual approaches are sometimes implemented using the dialogue and drill components, while eliminating the conversation component of the original. In view of recent findings about second language acquisition, it may well be that the real communicative situations were an essential and productive aspect of the Army's method.

OTHER RECENT APPROACHES

New directions in thinking about second language acquisition unleashed by Chomsky (see Chapter 4), along with dissatisfaction about the state of language instruction, have led to the development of many new approaches to second language instruction. In general, second language instruction has moved away from the tight restrictions inherent in the audiolingual approach and now tends to focus more on the active involvement of students in the lan-guage acquisition process.

Modern approaches reflect the idea that language acquisition is a natural and creative process that involves the student in thinking in the new language. Production of the new language arises naturally when a student is ready to begin to speak. There are several new approaches that have caught the attention of dual and second language instructors. Some may be surprising, since they represent a departure from the language teaching most of us have experienced. These approaches focus on providing language instruction in nonthreatening environments and emphasize communication rather than cor-rect form or knowledge of rules. The following brief descriptions will provide a flavor of recent innovative approaches to second language instruction.

Total Physical Response (TPR). Developed by James Asher, TPR is based on the assumption that a second language is internalized through a process of codebreaking similar to first language development and that the process allows for a long period of listening and developing comprehension prior to production. Students are given a period of several weeks or months during which they are not asked to produce language and need only respond to commands that require physical movement (Asher, 1982).

Suggestopedia. Developed by Georgi Lozanov, Suggestopedia relies on the assumption that it is possible to increase our ability to learn language by tapping the paraconscious reserves of the brain. Lozanov's method provides a rich acquisition environment; careful attention is paid to the affective dimension of language acquisition. Lessons take place in a pleasant and informal setting.

The culminating component of each Suggestopedia session is unique. Instructors, trained in psychology and art, read language selections in careful synchronization with musical selections. Students prepare for the session by engaging in relaxation techniques derived from yogic meditation and breathing exercises. These exercises activate the subconscious mind and allow students to tap reserves of super memory (Lozanov, 1982). While many aspects of Suggestopedia would be difficult to implement in the public school setting, innovative aspects of this approach have been incorporated into second language teaching programs with excellent results (Bancroft, 1978).

Counseling-Learning. Developed by Charles Curran, the Counseling-Learning approach is actually an instructional theory that is applicable to a wide variety of subjects. The approach suggests that basic precepts of counseling are broadly applicable to all learning situations. Curran chose to apply his thinking to language teaching, since it appeared to be an area where many techniques were unsuccessful. In addition, language teaching is a fruitful area for research because gains can be readily tested.

Counseling-Learning assumes that there are parallels between a counseling situation and an instructional situation. The learner, or "client," may feel threatened and insecure and may experience conflict and frustration. The role of the teacher or "counselor" is to empathize with the student (client) and to provide the learner with skills that will eliminate frustration. Students work in small groups and initiate conversations in their native languages, which are then translated by language experts who sit outside the circle. As students become less anxious and more proficient, conversations become more personal and more linguistically complex, and students require less translation assistance from the experts. Tape recordings of the sessions and brief sessions on points of grammar provide opportunities for review and clarification.

Curran's research indicates that students who attempted new languages with the counseling method made favorable progress when compared with students who participated in traditional college language classes (Curran, 1982).

The Notional-Functional Approach. Although TPR, Suggestopedia, and Counseling-Learning have been called *interpersonal approaches* (Brown, 1980) and reflect a strong concern for the importance of the affective variable in second language learning, the Notional-Functional approach considers the pragmatics of language. A Notional-Functional syllabus organizes instruction around the functions of language. Students learn appropriate communication strategies for a variety of situations. For example, a Notional-Functional syllabus might provide students with opportunities to learn to agree, argue, question, or compliment.

The Natural Approach. Stephen Krashen's theory of language acquisition (see Chapter 4) inspired the development of the Natural Approach (Krashen & Terrell, 1983) to second language teaching. The Natural Approach is of particular interest to instructors at the primary level, since it has greater practical applicability at the elementary level than many of the other new communication-based approaches, such as Suggestopedia. We will, therefore, outline the Natural Approach in some detail.

According to Krashen, language acquisition will occur when certain conditions are met. The Natural Approach (Terrell, 1981) meets those conditions by:

- Providing comprehensible input.
- Focusing on communication of messages.
- Creating low anxiety situations.

The Natural Approach assumes that speech emerges in four natural and distinct stages:

- Preproduction, when students communicate primarily with gesture and actions.
- Early production, when students begin to use one- or two-word utterances, or short phrases.
- Speech emergence, when students use longer phrases or complete sentences.
- Intermediate fluency, when students can engage in conversation and produce connected narratives.

Instruction in the Natural Approach is organized according to these progressive levels of language acquisition. At the outset the teacher supplies a lot of comprehensible input, but does not demand production from the students. As students progress, the teacher introduces new receptive vocabulary and encourages higher levels of language use. Reading and writing activities are incorporated into the curriculum when students have reached intermediate fluency.

The Natural Approach promotes basic proficiency and is particularly appropriate for primary levels. However, overreliance on approaches that do not explicitly address syntax may result in fossilization or the internalization of incorrect forms. As students advance in their second language, therefore, teachers generally supplement the Natural Approach with instruction in language arts areas such as reading, writing, and critical thinking.

Integrating Language and Content: Specially Designed Academic Instruction in English

Recently, educators have begun to understand that language learning is most meaningful when it is tied to content instruction. Snow, Met, and Genesee (1989) suggest that language development is facilitated when it is combined with content area instruction because:

- Cognitive development and language development are inextricably tied, especially for young children.
- School subjects are what children need to talk about in school, so content area provides both the motivation and the opportunity for meaningful communication.
- Tying language development to content area allows students to develop the kind of language that is used in school. (See Chapter 6 for a discussion of Cognitive Academic Language Proficiency.)

Increasingly, teachers are utilizing an approach called *Specially Designed Academic Instruction in English (SDAIE)* to assist second language learners in developing their abilities in English while they master the concepts and skills in the required curriculum.

SDAIE is particularly useful in situations that arise where primary language instruction is difficult or impossible—for example:

- Bilingual staff is unavailable to meet all students' needs, and/or
- The classroom contains students with a variety of primary languages other than English.

In general, SDAIE combines the important components of quality teaching with approaches based on second language acquisition theory. Properly implemented, SDAIE addresses all areas of instruction, including planning, classroom management, lesson delivery, and assessment.

PLANNING

Recent research (Short, 2002), demonstrates that teachers, even teachers with training in second language instruction, emphasize content and tasks over language. In SDAIE, however, language is seen as the vehicle for content, and vice versa. Consequently, teachers should plan each lesson to meet not only the curricular objectives related to content, but also to include appropriate language objectives. Met (1994) distinguishes between content-obligatory and content-compatible language objectives. *Content-obligatory objectives* are those that must be included to make a lesson comprehensible for students. So, for example, second language learners studying the Civil War need to be familiar with words like *enslavement, federalism,* and *emancipation.*

Content-compatible objectives are those that can be tied into the subject matter to assist students in language growth and development but aren't mandatory for students to understand the subject at hand. In the case of the Civil War, a teacher could, for example, emphasize the use of conditional phrases: "What would have happened if John Wilkes Booth had failed to assassinate the president?" Use of the conditional can be incorporated into almost any subject area and isn't required for students to learn about the Civil War. Based on an assessment of students' language development and needs, however, a teacher might want to include this content-compatible objective.

CLASSROOM MANAGEMENT

Classroom management is an important component of SDAIE. If we accept current analyses of the ways that students develop in their second language, we can assume that we need to provide safe, comfortable classroom environments and organize instruction to provide opportunities for students to interact around meaningful activities. Cooperative grouping, described in Chapter 6, is one useful approach. Buddy systems and peer-tutoring systems also allow students to try out their language in a nonthreatening environment while completing academic tasks.

LESSON DELIVERY

Sheltered English. One important methodology within SDAIE is *sheltered English.* In a sheltered classroom, English is used as the medium of instruction in the content areas, and teachers use strategies to encourage English acquisition through comprehensible input and contextualization. Such strategies might include:

- Slow but natural levels of speech.
- Clear enunciation.
- Short, simple sentences.
- Repetition and paraphrasing.
- Controlled vocabulary and idioms.
- Visual reinforcement through the use of gestures, props, pictures, films, demonstrations, and hands-on activities.
- Frequent comprehension checks.

Teachers in a sheltered English classroom maintain a setting with a low level of anxiety, stressing comprehension prior to eliciting production and emphasizing communication over correctness. Activities are selected that encourage hands-on, active engagement with the material, as well as social interaction among students.

Sheltered methodology responds to the idea that the language of classroom discourse (CALP) differs significantly from language used for everyday purposes (BICS). If students are asked to "list the factors that contributed to the Civil War," a teacher in a sheltered setting might review the words *list* and *factor*. As Corson (1995) notes, "Academic . . . words are mainly literary in their use . . . the words' introduction in literature or textbooks, rather than in conversation, restricts people's access to them" (p. 677).

Thematic instruction has particular utility in sheltered classrooms, because students encounter familiar language across several subject areas. Thematic instruction organizes teaching and learning around a key concept or big idea, allowing students to think critically and use oral language, writing, and reading across multiple disciplines or subject areas. One teacher in Santa Clara County organizes each school year around a single theme. In 1993, for a combination fifth/sixth/seventh-grade class, the central theme for the school year was titled "Kokopelli's Flute—A Song of the Southwest" (Perssons, 1993). The school year started with "Story of the Earth," in which students read, illustrated, and dramatized ancient myths, and culminated with a field trip to the Southwest, organized in great measure by the students themselves.

Students in sheltered settings should have an intermediate command of English and should be grouped within the classroom according to their English ability. It is important to remember, however, that it is not the objective of a sheltered classroom to provide remediation in subject areas. The subject content and objectives of a sheltered classroom should be identical to those of a mainstream classroom in the same subject.

ASSESSMENT

Assessment is a key part of any instructional approach. Genesee and Hamayan point out (1994) that when language instruction is integrated with content instruction teachers need to use a variety of assessment techniques that distinguish between students' language abilities and growth and their mastery of subject matter.

Standardized testing has traditionally been the backbone of classroom assessment of student achievement, but teachers are turning increasingly to what have been called *alternative assessment approaches*. One form of alternative assessment is performance assessment. In performance assessment, "a student completes an assignment alone or with other students, often in a content area, and prepares a summary or interpretation of the activity" (O'Malley & Valdez Pierce, 1991, p. 2), which is then evaluated by the teacher. Many teachers are now combining the results of traditional and alternative assessments into portfolios.

Portfolios allow students to present work in their native language, or in ways that are not exclusively language bound, such as photographs and videos. They help students track their progress in language development over time. Portfolios also allow parents of second language learners to see what

In Your Classroom
Instruction that Supports Second
Language Learners

Strategies that support language development and scaffold content for second language learners require attention to all areas of instruction, including classroom management, lesson planning and delivery, and assessment. Based on what we know about how students learn a new language, here are some basic ideas to help you get started:

Language is best learned in a comfortable, low-stress environment. Students need to feel safe as they try out their newly acquired language skills. One simple way to create a secure environment is to establish routines. Routines allow students to know what to expect, even if they don't understand everything you say, and also provide an opportunity for them to begin to attach the language you use to what's happening around them. You can build your routines around the calendar and the weather. "Let's all bring our chairs and sit in a circle. Who can tell me what day today is?"

Language is learned through communication (i.e., real interaction about real events, tasks, needs that have meaning to the participants). Don't expect and certainly don't require a quiet classroom. Set up students' desks to facilitate conversation and create activities that require students to interact. Groups of four allow for pair-share and crosstalk.

Every individual has different abilities. Give careful thought to how you group your students. Consider students' language abilities and their social skills so that your groups have balance. Remember, all your students have strengths, and all your students are growing and changing. Groups don't have to stay fixed for a whole year. Regroup students as they develop their abilities, and create opportunities to utilize their strengths.

Not every language learner is ready to talk in class. Our receptive language abilities are generally greater than our productive abilities, and new language learners may be reluctant to express themselves publicly at first. Create opportunities for nonverbal responses. For example, young children can make "lollipops," with one green and one red side to hold up in response to yes /no questions. Create opportunities for verbal participation that don't create discomfort. Group recitation and group singing are fun for young children and allow them to practice language without discomfort.

Real communication is meaningful. Give your groups tasks that require interaction. For example, if each student in the group becomes an "expert" in one aspect of an assignment, and every student in the group needs to produce a paper about the whole assignment, everyone will be drawn into the conversation.

In all areas of learning, we build on prior knowledge. Thematic instruction allows students to use language they have already learned to address new tasks and solve new problems. If you are reading *The Very Hungry Caterpillar* (Carle, 1969), your students can count caterpillars, butterflies, and fruits. You can use the story as the basis for a science unit on caterpillars or on nutrition, a math unit on measurement ("How far can a caterpillar of a given length travel?"), or as a way to introduce concepts related to change. The possibilities are as unlimited as your imagination, and that's just one story and one theme!

Young students need to be taught to work collaboratively. Don't assume that students will naturally know how to function in a group. Engage your students in creating a safe learning community by developing rules for respectful interaction. Define roles and tasks for group assignments and monitor group interactions.

Modify your spoken language to make it accessible to new language learners. Speak slowly and clearly, and avoid idiomatic expressions.

Scaffold instruction with as many real experiences, demonstrations, and illustrations as possible. Especially for beginners, concrete objects and pictures are essential to understanding content and developing language.

Check for understanding in a variety of ways. It is ineffective with *any* group of students to ask, "Did you understand?" In general, people who don't understand aren't clear about whether they understand or not, so the question is not a useful assessment tool. Check for understanding by soliciting demonstrations of learning. Think of ways that new language learners can show you they understand by doing. For example, ask them to point to a location on a map or solve a math problem on the board.

their students are doing in school (Genesee & Hamayan, 1994; O'Malley & Valdez Pierce, 1992).

Literacy and Biliteracy

WHAT IS LITERACY?

Speaking to me, a student who was entering high school from eighth grade expressed surprise that he had to take a class in English.

"Why do I have to take English in high school?" he said. "I speak it already!"

"Because you've got to read Shakespeare, and where else will you do it if not in high school?!" I replied.

My reply was only half-joking: As a modern, literate society we share the assumptions, correct but usually unexplored, that language development continues through adolescence and young adulthood and that full language development includes literacy. Consequently, we require English speakers to take English in high school and through college.

In other words, literacy means more to us than simply mastering the ability to decode the written word. As one author puts it, "Literacy can be viewed . . . as the ability to think and reason like a literate person, *within a particular society*" (Langer, 1991, p. 11).

Furthermore, literacy has political implications. Since the earliest times of our republic, literacy has been seen as crucial to participation in a representative democracy. In a literate society, the ability to read is the key that unlocks the doors to the knowledge base of the culture of power and to the political system. Williams and Capizzi Snipper define *critical literacy* as the ability to determine "what effect a writer is attempting to bring about in readers, why he or she is making the effort, and just who those readers are" (1990, p. 11). In common parlance, a critical reader can read between the lines. It is not surprising, therefore, that the most repressive regimes in the world are the ones that offer the least opportunity for schooling or support for literacy.

BILITERACY

Often, when people discuss bilingualism and bilingual education, their attention is focused on the ability to speak a language. A preservice student teacher in a class on bilingualism once asked, "If children come from Spanish-speaking families, why do they need to study Spanish in school? Won't they learn it at home?" Children in Spanish-speaking households learn Spanish just like children in English-speaking households learn English.

But much as we assume that English speakers will develop literacy in their language in school, so speakers of other languages benefit from the language development that a school setting offers. And much as we expect an English speaker to be familiar with the great works of English language literature (abbreviated as "Shakespeare" in my reply to the eighth grader), or to write research papers and business letters in an appropriate format, so an educated Spanish speaker needs formal instruction to perform comparably in Spanish. Biliteracy, then, includes the development of the full range of understanding and skills appropriate for an educated speaker of two languages.

HOW CAN TEACHERS SUPPORT BILITERACY?

Theoretically, literacy is most readily achieved in a student's first language. Note that this generalization may not apply in American schools to speakers of some Asian languages such as Chinese. Mastery of the Chinese writing system is arduous, and youngsters may more readily learn to read in English, assuming that they have acquired some oral proficiency.

In general, however, as we have already seen, most of the concepts and skills that support our ability to read transfer readily from one language to another. Once we are literate in any language, we are literate. While we need to learn specific features of a new writing system, we don't need to learn to read each time we learn to read a new language.

Also, contrary to earlier thinking that students should not be introduced to reading in their new language until they are literate in their home language, it appears that bilingual students often become biliterate in both languages at about the same time and without the benefit of targeted instruction. De la Luz Reyes analyzed the work of four second-grade students who had been in bilingual classes from kindergarten on. Despite the fact that they each had only received literacy instruction in their dominant language, all achieved a

Several states permit automobile owners to create their own license plate numbers. Look at the following examples of so-called "vanity" license plates:

VET4ME	JANS BUG	AUIYQ
MOM ROX 2	XQQSME	EDUK8TR

You can probably read these license plates, and in some cases you may even know the make of the car or something about the owner. Think about how you are able to come up with this information. The letters and the sounds they make provide important clues, but clearly your ability to do so goes beyond graphophonic knowledge, the ability to connect letters and sounds.

You can decipher these license plates because you can draw on a reservoir of prior experiences and understandings about language (English in the examples above) and about the world. You know for example, what a license plate is, and that sometimes people use language on them in special and often playful ways. You know that sometimes letters or numbers on license plates stand in for syllables or entire words. You know that the plates often refer to the cars people drive, or the people themselves, and that cars have nicknames.

Reading is supported by our knowledge of content, our knowledge of meanings (semantics), and our cultural understandings. When you read in a second language, depending on your proficiency, you may not have the context knowledge that a native speaker has, so you may read more slowly and rely more heavily on graphophonic clues.

When you read with your English language learners or before you ask them to read on their own, spend time developing context. Students can read about new and unfamiliar situations. That's exactly what the world of reading is for. But you need to build a foundation for your students so they can extract meaning from the text.

You can support second language readers before, during and after reading a story with many different kinds of activities. For example, you can:

- Show students real examples of key objects that appear in the text and talk about them. Where realia are impractical, bring in good illustrations. If a story includes a guitar, maybe you can play the guitar for your students or you know a colleague or a student who can. That may not be practical, but you can always bring in a picture and a sound recording to share.
- Build a semantic web around key words in the text. Start with a word, and ask students to add meanings they associate with that word. Think, for example, about the words you might associate with *guitar*. As students build the web, they may suggest or you can add other related words that appear in the text.
- Build a cultural web. If your students come from different cultures, ask them to tell the class about stringed instruments from their cultures, or find examples and illustrations of instruments from the cultures represented in your classroom and beyond. For example, there's an enormous variety of stringed instruments around the world, including but hardly limited to charangos, ukeleles, balalaikas, ouds, sitars, erhus, harps, dulcimers, and kotos. Images and even audio samples of many of them are readily available on the web.
- Transform the genre: Ask students to act out a section of the story or text, perhaps using puppets, or to create a tableau, or "still" image from the text. Imagine a tableau of "The Cat and the Fiddle."

significant degree of biliteracy by second grade. De la Luz Reyes asserts that the children's "spontaneous biliteracy" was the result of "a learning environment that fosters and nurtures the learners' cultural and linguistic resources" (2001, p. 113). She also notes that the children's social play, which emerged in activities related to classroom activities, revolved around reading in both Spanish and English.

Riches and Genesee (2006) in their review of research on the relationships between first and second language and oral and written language conclude "L1 literacy does not detract from L2 literacy but rather contributes to and supports its development" (2006, p. 81). They further note that English language learners who are successful readers and writers use all the language tools at their disposal, using their knowledge of language in general and of their specific languages to help them make sense of text. This supports the concept of a reservoir of deep underlying language proficiency and suggests yet again that for academic purposes, bilingual is indeed better.

LITERACY AND THE SECOND LANGUAGE LEARNER

The process of becoming literate involves the construction and creation of meaning through text. Current theorists suggest this interaction with text to engage meaning is both cognitive and social (Hudelson, 1994; Riggs, 1991). Citing Goodman and Goodman, Riggs asserts that "in a literate society, using written language is as natural as using conversation, and the uses of written language develop as naturally as do the uses of oral language" (1991, p. 524).

Many of the strategies that teachers use to develop native literacy are useful for assisting students to develop literacy in a new language. Hudelson (1994) suggests that teachers create a print-rich environment, provide opportunities for collaboration, and organize instruction so that students engage literature in a meaningful way and write purposefully.

It is important to remember, however, that text is embedded in cultural and social contexts, which may be unfamiliar to second language learners. Escamilla (1993) points out that students can answer many conventionally structured comprehension questions by quoting directly from a text without any real understanding. Harman (1991) provides an excellent example of how this is possible with a nonsense sample text: "The three blugy chinzles slottled prusily on the flubbish werlies." By referring to the text, it is possible to answer the question "How did the blugy chinzles slottle?" (p. 144) without any real comprehension. Teachers of second language learners need to develop strategies for evaluating whether students have engaged the real meaning of a text.

HOW CAN SCHOOLS PROMOTE BILITERACY?

In the American context, the development of fully bilingual and biliterate students requires a rethinking of language education. First, we must promote

In Your Classroom
Using Technology to Teach a Second Language

As access to technology increases, teachers may want to mediate language instruction. Technology can:

- *Motivate:* Today's students are often familiar with contemporary technology, even at fairly young ages, and are often excited to work on classroom computers.
- *Use visual approaches:* Animations and videos are especially useful with young students who have not yet developed literacy skills.
- *Differentiate:* Use technology to provide individualized instruction or to provide activities for independent groups.
- *Provide input and monitor output:* As traditional language laboratories have done for years, technology can allow students to listen to their new language and record and listen to their own language production.

But while drill-and-practice on language skills may be helpful, it can easily devolve into mechanistic "drill-and-kill." Teachers should organize assignments and select software that encourage interaction and problem solving.

Research and literature on how to use technology effectively when working with English language learners is still emerging. One good resource for teachers is *Technology and Teaching English Language Learners,* by Mary Ellen Butler-Pascoe and Karin M. Wiburg (Boston: Pearson, 2003).

maintenance bilingual education for language minority students and enrichment language instruction for native English speakers. Then we must extend our programming to include secondary and postsecondary education. For example, all too often, native Spanish speakers have little opportunity to develop skills in reading and writing Spanish. Courses specifically geared for native speakers are offered at some high schools and colleges, but they are still relatively rare. Expansion of our efforts will no doubt require that educators promote understanding of the dimensions and value of biliteracy.

Summary

Dual language instructional programs include a component for developing students' proficiency in a second language. Grammar-translation approaches have dominated second language instruction for centuries, despite their ineffectuality in developing communicative competence. The audiolingual approach, first developed for military purposes, relies heavily on habit formation and has proven somewhat useful.

Theories about second language acquisition have led to the development of approaches that attempt to develop communicative competence. Total Physical Response, Suggestopedia, and Counseling-Learning pay careful attention to the need to address the affective variables in second language learning. Notional-functional approaches respond to the pragmatics of language and organize activities around language functions.

Krashen's theory of second language acquisition has formed the basis for the Natural Approach, which attempts to provide rich, comprehensible input to students in a comfortable environment as they move through the stages of language development.

Specially Designed Academic Instruction in English (SDAIE) combines second language instruction with content instruction. SDAIE applies to all aspects of instruction, including planning, classroom management, lesson delivery, and assessment. It is useful for intermediate second language speakers and as a bridge for students about to make the transition to all-English classrooms.

Literacy and biliteracy are important considerations in dual language instruction. Literacy must be defined as *critical literacy,* and students should have the opportunity to develop their critical literacy skills to the fullest extent in both their languages.

Questions to Think About and Discuss

1. If you learned a second language in school, how were you taught? Was the approach effective? Why or why not? As best you can remember and discern, did it conform to any theory of second language acquisition with which you are familiar?
2. If you successfully learned a second language outside of a formal school setting, what were the factors that led to your success in gaining proficiency in that language?
3. What kinds of approaches and programs are used in your school to teach English as a second language? How do these programs measure up to what theorists tell us about the ways children learn a new language?
4. What is the prevailing approach to literacy in your school? How are second language learners introduced to literacy? Is the approach successful? Why or why not?
5. How can teachers create learning environments that support literacy beyond a mechanistic, skills-based approach? In other words, how can teachers encourage students to engage with text and learn to love reading?

Activities

1. Visit a primary level and a secondary/adult second language lesson. What kind of assumptions underlie the kind of approach in use? To

what extent are these assumptions in keeping with current second language acquisition theory?

2. Investigate commercial language teaching programs in your area. What languages are taught? What approaches are used? How much do the courses or programs cost? How many students are enrolled in the programs?

3. Develop a lesson plan in social studies, science, or mathematics appropriate for a sheltered English setting. Include content-obligatory and content-compatible language objectives. Describe how you plan to contextualize the material. Be careful to maintain the level of the material in the lesson while modifying the delivery for intermediate second language learners. Include an assessment component.

Suggestions for Further Reading

Asher, J. (1986). *Learning another language through actions. The complete teacher's guidebook.* Los Gatos, CA: Sky Oaks Productions.
   A handbook on Total Physical Response, this book provides background on how the approach was developed, documents its effectiveness, answers common questions about it, and provides a lesson-by-lesson plan for its implementation.

Blair, R. W. (Ed.). (1982). *Innovative approaches to language teaching.* Rowley, MA: Newbury House.
   Blair divides language teaching approaches into three categories: the comprehension approach, approaches to a rich acquisition environment, and rich learning environment approaches. Within those categories, the book contains articles by a number of authors, including Asher, Terrell, and Lozanov. The introduction to the book sets the development of language teaching in a historical context and also contains a paper presented by Krashen at Brigham Young University in 1979 that is an excellent introduction to his theories on language acquisition. The book's bibliography is particularly useful because it contains references divided by teaching approaches.

Carle, E. (1969). *The very hungry caterpillar.* New York: World Publishing.
   A children's classic, and a wonderful addition to any primary level classroom library, this book has been translated into many languages. Many teachers have used it in lots of ways, and a web search will provide you with excellent ideas and starting points.

de la Luz Reyes, M., & Halcón, J. J. (Eds.). (2001). *The best for our children: Critical perspectives on literacy for Latino students.* New York: Teachers College Press.
   This book looks at the sociocultural, sociohistorical, and sociopolitical contexts of literacy. The third section of the book provides an overview of creative and successful instructional approaches that support literacy for Latino students by engaging those contexts in meaningful and powerful ways.

Echevarria, J., & Graves, A. (2007). *Sheltered content instruction: Teaching English language learners with diverse abilities* (3rd ed.). Boston: Pearson.
   Following brief overviews of foundational information, this book has five chapters focused on classroom practice guiding teachers in strategies to shelter content to make it accessible to second language learners.

Freeman, D. E., & Freeman, Y. S. (2001). *Between worlds: Access to second language acquisition* (2nd ed.). Portsmouth, NH: Heinemann.

Combining descriptions of theory with practice and examples of student work, this book is useful to all teachers who want to support their second language learners. The book is particularly valuable because it speaks to the cultural and social contexts of second language learning and reaches beyond the classroom, showing teachers how to work with their students' families and communities. Appendices include bibliographies related to second language acquisition theory, methods of teaching, and resources for classroom use.

Hadaway, N. L., Vardell, S. M., & Young, T. A. (2002). *Literature-based instruction with English language learners.* Boston: Allyn and Bacon.

The emphasis on accountability has pressured many teachers into reductionist strategies for teaching reading. While these strategies may show immediate short-range gains on standardized tests, they do not necessarily develop students' literacy, construed in the broadest sense. Teachers will find this book useful in thinking about ways to develop reading around literature. This is particularly valuable for second language learners, because exposure to literature supports language acquisition.

Hamayan, E. V., & Perlman, R. (1990, Spring). *Helping language minority students after they exit from bilingual/ESL programs: A handbook for teachers.* Rosslyn, VA: National Clearinghouse for Bilingual Education.

This short publication enumerates and explains strategies that teachers can use to shelter their content-area instruction to assist their second language learners. The handbook provides detailed information about setting up and monitoring a buddy system that pairs second language learners with bilingual or monolingual English-speaking students.

Krashen, S. D., & Terrell, T. D. (1983). *The natural approach: Language acquisition in the classroom.* San Francisco: Alemany.

This book contains an explanation of Krashen's theory of language acquisition and develops the implications of the theory for classroom instruction. Several chapters are devoted to actual classroom activities for the implementation of the Natural Approach. The introductory chapter provides a historical overview of second language instruction, which provides the context for the development of this new approach.

Peregoy, S. F., & Boyle, O. F. (2005). *Reading, writing, & learning in ESL: A resource book for K–8 teachers* (4th ed.). White Plains, NY: Longman.

Providing clear directions for teaching reading and writing in English to English as a second language learners, this book includes activities and resources and addresses the daily concerns of classroom teachers.

Pérez, B. (Ed.). (1998). *Sociocultural contexts of language and literacy.* Mahwah, NJ: Lawrence Erlbaum.

Starting from the assumption that "Literacy is always socially and culturally situated" (p. 4), this book explores reading and writing instruction as they might be situated in a variety of cultural communities, and offers teachers perspectives and strategies to inform instruction in rich and productive ways.

Ramírez, A. G. (1995). *Creating contexts for second language acquisition: Theory and methods.* White Plains, NY: Longman.

This book is comprehensive, up-to-date, and useful. It includes a well-organized overview of current theory as well as useful directions for practice, with descriptions and examples of ways to teach listening, speaking, reading, and writing to second language learners. The book deserves special acknowledgment for attention to the dynamics of culture in second language learning.

Richard-Amato, P. A., & Snow, M. A. (1995). *The multicultural classroom: Readings for content-area teachers* (2nd ed.). White Plains, NY: Longman.

Following a collection of articles that define a theoretical framework and describe cultural considerations, this book addresses the specifics of classroom instruction in social studies, mathematics, science, art, physical education, music, and literacy development for second language learners.

Valdés, G. (2001). *Learning and not learning English.* New York: Teachers College Press.

The author follows four newly arrived middle school students through their English as a second language instruction, and through their experiences and perceptions, teases out the ways social and political dynamics affect the extent to which English language learners succeed, or more importantly, fail, despite their teachers' best professed intentions. As the author points out in this critical analysis (p. 155), "Individuals of good will are not aware that they have become instruments of dominant interests. They are seldom conscious of the fact that power is exercised both through coercion and through consent."

8

Aspects of Culture

Language and its use in the classroom are natural foci for the study of dual language instruction. Language, however, is inextricably bound with culture, and cultural factors have an important influence on educational outcomes for all students.

The history of the United States has always been characterized by cultural diversity, but never so much as in modern times. The last part of the twentieth century has seen unprecedented numbers of immigrants coming to the United States. In addition, changes in immigration law in 1965 opened the door to newcomers from every corner of the world.

Nowhere is the impact of continued and varied immigration felt more than in the public schools. Each day, teachers attempt to meet the needs of children from many different cultural backgrounds. This chapter will attempt to clarify definitions of culture and provide examples of its characteristics and manifestations. In addition, this chapter will consider multicultural education and its relationship to bilingual education.

Culture and Population

American culture is difficult to characterize because it is made up of many complex and changing subcultures. In fact, complexity and change are at the heart of American culture. The demographics of the United States are in flux at the current time for a variety of reasons.

THE IMPACT OF IMMIGRATION

Compelled by war or famine or lured by the prospect of life in a new and exciting world, people have been immigrating to the New World since before the inception of the United States as a nation. In the nineteenth century, social, political, and economic upheaval caused an influx of people from all over Europe. The Irish arrived, having fled the potato famines. German and Scandinavian farmers were attracted by the farmlands of the Midwest. Chinese laborers built our transcontinental railroad lines. Italians, Poles, and Czechs, attracted by the opportunities for economic success and freedom from oppression, all made their way to the United States in the late 1800s.

The nineteenth-century wave of immigration swelled into the twentieth century, reaching a peak between 1900 and 1920 when numbers of Italians and Eastern European Jews flooded East Coast ports, and Mexicans, displaced by the Revolution of 1910, immigrated northward to the Southwest and California.

Reaction to newcomers was swift and often vicious. *Xenophobia* (a fear of things that seem foreign) and racism led to attempts to limit immigration. The Chinese Exclusion Act of 1882 was the first federal attempt to limit immigration by nationality. The 1917 Immigration Act excluded Asians, and the National Origins Act of 1924 established quotas for nations outside the Western Hemisphere (The Immigration Project, 1981).

In 1965, however, President Lyndon B. Johnson signed legislation that altered national immigration policy. Prior to 1965, immigration law favored ethnic groups who were already represented in the U.S. population. Johnson's legislation placed an annual limit of 20,000 immigrants for each country. As a result, people are entering the United States in significant numbers from all over the world. In 1984 the United States admitted 600,000 legal immigrants.

Official numbers do not appear to exceed figures of the early part of the century, but illegal immigration adds significant numbers, perhaps doubling official counts ("Growth of a Nation," 1985). Not only has the number of immigrants increased, but the diversity of newcomers has increased as well, with the flow from Europe decreasing and the influx from Latin America and Asia increasing.

OTHER DEMOGRAPHIC FACTORS

While steady and varied immigration has an undeniable and dynamic impact on our profile as a nation, it is not the only factor that affects the demographic picture. Differential rates of growth among various groups also have a significant effect on our population. The "baby boom" that occurred after World War II was primarily a white middle-class phenomenon, and the rate of growth in that segment of the population has since decreased significantly. People of color in the United States are younger than white people and have higher birth rates (U.S. Bureau of the Census, 1997).

The changing demographic and cultural situation in our schools means that all teachers will have to develop skills to work with children who fall into the following categories:

- *Language minority children:* These are children who have a person who speaks a language other than English in their homes. They may be bilingual or may speak only English. In either case, they are likely to have links to an ethnic minority culture.
- *English language learners:* According to the National Clearinghouse for English Language Acquisition (NCELA), there were approximately 5.2

million English language learners in public schools in the United States (K–12) in 2004–2005. While public school enrollments rose about 2.6 percent between 1994 and 2005, the number of English language learners grew by an astonishing 61 percent. Enrollments of student with limited proficiency in English are predictably high in certain states. California, for example, which enrolls approximately 10 percent of the nation's schoolchildren, identified approximately 1.6 million English language learners in grades K through 12 in 2006–2007 (California State Department of Education, 2007). Other states with high enrollments of English learners include Arizona, Florida, Illinois, New York, and Texas. But enrollments are not limited to those areas, and increases in the English learner student population are large in places you might not expect. Georgia, for example, experienced an increase of 113 percent from 1999–2000 to 2000–2001. In the same period, Montana experienced an increase of 88.4 percent (Kindler, 2002). Looking at a longer time frame, in the decade between 1990 and 2000, 19 states experienced growth in limited English proficient student populations in excess of 200 percent (NCELA, 2003). Updated information about your state's student population is available from the National Clearinghouse for English Language Acquisition at www.ncela.gwu.edu. The website for the state department of education in your state is another useful source of up-to-date demographic information.

The school has traditionally been a gateway to mainstream culture for the diverse groups that make up American society. As the population changes, and indeed as our concept of mainstream culture is altered by the groups that enter it, teachers will need to develop a deep understanding of the nature of culture and the implications of diversity in the classroom.

What Is Culture?

Like language, our own culture is usually invisible to us. We tend to associate culture with things that are far away and exotic. A student of mine once commented, "I didn't know there was such a thing as American culture until I spent time in Central America." Away from home, amid people who operate under different assumptions, that student was able to perceive characteristics of her own culture. According to an old Japanese saying, "One sees the sky through a hollow reed." If we equate the sky to reality, then the hollow reed through which we view it may be likened to our culture. But what exactly is culture?

Definitions of culture abound in social science literature, and the search for a single definition can be perplexing and frustrating. As basic social science assumptions have changed over time, so have definitions of culture. The trend toward behaviorist thinking gave rise to definitions of culture that emphasized the observable patterns of behavior of a particular group. In the

1950s the thinking of cognitive psychologists influenced anthropologists, who began to conceptualize culture in terms of ideas and beliefs to the exclusion of observable behaviors.

One frequently cited definition describes *culture* as a system of standards for perceiving, believing, evaluating, and acting (Goodenough, 1971). Each culture has many complex and overlapping systems within which its members operate and through which they assign and extract meaning. When you encounter a culture different from your own, you try to figure out how things work (*cultural behavior*) and why they function as they do (*cultural knowledge*).

For our purposes, it is useful to accept a fairly inclusive approach to the concept of culture. One analysis (Arvizu, Snyder, & Espinosa, 1980) suggests that culture is "a dynamic, creative, and continuous process including behaviors, values, and substance learned and shared by people that guides them in their struggle for survival and gives meaning to their lives." Let us consider the components of this definition, that is, the characteristics of culture.

CULTURE IS DYNAMIC

Just as language changes over time to meet the needs of its users, culture changes over time as people adapt to changing circumstances. For example, people often think of Native Americans as people who live in tepees, wear feather headdresses, and hunt buffalo. That characterization might be historically accurate to a limited extent, but it no longer applies, despite pervasive media images to the contrary. While Native Americans today cherish and protect their traditional heritages, they are also likely to be part of mainstream U.S. culture.

CULTURE IS CREATIVE

The process of culture change is one of creativity. Each new environmental change results in a cultural adaptation. Old ways are replaced by the new in dynamic and creative ways. For example, economic circumstances in the United States have resulted in large numbers of women entering the wage-earning workforce. The result has been a change in our perception of family structure, in our belief system about the abilities of women, and in systems for caring for children outside the immediate family.

CULTURE IS CONTINUOUS

Changing circumstances produce new systems of action, belief, and perception, but the new systems contain traces of the old. Such traces are what we call *tradition*. Each successive generation passes on its cumulative culture to the next. Chinese Americans, for example, celebrate the Chinese New Year in the United States. While the traditional week-long celebration observed in

China is impractical in a modern U.S. setting, traditional foods are prepared and customs are still maintained.

CULTURE IS LEARNED

We are not born with our culture. A film called *Living on Tokyo Time* (Okazaki, 1987) tells the story of a young Japanese woman who immigrates to California and marries a Japanese American man in order to obtain legal immigration status. The movie recounts her experience and her surprise as she discovers that although her new husband looks like someone from Japan, he is unfamiliar with Japanese customs and even with Japanese food. Such characteristics as the color of our hair and eyes are genetically determined, but we learn our culture as we are socialized by the people and circumstances that surround us, in a process called *enculturation.*

CULTURE IS SHARED

Just as language is useful only if we agree on certain conventions, culture needs shared assumptions in order to function. Some of you, for example, may belong to an in-group or subculture that uses a particular handshake as a greeting. Members of that group rely on the handshake as a symbol for group membership and a way of opening a social interaction. Such a symbol is useful only if members of the group share an understanding of its meaning.

The assumption that culture is shared is operative even when a particular behavior or activity is not. For example, among mainstream Americans, people generally brush their teeth individually, in private. Despite the absence of others, we each usually brush our teeth according to shared culture knowledge about what to use and how to proceed, with certain shared assumptions about the value of dental care.

Every culture is extremely complex, and not every member knows all the systems and symbols involved. Conversely, most of us belong to more than one subculture and may be competent in the symbols and systems of several (Goodenough, 1971).

CULTURE IS A STRUGGLE FOR SURVIVAL

Each culture is an adaptive response to a particular environment. The symbols and systems of a culture evolve to allow a particular group to adjust to its circumstances. As mentioned before, we tend to have an inaccurate and stereotypical view of Native Americans, both as they are in the present and as they were in the past. Photographs, however, taken between 1896 and 1930 by Edward S. Curtis (Brown, 1972) reveal the astounding number and variety of Native American cultures that existed on the North American continent prior to European domination.

The hunting tribes of the Great Plains lived in tepees, which were made of readily available buffalo skins and easily transported in keeping with the tribe members' needs as nomadic hunters. Indians of the coastal Northwest, on the other hand, lived in reed houses and were skilled as fishermen. Each group developed a culture that met its needs for survival and responded to the resources and demands of its environment.

Culture and Language

The relationship of culture and language has been of interest to anthropologists and linguists since the early twentieth century. The debate centers around Edward Sapir's suggestion that speakers of different languages have different perceptions of the world; that is, language determines culture. This view, promulgated by his student Benjamin Lee Whorf, is sometimes called the *Whorf* (or *Sapir-Whorf*) *hypothesis*. The layperson's expression of the Whorf hypothesis is often stated in this way: "There are some things you can only say in Spanish," or whatever language the speaker holds dear.

One researcher (Chaika, 1989) has characterized language as "a mirror of its speakers' attitudes and ideas. A mirror reflects. It does not determine; it does not hold prisoners" (p. 295). As we saw in our discussion of the nature of language in Chapter 3, language changes and adapts to meet the needs of its speakers. While some languages may have more concise forms of expression for objects or concepts that exist in a particular culture, any language can express any idea that its culture requires. For example, Japanese has *wabi*, a word that describes the flaw that makes an object beautiful (Rheingold, 1988, p. 74). The German word *schadenfreude* describes the pleasure one person takes from another person's misfortunes. We don't have an English word for those concepts, but we can express the ideas. Actually, *schadenfreude* has been borrowed by English speakers and now appears in many English dictionaries. Apparently, while few of us might like to admit feeling it, the word for *schadenfreude* comes in handy!

The contemporary educational philosopher Neil Postman (1995) says that "we use language to create the world. . . . Language allows us to name things, but, more than that, it also suggests what feelings we are obliged to associate with the things we name. Even more, language controls what things shall be named, what things we ought to pay attention to" (pp. 83–84). The debate as to whether or not language determines culture or vice versa may continue, but it is inarguable that language and culture are inseparable, and learning a new language invariably entails learning a new culture.

In the motion picture *Born in East L.A.* (Marin & Macgregor-Scott, 1987), a native-born Mexican American is mistakenly deported from Los Angeles to Mexico. Trying to earn his way back to the United States, he takes a job with a *coyote* (people smuggler), teaching people English so they can blend in when they make their way across the border. His students are Asian immigrants trying to cross the border into the United States illegally. He quickly discerns what they will need to know in Los Angeles. He dresses them in bandannas, teaches them a "cool" walk, and begins their training in English with the words "*Orale vato*, wha's happenin'!" (Hey, buddy, what's happening?) It is clear from the outset that language learning must be accompanied by culture learning.

How Is Culture Manifested?

James P. Spradley (1972) commented, "The man in the street is a naive realist who lives in a world he can count on, a world he believes is much the same for everyone else" (p. 8). In other words, we usually assume that the qualities we perceive in the world around us and the meanings we assign to symbols and events are concrete and universal. On the contrary, people around the world have devised an infinite number and variety of social institutions, daily habits, and meaning systems in their quest for survival.

To get a sense of the vastness of the cultural enterprise we will look at a few of the many manifestations of culture. All of us are familiar with myriad examples of each culture area. Exemplification, however, sometimes leads to stereotyping. The examples presented here are meant to be illustrative, but may be somewhat oversimplified.

CLOTHING AND DECORATION

While we might immediately assume that the purpose of clothing is for protection against the weather, a closer look shows us that people use clothing for a variety of purposes such as gender differentiation, status display, and ritual.

For example, if you have ever planned a wedding, you know how much emphasis is placed on proper dress for everyone involved. In middle-class mainstream U.S. culture, brides often wear white. However, depending on the formality of the occasion or their previous marital status, they may wear another color and dress less formally. Attendants are carefully dressed, and the groom and his party must be attired in keeping with the nature of the event. Flowers are carefully selected and arranged. Stores even market mother-of-the-bride dresses, indicating that we have a particular cultural expectation of the bride's mother. Rites of passage and other ceremonial events require special dress and adornment that differs from culture to culture.

HOUSING

Again, it seems logical to assume that the purpose of housing is protection. As shelter, housing generally conforms to the resources and demands of each particular environment. Stone houses in New England are practical and serviceable in an environment with abundant large rocks in the soil and a cold climate. Such houses would be impractical and out of place near the equator, where the climate is always warm and humid, or for nomadic peoples who need shelters that can be dismantled and carried for long distances.

But housing, like clothing, serves purposes beyond the need for protection. A home may serve as a center for family or community life, and an analysis of housing often reveals social organization. Houses may also indicate status. For example, the President of the United States always resides in the White House for the duration of the term. While not necessarily the most opulent residence in the country, the White House has social and historical significance.

TIME ORIENTATION

Different cultures have different orientations to time. You may have encountered an overt reference to cultural time orientation if you have been invited to a party and were told that it would start at six o'clock in the evening *hora Latina* (Latin time). Such an invitation acknowledges the fact that in the Hispanic cultural context, a social invitation for six o'clock may indicate an event that will start no earlier than seven in the evening. If you were to appear at six, you would likely be the first to arrive and would find your hosts unprepared. Some people might suggest that Hispanics are not prompt or "have no sense of time." Such an ethnocentric view fails to understand that each of us knows when to arrive for a particular event within the context of our culture or subculture.

SPATIAL ORIENTATION

Each culture has its own patterns for the use of personal space. You may have noticed a proxemic pattern if you were born in the United States and have had a conversation with a person born in the Middle East. Middle Easterners have a different concept of appropriate distance from North Americans for nonintimate personal conversation, standing closer to each other than North Americans do. Such differences are often the cause of misjudgments and misunderstandings: one person assumes the other is moving in too close, while the other person judges the first as aloof or uncaring. Proxemic patterns also manifest themselves in architecture, arrangement of furnishings, and body language (Hall, 1966).

VALUES

Each culture has a frame of reference for identifying what is desirable or important to the group. The academic achievement of newly arrived Asian immigrants has led to speculation that their success is related to the Confucian value system and the value it places on scholarship (Butterfield, 1986). Without entering into a discussion of the merits of that suggestion, we note that it acknowledges the role of values in culture.

Values are harder to identify than the material aspects of culture, but they are of particular importance to teachers. All too often teachers acknowledge surface aspects of culture through ethnic heritage celebrations, classroom decor, and curriculum materials. While such acknowledgments of material or surface culture are worthwhile, they are not sufficient.

For example, it has been said that Navajo children from traditional backgrounds look down when they are addressed by a teacher. Teachers who fail to understand that the children are showing them respect within the context of Navajo culture often misinterpret their behavior and assume they are disrespectful or even sneaky. Mainstream American culture places a high value on direct eye contact, as manifested in expressions such as, "I looked him straight in the eye."

One teacher tells of his difficulty in trying to encourage Rosa, a Mexican American high school student in his remedial English class. In an attempt to express a genuine interest in her, he complimented her on a new hair style. Shortly thereafter, she began cutting class and finally revealed to a counselor that she thought the teacher was taking an inappropriate romantic interest in her (Wineburg, 1987). In that case, the values difference between Rosa and her teacher led to an uncomfortable and potentially serious misunderstanding. Misunderstanding of deep culture or value systems may result in discriminatory treatment of children from minority groups.

Bilingual Education and Multicultural Education

In practice, educators often refer to *bilingual/multicultural education*. Because the terms appear side by side, *bilingual* and *multicultural education* are erroneously construed as identical. The two are not one and the same thing, although there is a relationship between dual language instruction and multicultural education.

WHAT IS MULTICULTURAL EDUCATION?

Carlos Cortés, a leading exponent of multicultural education, begins his definition of *multicultural education* by describing what multicultural education is *not* (1990). He asserts that multicultural education is not the celebration of holidays or the inclusion of special history days or weeks in the curriculum, an approach that James Banks, another important multicultural theorist, refers to as "tepees and chitlins" and "heroes and holidays" (1977). Banks calls such approaches to multicultural education additive—they tack on bits and pieces to the existing curriculum, but they do not alter the basic structure of schooling. Cortés and Banks also agree that multicultural education is not the study of a particular ethnic group, although ethnic studies may contribute to multicultural education by generating the scholarship necessary to build an inclusive curriculum. Finally, multicultural education is not a compensatory program for students who are identified as "minority."

Multicultural education in its broadest sense entails educational reform or restructuring to empower students, provide all students with equitable

ℒetter from a Mother of a Native American Child

Dear Teacher:

Before you take charge of the classroom that contains my child, please ask yourself why you are going to teach Indian children. What are your expectations? What rewards do you anticipate? What ego needs will our children have to meet?

Write down and examine all the information and opinions you possess about Indians. What are the stereotypes and untested assumptions that you bring with you into the class-room. How many negative attitudes towards Indians will you put before my child?

What values, class prejudices and moral principles do you take for granted as universal? Please remember that "different from" is not the same as "worse than" or "better than," and the yardstick you use to measure your own life satisfactorily may not be appropriate for their lives.

The term "culturally deprived" was invented by well-meaning middle-class whites to describe something they could not understand.

Too many teachers, unfortunately, seem to see their role as rescuer. My child does not need to be rescued; he does not consider being Indian a misfortune. He has a culture, probably older than yours; he has meaningful values and a rich and varied experiential background. However strange or incomprehensible it may seem to you, you have no right to do or say anything that implies to him that it is less than satisfactory.

Our children's experiences have been different from those of the "typical" white middle-class child for whom most school curricula seem to have been designed (I suspect that this "typical" child does not exist except in the minds of curriculum writers). Nonetheless, my child's experiences have been as intense and meaningful to him as any child's.

Like most Indian children his age, he is competent. He can dress himself, prepare a meal for himself, clean up afterwards, care for a younger child. He knows his Reserve, all of which is his home, like the back of his hand.

He is not accustomed to having to ask permission to do the ordinary things that are part of normal living. He is seldom forbidden to do anything; more usually the consequences of an action are explained to him and he is allowed to decide for himself whether or not to act. His entire existence since he has been old enough to see and hear has been an experiential learning situation, arranged to provide him with the opportunity to develop his skills and confidence in his own capacities. Didactic teaching will be an alien experience for him.

He is not self-conscious in the way many white children are. Nobody has ever told him his efforts towards independence are cute. He is a young human being energetically doing his job, which is to get on with the process of learning to function as an adult human being. He will respect you as a person, but he will expect you to do likewise to him.

He has been taught, by precept, that courtesy is an essential part of human conduct and rudeness is any action that makes another person feel stupid or foolish. Do not mistake his patient courtesy for indifference or passivity.

He doesn't speak standard English, but he is no way "linguistically handicapped." If you will take the time and courtesy to listen and observe carefully, you will see that he and the other Indian children communicate very well, both among themselves and with other Indians. They speak "functional English," very effectively augmented by their fluency in the silent language, the subtle, unspoken communication of facial expressions, gestures, body movement and the use of personal space.

You will be well advised to remember that our children are skillful interpreters of the silent language. They will know your feelings and attitudes with unerring precision, no matter how carefully you arrange your smile or modulate your voice. They will learn in your classroom, because children learn involuntarily. What they learn will depend on you.

Will you help my child to learn to read, or will you teach him that he has a reading problem? Will you help him develop problem solving skills, or will you teach him that school is where you try to guess what answer the teacher wants?

Will he learn that his sense of his own value and dignity is valid, or will he learn that he must forever be apologetic and "trying harder" because he isn't white? Can you help him acquire the intellectual skills he needs without at the same time imposing your values on top of those he already has?

Respect my child. He is a person. He has a right to be himself.

Yours very sincerely,

His Mother

SOURCE: "Respect My Child: He Has a Right to Be Himself." Wassaja, February 1976. Reprinted by permission of *The Indian Historian*.

opportunities, and enable all students to function comfortably and effectively in a pluralist democracy (Cortés, 1990; Nieto, 1992). Current theorists favor a social reconstructionist multicultural approach. Social reconstructionists work toward empowering students to actively engage their own life circumstances and alter them in the direction of social equity and justice. This point of view is rooted in the educational philosophy of critical pedagogy.

Critical pedagogy rejects what Paolo Freire (1970) has termed the "banking" concept of education, where teachers make deposits of knowledge into their students, a system which assumes that teachers are experts and students are not. In critical pedagogy, students are encouraged to pose their own questions and seek their own answers. Critical pedagogy assumes that students are inquisitive and creative and can use themselves and their environments as sources for both problems and their solutions.

Critical approaches underlie programs such as *Como Ellos Lo Ven* (Lessow-Hurley, 1977). In that project, students from migrant farmwork families in Longmont, Colorado, created a documentary of their lives, using their own photographs and narratives based on those images to produce a book that was then incorporated into the reading program in their class.

In another project based in critical pedagogy, Flor Ada engaged Spanish-speaking parents in the Pajaro Valley in California in developing their children's literacy skills (Flor Ada, 1988). Through presentations and small group discussions, parents were introduced to Spanish language children's literature and to ways of encouraging their children to read and write. As a result of their participation, parents came to understand the value of their home language, to see themselves as essential participants in their children's education, and to develop their own critical literacy skills as a key to understanding their world.

Multicultural education broadly conceived touches every aspect of school life, from the books and materials students use to the distribution of power within the school community. Nieto (1992) asserts that multicultural education is basic and pervasive. Cortés sums up his definition of multicultural education as "a continuous, integrated, multiethnic, multidisciplinary process for educating all American students about diversity, a curricular basic oriented toward preparing young people to live with pride and understanding in our multiethnic present and increasingly multiethnic future" (p. 3).

In its fullest sense, multicultural education is not a program that is implemented on Monday, or in January, but a total rethinking of the way we do schooling in a diverse society with a democratic civic framework.

WHAT IS THE CONNECTION BETWEEN BILINGUAL EDUCATION AND MULTICULTURAL EDUCATION?

In the professional arena, bilingual and multicultural education have developed separately, with separate journals, professional associations, and constituencies. Bilingual education is often erroneously construed as compensatory education for speakers of minority languages, while multicultural education is often mistakenly conceptualized as a program for African American students. We have seen that both bilingual and multicultural education admit to much more inclusive and useful definitions than those with a compensatory or deficit focus. What then is the connection between these two concepts?

Both multicultural and bilingual education subscribe to the fundamental idea that schooling should utilize students' knowledge of the world as a starting point and resource for learning. For all students, language is perhaps the single most important aspect of culture, since language is the primary means by which each of us is enculturated, that is, brought into our particular communities of behavior and belief. For language minority students, primary language is a deep resource that schooling should validate and enhance. Using the students' first language is empowering, since it validates students' culture. It is equitable to the extent that it provides equal access to the curriculum. And when it develops and maintains students' primary language alongside English, it enhances their preparation to function in an increasingly pluralist environment. In other words, bilingual education that values and promotes bilingualism and biliteracy is multicultural as well.

Bilingualism is an asset in an increasingly multicultural society and a global economy. English-only students benefit from an education that allows them to learn in more than one language and prepares them to function effectively in a world characterized by diversity. When we provide a bilingual education to all students we meet many of the goals embodied in broad definitions of multicultural education. In sum, while bilingual and multicultural education are not necessarily identical, all students can benefit from an education that is bilingual and multicultural.

Summary

The demography of the United States is changing significantly, due both to immigration and to differences among ethnic groups in average age and birth rates. Schools are particularly affected by these demographic changes, so that teachers are working increasingly with children from diverse linguistic and cultural backgrounds.

Culture is something we all have but often find difficult to perceive. Culture, like language, is dynamic, changing to meet the needs of the people it serves. All cultures have coherent, shared systems of action and belief that allow people to function and survive. Culture is manifested in our behaviors and beliefs about food, shelter, clothing, space, and time, as well as our value systems. We learn our cultures, and second language learning involves culture learning as well.

Bilingual and multicultural education are not identical, but many basic dispositions, concepts, and skills are common to both fields, and student empowerment is a key concept in both.

Questions to Think About and Discuss

1. How would you characterize your own culture? What values would you consider part of your cultural identity? What kinds of things do you do that you would consider cultural expression? (Remember, that's just about everything!) If you identify with a particular ethnic or religious group, what values do you hold as part of that identity and what behaviors do you engage in as a result of your identification with that group?

2. Often, people develop their understandings of cultural difference through travel. If you have traveled outside the United States, think about your experiences. Were there differences in everyday assumptions and transactions? Were there interactions where you were able to negotiate the differences? Were there occasions when differing assumptions caused you inconvenience or discomfort?

3. Think about the assumptions and behaviors that are commonplace in American schools. Imagine that you are an immigrant youngster entering an American school for the first time. What will you find perplexing? What would help you negotiate your new experience?

Activities

1. Look up demographics for your local school district(s). Your state department of education may have the data. School districts may also have the information. Local newspapers sometimes report on demographic changes. How has the population changed in the last ten years? How many English language learners are there in your area? What language groups are represented? Make an illustrative chart or map to share with your colleagues.

2. Teachers working with Navajo children need to be careful about field trips to the zoo and to certain museums. Navajo children should not see bears or snakes, nor should they be allowed to view human skeletal remain. In the event that they do, they must participate in cleansing ceremonies, which are lengthy and often costly. Study an ethnic or cultural group in your area. Use personal resources as well as the library. What values and assumptions does the group have that differ from your own? What can you learn that will help you provide relevant, motivating, and effective instruction for your students?

Suggestions for Further Reading

The study of culture includes the study of just about everything. From an academic standpoint, culture is studied by anthropologists, educators, linguists, psychologists, sociologists, and cyberneticists. It is impossible, therefore, to provide a comprehensive list of readings on the subject. In addition to books about the concept of culture in general, an abundance of scholarly literature describes particular cultures as well as cross-cultural communication and conflict.

We cannot, in addition, exclude the realm of fiction. The works of Isaac Bashevis Singer, Maxine Hong Kingston, Ernesto Galarza, Toni Morrison, Amy Tan, Jumpa Lahirí, and Ntozake Shange are a tiny sampling of the possibilities. Tony Hillerman's popular series of mystery novels set on the Navajo reservation provides fascinating insights into Navajo and Hopi cultures. The list below reviews books that highlight points in this chapter. It serves as a starting point for additional reading.

Arvizu, S. F., Snyder, W. A., & Espinosa, P. T. (1980). *Demystifying the concept of culture: Theoretical and conceptual tools.* Los Angeles: Evaluation, Dissemination, and Assessment Center, California State University, Los Angeles.
An analysis of the nature of culture, with illustrative examples, this monograph contains clear, useful information for teachers in training.

Hall, E. T. (1959). *The silent language.* Garden City, NY: Doubleday.
Hall defines culture as communication and analyzes modalities of communication, including language, space, and time, from a cross-cultural perspective.

Hall, E. T. (1966). *The hidden dimension.* Garden City, NY: Doubleday.

An examination of people's use of space in public and in private from an anthropological perspective, this classic book contains fascinating explanations and examples of concepts of proxemics.

Igoa, C. (1995). *The inner world of the immigrant child.* New York: St. Martin's Press.

This is a first-person account of the author's experiences as a teacher of immigrant children and an immigrant herself. Through her story and the stories of her students, she describes how she developed her philosophy and her methodology. Each chapter ends with a summary that provides concrete suggestions for teachers working with immigrant students.

Levine, R. (1997). *A geography of time: The temporal misadventures of a social psychologist, or how every culture keeps time just a little bit differently.* New York: Basic Books.

According to the author's research, Boston is America's fastest moving city. This might come as a surprise to New Yorkers, or even Angelenos, and if you find this kind of information interesting, this is the book for you.

Olsen, L. (1997). *Made in America: Immigrant students in our public schools.* New York: The New Press.

The author spent two and a half years at a large, ethnically diverse high school in northern California's Bay Area. The resulting ethnographic study describes the students, their aspirations, and the challenges that face them in a system that ultimately marginalizes and excludes them.

Philips, S. U. (1983). *The invisible culture: Communication in the classroom and the community on the Warm Springs Indian Reservation.* White Plains, NY: Longman.

In this fascinating work, the author studies communication patterns among adults in the Warm Springs Indian community and then analyzes the mismatch between the expectations Warm Springs Indian children have in communication settings and what they encounter in classrooms.

Saravia-Shore, M., & Arvizu, S. F. (1992). *Cross-cultural literacy: Ethnographies of communication in multiethnic classrooms.* New York: Garland.

This is a collection of studies that use microethnography to analyze multiethnic classrooms and schools in the context of their communities. The introduction provides an excellent overview of anthropological approaches to studying education. Articles included cover a broad scope of community and school settings as well as ethnicities.

Spradley, J. P. (Ed.). (1972). *Culture and cognition: Rules, maps, and plans.* San Francisco: Chandler.

The central theme of this book is the nature and structure of culture. Articles from the fields of anthropology, economics, linguistics, psychology, and sociology provide a wide variety of perspectives and examples.

Valdes, J. M. (1986). *Culture bound: Bridging the cultural gap in language teaching.* New York: Cambridge University Press.

Part 1 of this book presents a theoretical foundation about the relationship of culture, thought, and language. Part 2 describes cultural traits of several groups to alert language teachers to the characteristics of their students. Articles in Part 3 relate to classroom applications and present practical suggestions for working with non-native speakers of a language.

Culture and Schooling

—Culture and Academic Success

Differential achievement, or "the achievement gap," as it is commonly called, refers to the persistent differences between the achievement of students of color and white students, generally as measured on standardized achievement tests. The National Assessment of Educational progress, which calls itself "the nation's report card" (nationsreportcard.gov), tests a representative sample of students nationwide in grades 4, 8, and 12 in reading and mathematics. Results of its 2007 tests indicate that overall, scores are rising. The gap between African American students and white students has gotten somewhat smaller but is still large, and the gap between Latino students and white students persists without much change.

Analyses of the differences between cultures are often used to attempt to explain differences in educational performance among ethnic groups. Differential achievement has been viewed from a variety of perspectives. Some theorists have proposed that different groups have varying abilities that are genetically determined. Others have suggested that some cultures are inadequate or lacking in basic ingredients that are necessary for children to succeed in school.

A third viewpoint that has gained popularity is the cultural mismatch view. Mismatch theorists suggest that different groups have communication and learning styles that don't fit with mainstream styles usually found in classrooms. The mismatch model does not address the entire problem, but understanding communication and learning styles is essential for teachers.

It has been suggested that analysis of differential achievement among groups must go beyond analysis of teacher and student interaction in the classroom and has to be seen in the political and social context of the wider society. The contextual interaction model will be discussed here.

GENETIC INFERIORITY

The genetic inferiority model assumes that certain groups are inherently incapable of intellectual achievement. Rooted in nineteenth-century colonialism, genetic inferiority was a convenient way of justifying cultural domination and enslavement. In current thinking, it has similar convenience value: It blames the victim and eliminates the need for any transformation of our education systems—if heredity is at fault, there simply are no solutions.

The current debate on the relationship between heredity and academic ability was sparked by an article by A. R. Jensen published in the *Harvard Educational Review* in 1969. In that article, Jensen suggested that a person's intellectual ability is determined 80 percent by heredity and 20 percent by environment—hence, most differences in achievement between groups are based in genetic factors. Scholars have criticized Jensen's work extensively (Cortés, 1986; Feuerstein, 1978; Ogbu, 1978), and research generally disproves the notion that intellectual ability is genetically determined and inalterable. This unfortunate perspective has remarkable staying power, however. For example, in a 1988 survey of science teachers, 26 percent of the 200 respondents replied "definitely true" or "probably true" to an item that stated, "Some races of people are more intelligent than others" ("Study Reveals . . . ," 1988).

In *The Bell Curve,* Charles Murray and Richard J. Herrnstein (1994) reasserted the idea that white people are more intelligent than black people as a result of genetic factors. Despite widespread criticism (Beardsley, 1995; "Reacting to *The Bell Curve,*" 1995; Kamin, 1995) of Murray and Herrnstein's assumptions and methodology, the book captured the attention of a public frustrated by the perceived inefficacy of government programs and the failure of schooling to address the problem of underachievement among minority groups.

CULTURAL DEFICIT

The cultural deficit or deficiency model suggests that ethnic minorities fail in school because their cultures are inadequate in some way. The deficit view gained popularity in the 1960s, when it was suggested, for example, that black children suffered from language deprivation as a result of inadequate language development in their home backgrounds (Bereiter & Engelmann, 1966).

As we have seen, all cultures are rich and complex and, like languages, evolve to suit the needs of particular groups. African Americans, like other groups, have a coherent culture. Black American culture in particular includes a vibrant and dynamic tradition of oral language, as witnessed for example by the richness of the black preaching heritage. The notion that black children are deprived somehow of language experience is clearly a case of cultural tunnel vision.

The cultural deficit view blames the victims, but assumes that the deficit is correctable and offers the possibility of solutions through remediation. Critics, however, suggest that remediation efforts have proven ineffective and that, furthermore, the deficit view fails to account for the social and political context of schooling (Boykin, 1984).

CULTURAL MISMATCH

The cultural mismatch model suggests that members of minority groups do not succeed in school because the characteristics of their cultures are incongruent with those of the mainstream group and the school system. This view is supported by the work of researchers who have analyzed learning styles. Culture traits that are part of learning style and that may affect classroom dynamics include cognitive styles, communicative styles, and interaction styles—features that often overlap.

While differences in learning styles may not be the entire explanation for differential achievement among groups, they warrant a detailed look. Such traits are part of what might be called *invisible* or *deep* culture. Teachers need to understand and acknowledge aspects of culture beyond material manifestations.

Cognitive Style. Cognitive styles are ways of thinking or problem solving. For example, sometimes we acknowledge that a person is particularly good at understanding "the big picture." On the other hand, we might refer to a friend or a colleague as "detail oriented." In these examples, we are making reference to a person's cognitive style.

Similarly, it has been proposed that some people are field dependent or field sensitive, whereas others are field independent. Field sensitive students prefer to work cooperatively; field independent students prefer competitive learning situations. Field sensitive students are motivated by their relationship to their teacher; they seek social rewards. Field independent students are task-oriented and motivated by nonsocial rewards.

Ramírez and Castañeda (1974) suggested that Mexican American students tend to be more field dependent than their European American counterparts or European American teachers as a result of cultural values and socialization practices. Lack of congruence between the cognitive styles of Mexican American children and the expectations of the school environment was offered as an explanation for their failure to achieve in school. The children who succeeded had become bicultural—that is, bicognitive, or able to cope with the differing demands of more than one culture.

The notion of biculturalism as bicognitivism was thought-provoking and controversial. Critics, however, have suggested that the rate and manner of cognitive development are demonstrably the same for Mexican American children and European American children. Also, recent demographic analyses of U.S. Hispanics has spotlighted the complexity of Hispanic culture and demonstrated that many previous commonly held assumptions about how Hispanics live were false. Consequently, the cognitive style analysis has been seen as an oversimplification of issues affecting the achievement of Mexican American students.

Subsequent research into patterns of interaction and communication, however, demonstrates that there are discernible differences between parental and community socialized behaviors and expectations that minority children bring to school and the environment they encounter there.

Communication Style. The common assumption that all parties to a particular interaction are assigning similar meanings to the subject at hand often leads to miscommunication. Awareness of the possible pitfalls in cross-cultural communication has led to books and articles that analyze cultural differences for the benefit of business people involved in international negotiations (Pfeiffer, 1988). Handbooks in the popular press present do's and don'ts for travelers to avoid misunderstandings in foreign countries.

However, subtleties of communication style differences often go unnoticed in classroom situations, and they may cause misunderstandings that affect children's ability to achieve and succeed. One study (Gumperz, 1981) analyzed the difference between black and white children's reactions to a classroom task. Black children appeared slower to settle down, were more likely to ask for help, and said things like "I can't do this" or "I don't know" even after they had received instruction. Researchers noted that their comments repeatedly had an identifiable pattern of intonation.

Black adult judges were asked to analyze tape recordings of the black children's verbal responses. Their understanding of the children's comments was that the children were expressing a desire for company while they worked, rather than an actual inability to do the work itself. Failure on the part of a teacher to understand the intention of the children's remarks might lead to the assumption that the students were incapable of understanding or completing the assigned task, which was not the case.

Interaction Style. Patterns of classroom interaction determine who participates, how they participate, and when. For example, a teacher can interact with all students as a group. In that format, a teacher can address all the students, or address individuals while the rest look on. Students may be asked to respond as a group or individually. Sometimes students respond voluntarily; other times they are called on. In these kinds of situations, the teacher generally structures the interaction.

In other patterns, the class may be divided into small groups, with one group interacting with the teacher while others work independently. In some cases, all the students in a class may work independently, with the teacher functioning as a monitor or a resource. Students may also work in small groups, with selected individuals taking leadership roles. Variations of this format are gaining popularity as cooperative-learning-based curricula are developed. (See Chapter 6 for a discussion of cooperative learning.)

The way in which interaction is structured has an impact on student participation. It has been noted, for example, that Native American children seem to be unable or unwilling to participate verbally in classroom interactions. Analyses of classroom interaction styles indicate that patterns of classroom interaction are often incongruent with traditional Native American interaction patterns.

Susan Philips (1983) studied the interaction styles of school children from the Warm Springs Indian Reservation in Oregon. Philips also examined communication patterns among adult members of the community to determine their interaction styles. She found that Warm Springs children's patterns of discourse and interaction differ from the usual communication patterns found in their classrooms. The children have been socialized to interact in patterns appropriate for their community.

According to Philips, "Indian organization of interaction can be characterized as maximizing the control that an individual has over his or her own turn at talk, and as minimizing the control that a given individual has over the turns of others" (p. 115). Consequently, Native American children were much less likely than non–Native American children to respond in situations where they were called upon involuntarily, or where they were singled out. On the other hand, the Native American children in the study participated verbally in small group situations where students were allowed to control their own interactions.

In another study of Native American classrooms (Mohatt & Erickson, 1981), researchers analyzed the differences between a Native American and a non–Native American teacher in an Odawa school in Canada. The researchers noted differences in pacing, the directiveness of the teachers, and the structures used to stimulate participation. The Native American teacher's classroom was organized at a slower pace and seemed to be more responsive to the students' readiness to move to a particular activity. The Native American teacher paused longer to wait for responses and engaged in more face-to-face private interactions than the non–Native American teacher. The Native American teacher used small group work to a far greater extent than the non–Native American counterpart.

Interaction during reading instruction was analyzed in the Kamehameha Early Education Program (KEEP) in Honolulu (Au & Jordan, 1981). As a result of that research, KEEP has successfully developed reading skills with Hawaiian children by structuring lessons to make them similar to Hawaiian talk stories, a traditional form of didactic storytelling.

Studies of interaction style are of particular interest. In many cases the children involved are English speaking or even English monolingual, but still experience difficulties in classroom settings that are culturally inappropriate to their experience. This leads us to the conclusion that we must consider factors beyond language in dual language instructional settings.

Cultural Mismatch: Does It Answer the Question? The cultural mismatch perspective does not assign responsibility for school failure to anyone in particular. It does suggest that members of ethnic groups need to acculturate and become more "Americanized," while, at the same time, schools need to recognize and accommodate children's cultural differences.

Cultural mismatch is an attractive perspective in that it offers tangible solutions. Critics, however, suggest that this view is oversimplified. If differential achievement is a matter of miscommunication, why don't students and teachers negotiate solutions among themselves? People generally overcome obstacles to communication, even in complex situations, altering their communicative style and sometimes developing whole new languages to interact with others (McDermott & Gospodinoff, 1981).

Is it possible that minority children in school fail to negotiate miscommunications because they resist the notion of acculturation? Acculturation, after all, implies the superiority of a particular group (Sue & Padilla, 1986). Wolcott (1997), describing his experiences teaching Kwakiutl children in British Columbia, adopts the metaphor "teacher as an enemy." For the students, he observes, cooperating with the instructional program "may mean selling out, defecting, turning traitor, ignoring the succorance and values and pressures of one's peers, one's family, one's own people" (p. 89). Overall, the cultural mismatch view, while revealing in individual classroom situations, fails to take into account the larger social and political context of education (Cummins, 1984).

CONTEXTUAL INTERACTION

Cross-cultural miscommunication has attracted interest, for example, in the area of business, where it has been noted that failure on the part of U.S. citizens to understand differences in communication styles has been embarrassing and costly. In the area of education, dual language classrooms eliminate obvious language barriers to understanding and accomplishment. And, as previously discussed, microstudies of classroom interactions allow us to develop strategies to maximize opportunities for culturally diverse students to participate and succeed.

But interaction patterns within individual classrooms account only for the teacher–child relationship, which is but one small segment of the entire network of relationships that affect children in school. Critics of the cultural mismatch theory suggest that the mismatch view is too narrow and that it fails to explain why some groups of language minority children do well in school despite cultural difference and language barriers (Ogbu & Matute-Bianchi, 1986).

Koreans are a case in point. Korean students, descendants of forced laborers brought to Japan in the 1930s, do not do well in Japanese schools, where they are a minority. In the United States, on the other hand, Korean students, like many other Asian students, have a tendency to excel. This example is not unique—comparable patterns arise in many places around the world. Why, then, do some minorities do poorly in some settings and well in others?

The contextual interaction model recognizes that there are differences between ethnic minority cultures and mainstream values that may be prevalent in schools. Unlike the mismatch model, however, contextual interaction suggests that there is a dynamic power relationship between minority cultures and schooling that must be analyzed from a broad social and political perspective (Cortés, 1986).

JOHN OGBU'S TYPOLOGY

Some minorities do well in school; others do not. Some reasons for this inconsistency become apparent if we recognize that not all minorities have the same political and social status. John Ogbu (1978) has categorized minorities into three distinct groups which are described in the following sections. Success in school, according to Ogbu, is different for members of each of these groups, in keeping with the characteristics he has described.

Autonomous Minorities. Jews and Mormons are examples of autonomous minorities in the United States. While they are definitely minorities in the numerical sense, they are not perceived as second-class citizens. They maintain a distinct cultural identity, but are not socially or politically isolated.

Immigrant Minorities. Immigrants have moved to the United States for a variety of reasons, but to some extent it is possible to say that they have come here voluntarily. While they may be socially and politically subordinated and economically disadvantaged, they maintain a positive self-concept.

Some immigrants have come from societies where they were socialized as majority group members and have internalized a sense of their own power. They perceive the disadvantages in their new setting as temporary and alterable. Cubans who took refuge in the United States after the Cuban revolution, for example, were often highly educated professionals and business people who quickly entered the U.S. mainstream.

Many immigrants feel that despite the inconveniences of their new circumstances, their situation has improved in the United States. A woman living in a two-room shack with four children told me that her life is better in the United States than in her country of origin because "back home with all of us working we ate meat once a week. Here we can eat meat every day."

Suarez-Orozco and Suarez-Orozco (1993) used the Thematic Apperception Test to study the attitudes of immigrant high school students from Central America. They concluded that the students they worked with were motivated to work hard in school as a compensation for feelings of guilt, resulting from having left families behind, often to endure hardships so that they themselves might have better opportunities.

Castelike Minorities. Sometimes called *indigenous* or *traditional minorities,* castelike minorities "have become incorporated into a society more or less involuntarily and permanently through slavery, conquest, or colonization and then relegated to menial status" (Ogbu & Matute-Bianchi, 1986, p. 90). Castelike or indigenous minorities in the United States include African Americans, who were brought here as slaves, and Native Americans, who were subordinated by conquest. Mexican Americans were originally a conquered people, and newly arrived Mexican immigrants acquire subordinate status as they enter the preexisting infrastructure that makes Mexican Americans a castelike minority.

Secondary Cultural Differences. Ogbu (1994) points out that attempts to rectify inequality between minority and dominant culture groups are most often implemented at the instrumental level, that is, by attempting to provide equal access to educational and material resources. Such attempts, ineffective in and of themselves, also ignore relational differences between groups.

For example, minority groups develop a set of cultural characteristics that arise in contact with the dominant culture, which allow minority group members to function in social settings where they are subordinated (Ogbu, 1992).

In Ogbu's view, members of castelike groups may in fact engage in what he calls *cultural inversion,* or "the tendency . . . to regard certain forms of behavior, events, symbols, and meanings as inappropriate . . . because these are characteristic of White Americans" (Ogbu, 1992, p. 8). Among some black students, for example, succeeding in school is equated with "acting white" (Fordham, 1991). Richmond Community High School, founded in 1977 in Richmond, Virginia, recognizes the potential damage this attitude can do, and provides gifted African American students from low-income households "a safe and intellectually challenging place for disadvantaged kids to be smart" (Viadero, 1997, p. 33).

It should be noted that young women may avoid success in school because academic success contradicts the images they have internalized as feminine (Bell, 1991). In other words, being too successful might equate with "acting male." In early 1998, a Bay Area high school became the first in California to offer separate classes for boys and girls. The students in the special two-year pilot program enjoy coeducational lunch and class breaks, but attend separate classes for academic subjects during their first and second high school years. Supporters of this experiment maintain that separate classes will be particularly helpful in allowing girls to flourish academically and develop self-esteem (Aratani, 1998).

Foley (1994) notes that Ogbu's theory of oppositional culture is a negative characterization that fails to acknowledge the "positive, self-valorizing character of oppositional ethnic humor, dialect, musical, and street art forms" (p. 187). Referring to his own research in a South Texas high school, Foley notes that despite the historical and social context in that region, many Mexican American students have achieved success without relinquishing a sense of their own ethnicity. At least in the particular situation Foley studied, students whom Ogbu might characterize as involuntary or castelike minorities appeared to function in a manner more congruent with voluntary minorities. Foley encourages us to focus our research on why some involuntary minority students succeed, rather than why some fail.

STATUS, POWER, AND SCHOOL SUCCESS

People sometimes fail to realize the nature and amount of power that schools represent. Schooling in the United States is compulsory—all children must attend. For members of the economic and social mainstream, taking their children to the schoolhouse door is often emotional, but not necessarily intimidating or threatening. For people whose cultural, social, economic, or political perspectives differ from the mainstream, schools may represent a power structure that will indoctrinate their children away from the ways of living that their families value and cherish.

Choice in schooling is generally reserved for the more affluent members of our society, and awareness of options in schooling is most often the privilege of the educated. Most children attend the neighborhood public school; there is relatively little choice in the matter. Schools, therefore, become what Henry Giroux (1988) has called "contested sites"—arenas for political power struggles.

Such struggles take a number of forms. The debate, for example, regarding evolution versus creationism is a curriculum battle that has been waged furiously for over 70 years and continues unabated today. Other areas of tension are manifested in censorship battles, where texts or materials in the school library may be at issue; and home schooling conflicts, where parents or a group of parents may resist the notion of a majority-imposed curriculum (Arons, 1983).

Preservice teachers are often surprised by the disparity between the behavior of minority children at home, where they are required to carry out important responsibilities such as providing income and caring for younger siblings or elderly grandparents, and the behavior of the same children in school, where they may be irresponsible and even disruptive. The behavior of those children makes it clear that they do not respect or feel respected in the school environment.

The Role of Schools as Perceived by Minority Students. Members of autonomous and immigrant minority groups are more likely to succeed in school than members of castelike minority groups. Children are astute sociologists, quickly making accurate sense of the world around them. Children who are members of castelike minorities perceive that society has placed limitations on their aspirations and that schools serve as instruments for preserving the power status quo.

Ogbu and Matute-Bianchi suggest (1986) that the role of schools becomes part of folk culture, handed down from one generation to the next. Among castelike minority groups, school is not seen as a way of getting ahead. The motion picture *Stand and Deliver* (Menendez, Musca, & Olmos, 1988) tells the true story of Jaime Escalante, a Bolivian-born school teacher, and his first year in an urban high school in Los Angeles. Escalante's entire math class, with many students who could not manage basic mathematics at the outset, passed the Advanced Placement calculus test.

In one striking scene, a student asks Escalante for an extra book to keep at home so his friends won't see him looking studious. He is not yet ready to give up his identity in a social setting that assures him success, to take on the identity of a student, in a world he mistrusts and may not be able to master. The students who did pass the Advanced Placement test were accused of cheating and were required to take the test again. The students were subsequently vindicated, but the accusation corroborates the contextual interaction model and speaks to the accurate awareness minority students may have that they are not welcomed by the system.

Contextual Interaction as a Solution to Differential Achievement. Contextual interaction, unlike the genetic inferiority or cultural deficit views, does not blame the victim. And while it incorporates the notion of cultural mismatch as part of the explanation for differential achievement, it suggests that we have to seek solutions beyond the classroom door. Contextual interaction requires that we consider the complex network of factors that schooling involves.

McDermott (1997) suggests that failure is a social construction. He asks us to reframe our essential question:

> Instead of asking why half the individuals in a culture do less well than the others, we can ask why a culture would acquire so many individuals in failing positions. Instead of asking why so many individuals do not learn what they need to get around in the culture, we can ask why a culture would organize opportunities for individuals to learn to behave in ways that would make them look like failures. (p. 121)

Summary

Educators have devised several theoretical frameworks to explain differential achievement among diverse ethnic groups. The genetic inferiority model suggests that ability is innate and consequently inalterable. The cultural deficit model posits that some cultures are inadequate.

The cultural mismatch model proposes that children come to school with values and behaviors that don't fit the school environment. Cultural mismatch theorists have provided some significant insights into culture differences in communication, but the model does not account for the fact that some children succeed in spite of language and culture differences. The contextual interaction model suggests that the failure of some children to achieve in school can be explained only by taking political and social factors into account.

Questions to Think About and Discuss

1. Was there ever a time when a teacher or somebody important to you made you feel that you were not a capable person? How did you react to that? Is there anything in our present system of schooling that might suggest to some students that they are not capable of success?

2. In 1989, Peggy McIntosh published a ground-breaking article that contained the now famous "White Privilege Checklist." The checklist is widely available on the web. Working with a group of colleagues, read the checklist and use the issues to interrogate the questions of race and color in the United States. What other kinds of privilege can you identify? Do you feel privileged in some way? How do hidden assumptions of privilege affect schools?

Activities

1. Look up recent citations under *academic achievement, achievement gap,* and *minority achievement* in the publications prepared under the U.S. Office of Education by the Educational Resources Information Center (ERIC). Survey titles and abstracts to see which approaches researchers are using to analyze minority student achievement.
2. How is academic achievement reported in your state/district? What tests are used? How are scores grouped? What patterns can you discern? Testing information may be available from your state department of education or from local district offices. Test results are sometimes reported in local newspapers.
3. Investigate placement procedures for special education in your local district. How is cultural diversity accommodated in the process?

Suggestions for Further Reading

California State Department of Education (Ed.). (1986). *Beyond language: Social and cultural factors in schooling language minority students.* Los Angeles: Evaluation, Dissemination, and Assessment Center, California State University, Los Angeles.

This book was constructed as a companion piece for "Schooling and language minority students: A theoretical framework" and "Studies on immersion education: A collection for United States educators," edited by the California State Department of Education (see Chapters 1 and 6). "Framework" and "Immersion" address educational issues of first and second language. Beyond Language considers social and cultural factors that have an impact on the education of language minority students. The book provides theoretical analyses and data that support the contextual interaction model. This book is basic reading for those concerned with the relationship of sociocultural factors and schooling.

Ogbu, J. U. (1978). *Minority education and caste: The American system in cross-cultural perspective.* New York: Academic Press.

Ogbu presents a structural argument for the underachievement of minority children in school. The contextual interaction model owes much to his analysis of schooling for minority children in cross-cultural settings. Articles by this author are included in Beyond Language *and* Language, Literacy and Culture.

Trueba, H. T., Guthrie, G. P., & Au, K. H. (Eds.). (1981). *Culture and the bilingual classroom: Studies in classroom ethnography.* Rowley, MA: Newbury House.
The studies in this volume use microethnography to focus on patterns of interaction between teachers and ethnically diverse students in schools and classrooms. Included are a study of teaching styles in an Odawa school (Gerald Mohatt and Frederick Erickson) and a discussion of the KEEP reading program for Hawaiian students (Kathryn Hu-Pei Au and Cathie Jordan), both of which are often mentioned in analyses of teaching and interaction styles in cross-cultural settings. A section on theoretical and methodological issues is useful to the beginning student of ethnography.

chapter 10

Legal Foundations of Dual Language Instruction

As we saw earlier, dual language instruction was widely available in the United States in the nineteenth century but became unpopular in reaction to large-scale European immigration. Anti-German feeling was particularly powerful, peaking with the advent of World War I. Because of the strong anti-foreign feelings the war engendered, there was little support for instruction in languages other than English in the period between World War I and World War II.

World War II marked the beginning of the American civil rights movement, initially among African Americans. The civil rights movement came to have significant impact on education in general and bilingual education in particular. This chapter will review the events that laid the groundwork for the legal foundations of dual language instruction.

The educational rights of limited English proficient children are protected by law in the form of legislation, court decisions, and administrative implementation and enforcement regulations. There is no single piece of legislation or court decision that requires dual language instruction for *all* limited English proficient children. Instead, there is a complex mesh of statutes and case law that defines the educational entitlements of limited English proficient students and affects the ways programs are funded for them. This chapter will review federal and state legislation and case law regarding dual language instruction and describe their impact on policy and program implementation.

The Historical Context for Dual Language Instruction: World War II and Beyond

WORLD WAR II AND FOREIGN LANGUAGE INSTRUCTION

Fueled by reactions to large waves of immigration and the imminence of World War I, the popularity of dual language instruction in the nineteenth century dwindled rapidly as antiforeign and anti-German sentiments reached a fever pitch. Nor did the Armistice end the disfavor into which dual language instruction had fallen. Following World War I, dual language instruction in general fell into disfavor, and even traditional foreign language instruction was viewed with distaste. The state of Nebraska went so far as to outlaw the teaching of foreign languages altogether, but that effort was deterred by a United States Supreme Court decision (*Meyer v. Nebraska,* 1923) that held the prohibition unconstitutional, making a case that is based on the Fourteenth Amendment.

The court case did little to inspire an increase in dual language and foreign language instruction, which remained in public disfavor and suffered from disinterest until World War II. With the onset of that war, a renewed interest in foreign language instruction was triggered by the immediate need for expertise in a variety of languages in order to communicate with our allies and maintain effective intelligence efforts.

The value of bilingualism to the war effort was demonstrated dramatically when the U.S. Marine Corps began using the Navajo language for radio communications. After the Japanese had deciphered all military codes, 400 Navajo marines volunteered to transmit top secret information in their first language. Ironically, the "code talkers" had been forbidden to speak their language in many places at home. Carl Gorman, the oldest of the group, who died at the age of 90 in 1998, "recalled that as a student at a mission school he had once been chained to an iron pipe for a week because he insisted on speaking his native tongue" (Thomas, 1998). The Japanese were never able to break the "code," and the Navajo effort made a significant contribution to U.S. military success in the Pacific. Many American lives were saved as a result of the contributions of the Navajo code talkers.

U.S. servicemen who were fluent in German, Italian, and Japanese were considered extremely valuable. To increase the number of military personnel who could be useful for intelligence gathering, the U.S. Army took a leadership role in developing methodologies for fast and effective foreign language instruction, as discussed in Chapter 7. After World War II, the federal government passed the National Defense Education Act (1958), which included support for foreign language instruction. The experiences of World War II taught the United States that the nation needed expertise in foreign languages as part of our national defense.

WORLD WAR II AND CIVIL RIGHTS

In addition to an awareness of the need for expertise in foreign languages, World War II affected many Americans' consciousness about their own status and rights. For indigenous minorities, as well as the children of immigrants, serving in World War II bolstered a self-concept of "Americanness." Having proved their commitment to the United States by offering their lives for their country, members of minorities were no longer willing to be regarded as outsiders or second-class citizens.

For many, military service provided the first opportunity to travel outside the United States (or even outside their home towns) and to experience cultures and lifestyles different from their own. Many Americans returned from Europe and Asia, where cultural diversity and multilingualism were the norm, with a more sophisticated view of themselves and American society.

The awareness gained through exposure to different cultures and viewpoints extended beyond acceptance of cultural and linguistic diversity. U.S. military personnel were viewed as liberators, and their presence was greeted with great excitement and gratitude. People literally crawled out of concentration camps in Europe to kiss the feet of American G.I.s. It mattered not at all to the Nazis' victims whether the feet and the people they belonged to were black or white or brown.

It is difficult to imagine how U.S. war veterans felt, having served their country and hailed as liberators, only to suffer the indignities of legalized segregation and discrimination on returning home. In 1948, when local authorities in Three Rivers, Texas, refused to bury a Mexican American war hero in the local veterans' cemetery, World War II veterans in Corpus Christi, Texas, founded the American G.I. Forum. The American G.I. Forum became an organization devoted to fighting discrimination in all areas. The incident in Texas was not the first or only demonstration of racism in our history, and the American G.I. Forum is not the first or only organization devoted to antidiscrimination, but the event shows how World War II had raised the consciousness of minority groups in the United States.

BROWN V. THE BOARD OF EDUCATION (1954)

This changing American consciousness provided the backdrop for the civil rights movement, which reached its most important legal expression in the U.S. Supreme Court decision in *Brown v. the Board of Education* of Topeka in 1954. The *Brown* decision established the principle that separate facilities that were the product of intentional segregation were inherently unequal, reversing a decision by the Court 58 years earlier that separate but equal facilities, or segregation, constituted equality (*Plessy v. Ferguson*, 1896).

The *Brown* decision was a landmark in U.S. history and had a significant impact on all forms of segregation. For example, it was used to break down segregation on buses, trains, restaurants, and (eventually) housing. But the immediate concern of *Brown* was schooling, and to this day schooling remains an arena in which the impact of *Brown* is continually felt.

Judicial efforts to desegregate the schools have been slowed and often stalled due to the resistance of state and local governments. De facto segregation continues to plague public schools today. Efforts to speed school desegregation included the Civil Rights Act of 1964, which contained provisions strengthening the federal government's ability to enforce desegregation and integration. Title VI of the Civil Rights Act plays a key role in the establishment of the rights of language minority children, as we will discuss later in this chapter.

THE CIVIL RIGHTS MOVEMENT AND DUAL LANGUAGE INSTRUCTION

Overall, the climate of the times in the late 1950s and early 1960s favored the establishment of dual language programs. As described in Chapter 1, the influx of Cuban refugees and the establishment of bilingual programs for Spanish-speaking children in Florida catalyzed the demand for programs for other non-English-speaking children. The success of the program in Florida, combined with increased ethnic self-awareness among minority groups and the philosophical impetus of the civil rights movement, led to legislation and litigation that established the educational rights of language minority children.

Who Governs Education?

The rights of language minority children are protected by legislation, case law, and other governmental actions. Because much of what we shall discuss is rooted in federal law, it is important to understand the avenues by which the federal government acquires jurisdiction over schooling.

The U.S. Constitution gives the federal government, among other things, the power to coin money, to declare war, and to regulate patents and copyrights, and prohibits individual states from acting in those areas without the consent of Congress. The functions not allotted to Congress or prohibited to the states are reserved to the states.

Under this constitutional arrangement, education, which is neither specifically assigned to the federal government nor prohibited to the states, is a state government function. The result is variety in education systems across the states.

For example, organization of school governance varies. Hawaii has one school district; California has over a thousand, some consisting of only one school and some consisting of many. Curriculum and funding mechanisms differ from state to state. If you are a certified teacher who has moved from one state to another, you have encountered the lack of uniformity in educational systems and have discovered that each state has its own certification requirements.

FEDERAL INVOLVEMENT IN EDUCATION

Despite the fact that education is theoretically reserved to the states, the federal government exerts powerful influence on schooling through funding, legislation, and judicial action. The federal government apportions funds for education at all levels and supports services that could not be sustained by state budgets. In 1998, PL 105-78 provided $29.4 billion in discretionary funds for the Department of Education. The bill allotted nearly $200 million dollars for instructional services to LEP students, $150 million for instructional services for immigrant children, funds for financial assistance for college students and after school programs, as well as support for school reform and technological innovation in schools.

In addition, federal agencies such as the National Science Foundation, the Department of Agriculture, the U.S. Information Agency, and others spend substantial sums for educational programs. Federal spending is accompanied by federal regulation. Federal dollars imply federal influence in the area of education.

The influence of federal spending on education is doubly felt because Title VI of the Civil Rights Act of 1964 prohibits institutions that receive federal assistance from discriminating on the basis of race, color, or national origin. Any institution failing to comply with the Civil Rights Act may lose all its federal funding. Most institutions receive federal funding and must therefore support the government's agenda of protecting minorities.

As we have already seen, the federal government also influences education through judicial action. It might be said, in fact, that the U.S. Supreme Court is the government's most powerful educational decision maker. Almost every analysis of law or policy in education must include consideration of the high court's decisions, which have had a strong impact on areas such as desegregation, religion in schools, student discipline, rights of handicapped and gifted students, and private schooling, to name just a few.

We have considered the impact of the federal government on education in some detail because it has bearing on the education of limited English proficient students through all three areas of influence. Funding, Title VI of the Civil Rights Act, and the U.S. Supreme Court, along with other federal legislation, case law, and regulation, provide a firm foundation for the rights of students who don't speak English.

The Bilingual Education Act (Title VII)

In 1968 Congress passed Title VII of the Elementary and Secondary Education Act, or the Bilingual Education Act, and in 1969 appropriated $7.5 million dollars to support its programs. Title VII was directed at children from environments where the dominant language was not English and at those whose families had incomes of less than $3,000 per year. Seventy-six projects were funded during the first year of appropriations, serving 27,000 children (Castellanos, 1983).

The 1974 reauthorization of the act broadened the definition of the children served to include those of limited English-speaking ability and eliminated the income requirements. In 1978 the population to be served was again redefined to include children of limited English proficiency (1978). This is important because proficiency is broader than speaking ability and implies that children should not be exited from programs based on speaking ability alone. The 1984 reauthorization included provisions for family English literacy programs for families of children served and for developmental (two-way) bilingual programs.

Over the course of 25 years, expansions of Title VII provided funding for a wide range of activities associated with dual language instruction. Basic services to children, preservice and in-service training for teachers and trainers of teachers, research activities, program evaluation, and nationwide dissemination of information on bilingual education were all funded through Title VII.

DISCRETIONARY FUNDING

Some forms of government funding are available to individuals who are members of a defined class. For example, Chapter 1 support for academic assistance is available from the government for any child who meets the established academic and income criteria. Other forms of government funding are not automatically available to defined classes of people, but are awarded on a competitive basis. Title VII did not require dual language instruction for every student who is limited English proficient, nor did it provide monetary assistance for every individual who qualified.

Instead, local school districts, universities, or state agencies applied for Title VII funds by submitting a grant application to the federal government. Applicants were required to describe the proposed program, indicate the need for it, describe the qualifications of the personnel involved, and provide an evaluation plan.

The funding process was competitive; thus, not all applicants received funding. Title VII was intended to help educational agencies to establish mechanisms for delivering services for limited English proficient students that would then become part of the agency's regularly funded and supported activities.

TITLE VII AND POLICY

Title VII did not mandate dual language instruction for all students or any students. Such a mandate would be out of keeping with the federal role in education. Title VII did, however, set national policy regarding services for limited English proficient children. It did so in two ways.

The first was through legislative language. The act acknowledged that there were large numbers of children who would benefit from instruction in their primary language using bilingual educational methods and techniques and went on to say:

> Congress declares it to be the policy of the United States, in order to establish equal educational opportunity for all children, to encourage the establishment and operation, where appropriate, of educational programs using bilingual educational practices, techniques, and methods. . . .

The second way Title VII influenced policy was through infrastructure. Title VII funding provided for the establishment of basic programs and also supported training for school personnel in the area of dual language instruction. In addition, money provided for basic research and program evaluation allowed educators to develop the theory and methodology necessary to properly serve children in dual language programs. National networking disseminated information, making it possible for educational agencies to benefit from each other's experiments and expertise. To the extent that funding permitted, programs, training, and research resulted in a knowledge and advocacy base that created infrastructure for dual language education.

Lau v. Nichols (1974)

As mentioned earlier, the U.S. Supreme Court has played a decisive role in many areas of education, and dual language instruction is no exception. In 1969, plaintiffs representing 1,800 language minority children in the San Francisco Unified School District sued the district, claiming that limited English proficient children were being denied equal educational opportunity in English-only classrooms.

Overturning the decision of a lower court, the Supreme Court decided in favor of the plaintiffs under Title VI of the Civil Rights Act. The language in the decision was strong. Justice William O. Douglas wrote:

> There is no equality of treatment merely by providing students with the same facilities, textbooks, teachers, and curriculum; for students who do not understand English are effectively foreclosed from any meaningful education. Basic skills are at the very core of what these public schools teach. Imposition of a requirement that before a child can effectively participate in the educational program he must already have acquired those basic skills is to make a mockery of public education. We know that those who do not understand English are certain to find their classroom experiences wholly incomprehensible and in no way meaningful.

INTERPRETATION OF *LAU*

The Court held for the plaintiffs in the *Lau* decision, and the case undoubtedly represents a victory for the rights of language minority children. There are several points, however, that should be borne in mind when considering *Lau* and its effects.

The *Lau* decision was an interpretation of the Civil Rights Act. At the time the Supreme Court agreed to review *Lau*, they refused to review *Serna v. Portales* (1974), a similar case that was argued on the basis of the equal protection clause of the Constitution. In deciding *Lau*, the Court avoided the constitutional issue. A decision on constitutional grounds would have been stronger than the decision rendered on the basis of a statute. This is true because Congress could make *Lau* irrelevant by simply passing a different law. In contrast, a constitutional amendment would be necessary to overturn a Supreme Court decision interpreting the Constitution.

Another issue that was raised by the case was numbers. In his concurring opinion in the *Lau* case, Justice Harry A. Blackmun observed that for him numbers were "at the heart of this case," suggesting that he might have viewed the situation differently if smaller numbers of children had been involved.

Finally, it should be noted that in deciding *Lau* the Court did not specify any particular remedy. The Court held that districts failing to provide services for children who could not function in English were violating the civil rights of those children. And it did require that the San Francisco Unified School District take affirmative steps to eliminate the inequities suffered by limited English proficient children as a result of its policies. But there is no requirement in *Lau* that districts must establish bilingual programs.

EFFECTS OF *LAU*

The *Lau* decision had several dramatic and immediate effects. In 1975 the Department of Health, Education, and Welfare (HEW) and the Office of Civil Rights (OCR) of the federal government developed a document to provide districts with guidance for implementing programs in compliance with Title VI of the Civil Rights Act as interpreted in *Lau*. The document, known as the "*Lau* Remedies," established standards for identifying limited English speaking children, assessing their language ability, and meeting their needs. The *Lau* Remedies were never formally accorded regulatory status, but did serve as the basis for compliance reviews by the Office of Civil Rights, which meant that districts generally attempted to abide by the requirements in the document.

Lau had an impact on other court cases that were pending at the time. In New York, for example, Aspira, a Puerto Rican community group, had filed suit against the New York City Board of Education on behalf of the system's approximately 182,000 Spanish-speaking students (*Aspira of New York, Inc. v. Board of Education*, 1972). Shortly after *Lau* was decided, the parties to the suit entered into a consent decree in which the New York City Board of Education agreed to provide substantial bilingual services to children of limited English ability.

Also, soon after *Lau* a number of states, including California and Texas, passed laws mandating some form of bilingual education (McFadden, 1983).

While *Lau* did not require any specific remedy or form of program, it favored the establishment of bilingual programs as a way of avoiding civil rights violations.

Advocates for the rights of language minority children now rely less on *Lau* and instead base their arguments on the Equal Educational Opportunities Act of 1974.

Equal Educational Opportunities Act of 1974

Section 1703(f) of the Equal Educational Opportunities Act (EEOA) states:

> No state shall deny equal educational opportunity to an individual on account of his or her race, color, sex, or national origin by . . . (f) the failure by an educational agency to take appropriate action to overcome language barriers that impede equal participation by its students in its instructional programs.

Section 1703(f) of EEOA restates the underlying principle of the *Lau* decision in statutory form. There is a growing body of federal case law that interprets the statute (*Castañeda v. Pickard*, 1981; *Gomez v. Illinois*, 1987; *Idaho Migrant Council v. Board*, 1981; *Keyes v. School District No. 1*, 1983). The cases do not require bilingual education but they do require equal access to the curriculum. In other words, children may not sit in classrooms where they cannot understand what is going on. Affirmative steps must be taken to ensure that all children have a meaningful educational experience. As articulated in the case law, in order to properly serve students who are limited English proficient, districts must:

- Develop a program based on a sound theoretical rationale.
- Provide trained teachers and sufficient material resources to implement the program.
- Develop an evaluation system for the program and refine the program in accordance with information from the evaluation.

Federal law protecting the rights of language minority children is of particular importance in areas where states have weakened or eliminated their own requirements regarding bilingual education. Under federal law, children who lack sufficient English skills to succeed in English-only classrooms are entitled to an educational opportunity equal to that of their English-speaking peers.

No Child Left Behind

In January, 2002, President George Bush signed into law the current reauthorization of the Elementary and Secondary Education Act, the No Child Left

Immigrant Students' Rights to Attend Public Schools

Educators sometimes question whether undocumented immigrant children have the right to attend public schools. Educators should be aware that, as a result of the United States Supreme Court decision in *Plyler v. Doe*, [457 U.S. 202 (1982)], all children who reside in the United States have the right to attend public schools, regardless of their immigration status.

Under *Plyler*, public schools may not:

- Deny a student admission based on immigration status.
- Make inquiries of students or parents that would expose their status.
- Require students or parents to document their status.
- Require social security numbers of students.

The National Coalition of Advocates for Students (NCAS), a national nonprofit advocacy organization, has an annual campaign to alert educators, parents, and students to students' rights as a result of *Plyler*. According to NCAS, recent changes in the Student Visa Program do not change the *Plyler* rights of undocumented children. Furthermore, the Family Education Rights and Privacy Act (FERPA) prohibits schools from providing any outside agency with information from a child's school file that would expose the student's undocumented status without first getting parental permission, unless the agency has a court order.

Educators can look for updated information on the NCAS website at www.ncasboston. org. The School Opening Alert is published on the site in several languages and can be downloaded and used to inform parents of their rights.

Behind Act of 2001 (NCLB). Title III of the NCLB, the English Language Acquisition, Language Enhancement and Academic Achievement Act consolidates programs previously funded under the Bilingual Education Act (BEA) and the Emergency Immigrant Education Act (1984), an impact aid program designed to help states cope with newly arrived immigrant students.

The NCLB signals a shift in emphasis and support from the BEA, which funded programs that supported students' first languages, to programs that focus exclusively on English development. Unlike the BEA, the NCLB makes no reference to bilingualism. For example, the Act continues funding for an informational clearinghouse, but renames the National Clearinghouse for Bilingual Education (NCBE) as the National Clearinghouse for English Language Acquisition (NCELA).

NCLB FUNDING

Unlike the BEA, the NCLB is a formula grant program with a funding level trigger. Under NCLB, as long as Congress appropriates at least $650 million, the program is funded as a state formula grant, that is, categorical rather than discretionary funding. This will benefit states that have seen a sudden increase in the number of English language learners in their schools. Under the BEA, states like New York and California, with large numbers of English language learners and significant experience in offering bilingual programs, had the advantage in competing for Title VII funds. Now states where demographics are changing may be eligible for federal funds without having to compete with traditionally successful grant makers.

The federal government is likely to keep funding to serve English language learners at a reasonably high level, but the funding will provide a strong policy push toward English-only in the schools. Also, while overall funding levels may appear higher than previous appropriations under the BEA, the money will be spread more thinly, resulting in less money per child.

What the NCLB Requires.   The NCLB requires states to develop annual achievement objectives for English language learners and to include all LEP students in statewide assessments in the areas of reading/language arts and mathematics. In addition, science is added to the mandatory assessments in 2007–2008. Schools are to be held accountable for meeting annual achievement objectives and for ensuring that LEP students make adequate progress in all areas.

English language learners are not required to take the reading and language arts assessments during their first year in U.S. schools, but must take an English language proficiency test and a math assessment. States may make some accommodations for second language learners. English language learners may be assessed in their first language for several years if such assessments can be made available. Assessments in languages other than English must align with state standards. Other accommodations such as simplified or native language instructions are permitted under the law, but English language learners must take the reading and English language arts tests after they have attended schools in the United States for three consecutive years.

NCLB provides funds for English instruction, curriculum development, professional development for teachers, tutoring, teacher aides, and technology. Native language instruction is permissible under the act. However, the act requires that states implement language instruction based on scientifically based research on teaching limited English proficient students. Research on the effectiveness of bilingual education (or any other kind of educational program) is likely to be inconclusive, for good reasons. Program evaluation studies are difficult to design. Random assignment of students to programs is unethical. Furthermore, it's hard to determine the effectiveness of programs through comparisons because programs are generally not truly comparable: Communities and schools vary in myriad ways.

Finally, research about schooling is generally politically informed. Given the particularly acrimonious debate about bilingual education, the term "scientifically based research" has excited controversy across the educational community.

NCLB PROS AND CONS

Advocates for English language learners are not unified in their response to NCLB. Some analysts see potential benefit for second language learners in the requirements of the NCLB. According to the nonprofit advocacy organization Education Trust, "The accountability provisions require states to set clear timelines for improving student achievement, with particular emphasis on closing achievement gaps between low-income and minority students and their peers (2003, p. 2)." Mayer (2002) points out that NCLB requires states to implement a statewide accountability system for all students, and to measure the academic progress of LEPs along with all other students on an annual basis. A policy brief published by the Urban Institute concurs, suggesting that NCLB puts "English language learners on the map" (Consentino de Cohen & Chu Clewell, 2007, p. 1). This is viewed as a good thing; in other words, states have to keep track of what's happening academically to English language learners along with everyone else.

One positive outcome of the emphasis on accountability is the move to statewide uniform language proficiency testing. The standardized use of tests across entire states will provide teachers with language proficiency information that is comparable from child to child. California, for example, has developed and implemented the California English Language Development Test (CELDT), and CELDT scores are reported along with student scores on other state-mandated standardized achievement tests.

English language learners may well be getting increased attention. And it is inarguable that assessment of student progress can inform instruction and support student success. However, for accountability to be meaningful, resources have to be equitably distributed. As both the Education Trust and the Urban Institute have documented, the students with the highest needs generally receive instruction from the least-qualified teachers in settings with the least resources (Peske & Haycock, 2006; Weiner & Pristoop, 2006; Consentino de Cohen & Chu Clewell, 2006).

Furthermore, implementation of NCLB has narrowed the focus of instruction, A recent report published by the Center on Education Policy (McMurrer, 2007) notes that emphasis on reading and mathematics has increased, and there has been a decrease in the time spent on social studies, science, music, and art. It can be argued that students with the least economic and social privileges at home need the most enriched experiences in school since their parents are unlikely to have the resources to support extra activities.

James Crawford, a well-regarded advocate for second language learners, strongly agrees that NCLB has diminished the quality of education for underserved students. Crawford notes concerns that have been seconded by many classroom teachers regarding "excessive class time devoted to test preparation, a curriculum narrowed to the two tested subjects, neglect of critical thinking in favor of basic skills, pressure to reduce or eliminate native-language instruction, demoralization of teachers whose students fall short of unrealistic cut scores, demoralization of children who are forced to take tests they can't understand, and, perhaps worst of all, practices that encourage low-scoring students to drop out before test day" (Crawford, 2007).

State Laws Regarding Bilingual Education

Prior to *Lau*, the only state-mandated dual language program in the United States was in Massachusetts. Massachusetts's vanguard bilingual education law required a transitional program if 20 or more children in a school district on the same grade level were limited English proficient and had the same primary language. Many other states, to the contrary, required by law that instruction be delivered in English. The passage of the federal Bilingual Education Act in 1968 had a positive effect on the political climate regarding dual language instruction, but funded only a relative handful of programs to meet the needs of children with limited English abilities.

By the mid-1980s, 20 states had bilingual education requirements. The majority of those laws, however, required programs that were transitional and compensatory in nature. This was unfortunate, because compensatory programs are perceived by the general public as peripheral. Without wide popular support, dual language programs are at risk, especially since the population they attempt to serve is often disenfranchised by its lack of English proficiency. Two-way programs offering second language skills to all students are more likely to build a broader political base, but such programs are relatively rare.

The future of state-mandated bilingual education is insecure at the present time. Illinois repealed its statute in 1980 but reinstated it under community pressure. California, with a school enrollment of nearly a million and a half limited English proficient children, allowed its legislation to lapse in 1987, and in 1998 passed an initiative that outlaws nearly all primary language instruction. Arizona followed suit, passing similar legislation in 2000, as did Massachusetts in 2002.

It is worth noting that despite policy shifts in federal legislation, federal judicial protections of the rights of limited English proficient students are still in effect. In the face of increasing needs, communities will undoubtedly need to use them to support dual language instructional programming.

ummary

Legislative and judicial support for publicly funded dual language instructional programs is rooted historically in the civil rights movement. Support at the federal level resides in legislation that provides funding for bilingual programs, civil rights legislation, and case law that requires that limited English proficient students be served. Some states have laws requiring some form of dual language instruction for students who need it, but several key states have all but eliminated primary language instruction for second language learners. Two-way programming rarely receives legislative support. The future of requirements for bilingual education at the state level is more uncertain at the present time than it has been in recent decades.

Questions to Think About and Discuss

1. Should the United States have one set of educational standards and assessments for all public schools? Why or why not?
2. If you are of the opinion that all the public schools in the United States should have one set of standards and assessments, who should determine what those standards and assessments would be?

Activities

1. Speak to the person in your local school district who is in charge of federally funded projects. How much federal money does the district receive annually? What kinds of activities are funded by federal dollars?
2. Does your state have a bilingual education statute? What kinds of programs are mandated? How are they implemented?

Suggestions for Further Reading

Readings on the legal foundations of bilingual education are difficult to identify, since statutes, court cases, and their interpretations are generally available in formats appropriate for legal professionals, while failing to meet the needs of lay readers. In today's world, readers who wish to stay abreast of law and public policy will find the most up-to-date information on the web. National organizations such as the National Association of Other Languages, www. nabe.org, and Teachers of English to Speakers of Other Languages, www.tesol. org, address legislation and policy on their websites and are excellent sources of current information.

11

Language Policy and Planning

$\mathcal{I}$n preceding chapters we have considered language and culture and have also built an educational rationale to support primary language instruction for limited English proficient students and second language enrichment for monolingual English speakers. While we have generally emphasized the benefits of dual language instruction for individual students, schooling exists within a larger social and political framework. Teachers don't generally think of themselves as government agents. But when we make decisions about language use in public school classrooms, we are also implementing government-sponsored language policy.

Shirley Brice Heath (1983), a prominent sociolinguist, defines language policies as "what the government says and does through its laws, legislative statues, regulations and bureaucratic practices that affect the choices and uses of one or more languages used by the people it represents" (p. 156). Sometimes a nation's policy is stated in the form of recognition of official languages, either through legislation or in a national constitution. At other times, language policy is established by legislation and regulation of language use in courts, schools, and other government agencies, or through a government body such as a language academy.

This chapter will discuss how governments can promote or suppress languages. In other words, we will look at aspects of language policy and language planning.

——Language Support

Language support includes graphization, the creation of a writing system; standardization, the creation of an orthography and grammar; modernization, expansion of the vocabulary; and dissemination, usually through teacher training and support in the schools.

The University of Hawaii, for example, with the support of the government of the Trust Territory of the Pacific Islands, has provided support for the languages of the Trust Territories (now the independent countries of the Federated States of Micronesia, the Republic of Belau, the Commonwealth of the Marianas, and the Marshall Islands). The university's support for local languages has included the development of orthographies, the publication of dictionaries and grammars, and teacher preparation to support dissemination of orthographies and to encourage primary language literacy in schools.

Language planning strategies are easy to formulate on paper. In practice, however, they are complicated by historical and social factors. In the case of the Trust Territories, for example, new orthographies are difficult to establish. Except for the Bible, published in vernaculars by missionaries, there was little printed matter in local languages prior to World War II. Old habits die hard, and the old-fashioned printing methods still in use in these remote areas are cumbersome to retool for new writing systems.

New writing systems are difficult to disseminate for other reasons. After a century of colonial domination by a series of foreign powers, teachers in the Pacific Islands have internalized the idea that primary languages should not be used for instruction, and they associate modernization and economic success with the use of English. And while some teachers have become convinced that primary language instruction is valuable, materials in local languages are limited. Basic instructional materials have been created in local languages, but the development of primary language literacy skills has been hampered by the fact that local languages generally have oral traditions. There is, for example, no backlog of written children's literature as we know it in English, and teachers cannot easily find children's books to supplement skills development.

Language Suppression

It is possible for a government to suppress a minority language in a number of ways. Governments can ban the use of minority languages in the media and in public life. Basque, for example, was vehemently suppressed during the Franco regime in Spain but has been restored to the status of an official provincial language under the current liberal monarchy (Grosjean, 1982).

Another way to suppress a minority language is to promote the idea that it is a substandard dialect of a majority language. Catalan, the language of Catalonia in northeastern Spain, is similar to Spanish in several ways, but linguists and speakers alike agree that Spanish and Catalan are different languages. Catalonia resisted the Franco regime, and in an attempt to silence Catalonian resistance, Franco's government deemed Catalan a dialect and made attempts to eradicate it.

Catalan was restored to the status of an official language after Franco's death, and a provincial government agency was established to stimulate its reinstitution (Woolard, 1985). The program to normalize Catalan, as it was called (Miller & Miller, 1996), has been fairly successful, but has had its challenges. Initial attempts to impose Catalan as the only language of instruction in the schools as an attempt to undo the previous damage under Franco's rule met with resistance from some Spanish-speaking parents of school children, who went to court to block the government's implementation of it (Battle in Spain, 1993). Also, as a result of years of language suppression, it was difficult to find qualified bilingual and biliterate teachers (Siguan, 1991).

Currently, students attend school in both languages in a variety of models and settings. While Catalan appears strong at the present time, in an increasingly globalized marketplace the value of Spanish as a world language may yet take its toll.

LANGUAGE SUPPRESSION AND THE MEDIA

Lippi-Green (1997) points out that the media have a role in what she calls the "language subordination process" (pp. 67–69). Her analysis of 371 characters in 24 animated feature films produced by the Disney Corporation indicates that characters with foreign accents are more likely to be "bad guys" than characters who speak either British or American English (Lippi-Green, 1997). Lippi-Green proposes that socialization through the media and the schools teaches children to adopt deprecatory attitudes toward English speakers with foreign accents.

At a macro level, the overwhelming presence of English in the media has a tendency to overpower other languages and even eliminate smaller, less powerful ones. A quick Google search of "English Dominance + Web" turns up multiple "hits" that indicate concern over the fact that English does, in fact, dominate in cyberspace.

ENDANGERED LANGUAGES

The ultimate outcome of language suppression is the disappearance of languages. According to Krauss (1992), an expert on indigenous languages at the Alaska Native Language Center, 40 percent of the world's languages are endangered, and another 50 percent are moribund, literally at death's door, because they are spoken only by adults who are not transmitting them to children. "Languages no longer being learned as mother-tongue by children are beyond mere endangerment, for, unless the course is somehow dramatically reversed, they are already doomed to extinction, like species lacking reproductive capability" (p. 4). Speaking at the turn of the twenty-first century, Krauss highlighted the gravity and immediacy of language death, reflecting, "I consider it a plausible calculation that—at the rate things are going—the coming century will see either the death or doom of 90 percent of mankind's languages" (p. 7). Nothing in the literature to date would indicate that his alarming prediction was wrong.

DOES LANGUAGE LOSS MATTER?

Whether through active suppression or the unintended consequences of mass communication, the world's languages are disappearing at an alarming rate. The world's leading language scholars insist that we should all be deeply concerned about language loss. Crystal (2000) reminds us that diversity is essential to human experience and that "language lies at the heart of what it means to be human" (pp. 33–34).

Some scholars propose that language, culture, and the biosphere may be inextricably linked (Skutnabb-Kangas, 1998). This idea is based on the theory that languages are not simply sets of labels superimposed on the material world, but rather "every language reflects a unique world-view and culture complex mirroring the manner in which a speech community has resolved its problems in dealing with the world, and has formulated its thinking, its philosophy and understanding of the world around it" (Wurm, 1996, p.1).

In other words, languages encode complex relationships with and understandings of the world we inhabit. Each culture relates to the environment in a different way and forms part of the world's ecological whole. Homogenizing the world's languages, and by extension, its cultures, limits the ways that we interact with our environments, and ultimately disturbs the balance that biological, cultural, and linguistic diversity create.

Along with the idea that losing a language costs us the knowledge embedded in a particular code and the way of seeing and expressing the world that the code embodies, we should also be concerned about the loss of the ultimate dynamic richness of language in general (Dalby, 2003). All languages are rich and full, and each language gains from its contact with others. Crystal reminds us that "languages are interesting in themselves" (2000, p. 54). And as Dalby eloquently states, the price we pay when we lose a language is that the "creativity and flexibility that our descendants will need in their language, if they are to survive and prosper, will in due course wither away" (2003, p. 287).

——Language Policy and Schooling

It has long been recognized that one potent way to suppress a particular language is to establish laws or policies forbidding its use in schools. Examples of this practice are numerous. During the Spanish colonial period in Latin America, missionaries were directed to provide instruction for Indians in Castilian in an attempt to replace indigenous languages (Weinberg, 1977). During the Japanese colonial period in the Pacific Islands between World Wars I and II, schooling was compulsory and all instruction was delivered in Japanese.

United States colonial policies have included attempts to use schools as a tool for replacing local languages with English in Hawaii, the Philippines, and Puerto Rico. Replacement of Native American languages through forced schooling played a significant role in debilitating Native American societies and destroying indigenous North American cultures.

The use of Spanish in the United States has traditionally provoked repressive reactions. Spanish is indigenous to the Southwest, and its continued use there is supported by substantial and continuing immigration by Spanish speakers. Our proximity to Mexico and a thousand miles of border make Spanish a viable southwestern language. On the East Coast, there are large numbers of Puerto Ricans who are citizens by birth and native Spanish speakers. The United States is the logical destination for Spanish-speaking refugees and immigrants from all of Latin America and the Caribbean. As a result, Spanish is widely spoken in the United States and seems to have staying power. There have historically been rigorous and ongoing attempts to suppress the use of Spanish in schools, including ridiculing, punishing, and expelling children for speaking it, even in play (Carter, 1970).

Ode to Sequoyah

The names of Waitie and Boudinot—
    The valiant warrior and gifted sage—
And other Cherokees, may be forgot,
    But thy name shall descend to every age;
The mysteries enshrouding Cadmus' name
Cannot obscure thy claim to fame.

The people's language cannot perish—nay,
    When from the face of this great continent
Inevitable doom hath swept away
    The last memorial—the last fragment
Of tribes,—some scholar learned shall pore
Upon thy letters, seeking ancient lore.

Some bard shall lift a voice in praise of thee,
    In moving numbers tell the world how men
Scoffed thee, hissed thee, charted with lunacy!
    And who could not give 'nough honor when
At length, in spite of jeers, of want and need,
Thy genius shaped a dream into a deed.

By cloud-capped summits in the boundless wet,
    or mightly river rolling to the sea,
Where'er thy footsteps led thee on that quest,
    Unknown, rest thee, illustrious Cherokee!

SOURCE: Sequoyah invented the Cherokee writing system. This poem in his memory was written by Alexander Lawrence Posey, a nineteenth-century Creek Indian poet. Used with permission of the Five Civilized Tribes Museum, Muskogee, OK 74401.

Schools have also been viewed as an avenue for language revitalization. One example is the successful revitalization of Hebrew in Israel. In a period of about 50 years, Hebrew, a language that had been used largely for liturgical purposes, was completely revitalized and established as the official language of a modern state. According to Spolsky, Hebrew was "vital in that it was passed on to children at home, vernacularized in that it was used as the daily spoken language of all classes, standardized in that it had not just dictionaries and grammars and an academy but a school system ranging from kindergarten to postgraduate university levels, and modernized in that it could be used to talk about sport or physics or politics or any topic" (2004, p. 192).

Spolsky notes that Israel is multilingual and that English is taught and widely spoken. This is as might be expected given that Hebrew is not a language of wider communication and that Israel has strong social, economic, and strategic ties to the United States. But from a language planning and policy perspective, the expansion of Hebrew from a language with limited uses to a language of everyday life is remarkable among efforts to revitalize minority languages. Unfortunately, as Dalby suggests, in many cases teachers are "powerful enough to kill the indigenous languages: they are not powerful enough to bring them back to life" (2003, p. 163). Ireland is a case in point. In 1922, with the establishment of the Republic of Ireland, the Irish language was recognized as the official national language (O'Riagain, 1997). The new government took a variety of measures to revitalize the language. All teachers were required to be proficient in Irish, and Irish instruction was required in the schools.

Revitalization efforts in Ireland have extended the social and geographic reach of the language (O'Riagain, 1997). Nevertheless, Irish has never achieved the status that was hoped for, and English is currently the prevailing medium

---

ℒanguage Suppression in Schools

The *Genius of Language* is a collection of essays written in English by writers for whom it is their second language. In his essay "Recovering the Original," Ngugi wa Thiong'o, the internationally known Kenyan writer, describes his experience as an elementary school student in Kenya in the 1950s, at a time when schools were directed to eradicate indigenous African languages:

He lay on his tummy on a high table in the assembly hall with all the students and the staff present. Two teachers held his head and legs and pinned him to the table and called him monkey, as the third whip lashed his buttocks. No matter how horribly he screamed and wriggled with pain, they would not let him go. . . . Eventually the shorts split and blood spluttered out, some of it on the shirts of those who held him down, and only then did they let him go. . . . His fault? He had been caught in the act of speaking Gikuyu in the environs of the school.

SOURCE: Thiong'o, N. (2004). Recovering the original. In Lesser, W. (Ed.), *The genius of language* (pp. 102–110). New York: Pantheon.

of communication in Ireland (Dalby, 2003). Given the growth and globalization of the Irish economy in the context of the European Union, Irish, a minority language at the outset of the Republic (O'Riagain, 2001), is likely to remain so.

Tollefson (2002) asserts the importance of a critical view of language planning that "explores the links between language policies and inequalities of class, region, and ethnicity/nationality" (p. 5). From that perspective, language policy in education must be seen as a factor in minority groups' struggle for social and economic empowerment. It is worthy of note then, that in the current political climate in the United States, there are few opportunities in public school settings to sustain or develop minority languages for speakers of languages other than English.

Therefore, most teachers in the present circumstances, whether they like it or not, are engaged in the development of students' English language skills to the ultimate detriment of students' home languages. There may be little any individual teacher can do to turn the tide of thinking about language in American educational policy. Nevertheless, understanding the dynamics of language planning and policy is key for teachers who work with second language learners.

Summary

Governments have language policies, or ways of promoting the use of particular languages for particular purposes. Governments can promote languages through standardization and dissemination or suppress them by prohibiting their use in public life. Language suppression leads to language loss, and language loss may have serious consequences for all people. Even though teachers do not see themselves as implementing language policy, schools are central institutions in the public sphere, and teachers have an important role in language planning.

Questions to Think About and Discuss

1. Should public schools support minority languages? Why or why not?
2. Should languages other than English be allowed for use in the workplace? In courts? In hospitals? Why or why not?

Activities

1. Interview a colleague, friend, or family member who has children and whose first language is a language other than English. Do this person's children speak their parents' language? How do parents (and children) feel about their language abilities?

Suggestions for Further Reading

Crystal, D. (2000). *Language death.* Cambridge, UK: Cambridge University Press.

Crystal describes the dynamics of language loss, communicates the urgency to address the issue, and turns our attention to strategies for revitalizing languages. The last chapter introduces the role of schooling and identifies the tensions that can arise when schools intervene in language policy.

Dalby, A. (2003). *Language in danger: The loss of linguistic diversity and the threat to our future.* New York: Columbia University Press.

This book will start you thinking about the consequences of language loss for us all. Written in a lively and conversational manner and full of interesting examples from a variety of languages, it's an excellent starting point for anyone interested in language policy and planning.

Fishman, J. A. (Ed.). (2001). *Can threatened languages be saved? Reversing language shift revisited: A 21st century perspective.* Clevedon, UK: Multilingual Matters.

According to the articles in this collection, the answer to the question posed in the title is a qualified "yes." Language shift can, in some cases, be reversed, but it's clearly an uphill battle. Chapters discuss French in Quebec, Quechua in South America, and Basque and Catalan in Spain, among others.

Haugen, E. (1987). *Blessings of Babel: Bilingualism and language planning.* Berlin: Mouton de Gruyter.

Not intended for the layperson or the beginner, this discussion of bilingualism in individuals and societies is nevertheless recommended as a synthesis of up-to-date thinking in the area of sociolinguistics. The author's personal observations as a bilingual person add a note of warmth and familiarity to abstract concepts of language contact, language shift, and language planning.

Robins, R. H., & Uhlenbeck, E. M. (Eds.). (1991). *Endangered languages.* Oxford, UK: Berg.

The first article in this collection, by Stephen A. Wurm, details the circumstances under which languages die or disappear. Following articles describe the condition of various languages around the world. Languages are dying at an incredible rate, and these scholarly analyses will fascinate and upset the reader who cherishes language and linguistic diversity.

Wurm, S. A. (Ed.). (1996). *Atlas of the world's languages in danger of disappearing.* Paris/Canberra: UNESCO Publishing/Pacific Linguistics.

This short volume will unsettle anyone concerned about the preservation of linguistic and cultural diversity. Wurm describes the ways that languages become endangered or moribund and catalogues some of the world's endangered languages. Maps by Theo Baumann offer disturbing images that highlight the extent of the problem. The editor comments, "The impression created [by this book] will be augmented and enhanced when the reader realizes that he or she is only looking at a sample and selection of the problem, and that the full truth is very much grimmer" (p. 17).

chapter

National Unity and Diversity

The United States in the Twenty-First Century

$\mathcal{O}$ur national motto is "E Pluribus Unum"—one out of many. Much of our political heritage has evolved from the tension implicit in the complex philosophy underlying those three words. While we hope to forge one nation from our many peoples and cultures, the nation we intend to create is one that protects our individual right to maintain our differences. As the nation progresses and grows, we try to make sense out of U.S. society. It is difficult to decide who we are, because U.S. identity is complex and constantly changing, and sometimes the debate, which ought to involve thoughtful negotiation, turns angry and acrimonious.

Current immigration trends have once again brought tension about culture and language difference to the forefront of debate at every level, from the United States Congress to the local coffee shop. This chapter will explore questions about cultural and linguistic assimilation in the American context and revisit the way these issues, especially those related to language, play out in public schools.

—Immigration

According to a working paper published by the U.S. Census Bureau, "The estimated size of the foreign-born population of the United States in 2002 was 32.5 million. . . . In absolute terms, this estimate represented an increase of 64.2 percent or 12.7 million over the estimated 19.8 million in the 1990 census, the largest foreign-born population living in the United States since record-keeping began in 1850" (Schmidley & Robinson, 2003, p. 1). Suarez-Orozco notes (2005) that the current wave of immigrants differs from previous immigrants in its intensity and diversity. "Until 1950, nearly 90 percent of all immigrants were Europeans or Canadians. Today, more than 50 percent of all immigrants are Latin American, and more than 25 percent are Asian" (p. 13).

Furthermore, newly arrived immigrants come from incredibly diverse backgrounds, from the highly skilled Asian Indians who find work in Silicon Valley to the uneducated and unskilled workers, many undocumented, who do farmwork, child care, housecleaning, and fly under the radar in any number of low-paid jobs (Portes and Rumbaut, 2006).

It's interesting to note that immigration to the United States is increasing, but the states that traditionally have been the destinations for new Americans (California, New York, Texas, Florida, New Jersey, Illinois) have seen a decline in the growth rates of their immigrant populations, while North Carolina, Georgia, Nevada, and Arkansas saw high growth entering the new millennium (Capps et al., 2002). The new diversity of immigrants, and their presence across the United States and especially in areas that have traditionally been homogenous, may well contribute to the current anxiety about immigration playing out in the political arena.

A HISTORICAL PERSPECTIVE

Suarez-Orozco comments that the United States is "arguably the only postindustrial democracy in the world where immigration is at once history and destiny" (2005, p. 70). Immigration is indisputably a constant in American history; equally constant is that immigration invariably provokes reactionary movements designed to limit the arrival of newcomers.

Many newcomers headed for American shores throughout the nineteenth century. As we saw in Chapter 1, the Irish, fleeing starvation and oppression, were one of the most significant groups seeking refuge in the United States, where they were greeted with open hostility. Their inability to speak English and their Catholicism were focal points for nativist attacks and gave rise midcentury to the Know Nothing party that sought to restrict immigration.

On the West Coast, nineteenth-century nativism focused on Chinese immigrants who came during the California Gold Rush and stayed to build the railroads and work in agriculture. The Naturalization Act of 1870 barred Asians from citizenship, and the Chinese Exclusion Act of 1882 denied citizenship to Chinese workers already in the United States while barring further entries.

In the early part of the twentieth century the country saw an enormous wave of European immigrants fleeing political unrest and persecution and seeking economic opportunity in the United States. Italians and Jews, along with many others, arrived at Ellis Island, Galveston, Baltimore, and other ports of entry, where they were received with the distrust and distaste that seems to greet all newcomers to our shores.

Mexicans, displaced by the Mexican Revolution in 1910, headed north in unprecedented numbers. Following the stock market crash of 1929 and the onset of the Great Depression, President Herbert Hoover, scapegoating Mexicans immigrants, initiated a repatriation movement. Concentrating on southern California and Texas, immigration officers conducted massive raids in parks, social halls, and workplaces and unceremoniously loaded literally thousands of people, irrespective of their status, onto trains headed for Mexico. Many deported in that fashion were American born and had never stepped foot on Mexican soil. Children were separated from their parents, husbands from their wives, people lost their livelihoods and their homes, and lives were irreversibly shattered in one of the most ignominious chapters in American history (Boisson, 2006).

Over the course of the twentieth century, various kinds of legislation limited immigration. In some cases, limitations were based on place of origin (McCarran-Walter Immigration Act, 1952) or political affiliation (Internal Security Act, 1950). Policy in the latter half of the twentieth century, however, keeping pace with changing public attitudes and economic conditions, took a new and somewhat less reactionary direction. The Immigration and Nationality Act (1965), which dramatically altered the shape of U.S. immigration policy, eliminated the national origin quota system and opened our doors to unprecedented diversity. Other kinds of legislation offer exceptions for refugees (Refugee Act, 1980). In 1986, the Immigration Reform and Control Act created an amnesty and offered an opportunity for undocumented residents to become citizens. The number of immigrants allowed into the United States annually was increased by the Immigration Act of 1990.

Current immigration reform efforts focus on undocumented immigrants. The estimated number of undocumented people in the United States and the impact of their presence on the economy, which is often the flashpoint for debate, vary dramatically, depending on who is counting and for what purpose. Generally, supporters of anti-immigration legislation target Mexicans, on the assumption that they comprise the largest number of undocumented entries to the United States. At this writing, the federal government has stalled in efforts to address the question of undocumented immigration through legislative reform. This failure has opened the door to any number of local initiatives, many of which trade on xenophobia and resemble the misguided nativist efforts of our past (Kotlowitz, 2007).

ASSIMILATION VERSUS PLURALISM

In the eighteenth and nineteenth centuries, political emphasis was placed on the concept of *unum*, crystallized at the beginning of the twentieth century as the "melting pot" (Gleason, 1984). The melting pot was envisioned as a process of ethnic and racial fusion, but it can also be seen as a call for Anglo-conformity. In the melting pot, a person was expected to "Americanize"—to emerge looking, sounding, and acting like a white person of northern European background. "Melting" was a misnomer in this context, because it did not involve a synthesis of all the elements involved.

As the various ethnic groups comprising the population of the United States have established themselves socially and politically, they have begun to view their ethnic heritages positively. Emphasis has moved to *pluribus;* a cultural pluralist view of American society has emerged, suggesting that it is possible to be unified while still maintaining diversity. The most common analogy for the cultural pluralist view is the salad bowl. All the ingredients in a salad bowl make contributions to the whole, but each one maintains its own distinguishable identity.

The salad bowl image is still a useful way to think about ourselves, but the question of American identity is further complicated by the emergence of new technologies. Unlike immigrants in earlier times, new Americans do not have to sever ties with their original homelands. The availability and low cost of email and other telecommunications make it possible to stay in touch across enormous distances. Transcontinental travel, once available only to the wealthy, is relatively inexpensive, and barring political barriers, people can, and often do, return regularly to their places of origin.

It's worth noting, as Suarez-Orozco points out (2005) that technological changes in communication and transportation create two-way streets. As American culture is changed by the arrival of newcomers, root cultures in today's world are changed by their exposure to American values, images, artifacts, and lifestyles. Often the conduit for that change is the immigrants themselves, who transmit resources, ideas, and political influence from the United States with every phone call or visit.

In any event, we are increasingly a nation of minorities and our identities play out across a spectrum of multiple hues and shades. At one end, American Amish live in separate enclaves, maintaining their own distinctive social organization and language. At the other end, many Americans function almost exclusively in the cultural mainstream, affirming their ethnicity only on special occasions, if at all, with traditional food, dress or rituals. Many of us are multicultural and don't readily fall into easily defined categories. In other words, ethnicity itself has been altered by the American experience.

Unity, Diversity, and Language

You've probably recently heard somebody complain that they can't understand customer service personnel who speak English as a second language. Or maybe you've heard somebody ask, "Why should I press 'one' for English?!" Nativist reactions to immigration invariably include language resistance.

Language resistance includes language parochialism, the attitude that multilingualism is not useful and may even be harmful, and language elitism, the attitude that bilingualism is desirable for individuals of elevated status but unacceptable for members of ethnic minority groups. Parochialism and elitism are costly—both economically and politically—and they set the stage for restrictionism. Language restrictionism is the attempt to formally promulgate a language policy that imposes restrictions on language use.

LANGUAGE PAROCHIALISM

Language parochialism might be characterized as an attitude about language that holds multlingualism in low regard and fails to acknowledge the benefits of language sophistication. Over 25 years ago, Paul Simon, at that time a congressman from Illinois, wrote a book titled *The Tongue-Tied American* (1980), which details the effects of language parochialism. Simon was ahead of his time in his insistence that American resistance to language learning and negative attitudes about bilingualism are costly to our nation. In the twenty-first century, the ability to speak languages other than English is critical both politically and economically.

International Trade. It is common wisdom that you can buy in any language but you should sell in the language of your customer. Around the world, salespeople are expected to be multilingual. U.S. business people, however, generally expect to conduct business in English, and our monolingualism and lack of cultural sensitivity has damaged our viability in the international marketplace. Simon (1980) has cataloged some of our more embarrassing attempts to advertise in foreign markets:

> "Body by Fisher," describing a General Motors product, came out "Corpse by Fisher" in Flemish. . . . Schweppes Tonic was advertised in Italy as "bathroom water." . . . "Come Alive With Pepsi" almost appeared in the Chinese version of the *Reader's Digest* as "Pepsi brings your ancestors back from the grave." (p. 32)

Translation errors are amusing, but the economic outcomes of our parochialism are not. A recent study evaluating the Fulbright-Hays programs that support research on language acquisition and language training is emphatic: "Growth in the language services sector has been explosive in recent years, reflecting similar growth in private-sector demand for language expertise. Large sectors of the economy—such as software, telecommunications, and financial services—are unable to penetrate foreign markets or . . . to develop products and services in the languages of their prospective customers, because of a shortage of language expertise" (Brecht & Rivers, 2000, p. xi).

National Security. During World War II, the military recognized the need for personnel with skills in foreign languages as essential to our national defense. As we discussed in Chapter 7, the U.S. Army took a leadership role in developing innovative language teaching strategies. After the war, the National Defense Education Act (1958) provided financial assistance to stimulate foreign language study. Funding for the act continued for a decade, and during that period of support, enrollment in high school foreign language courses in the United States increased from 16.5 to 27.7 percent (Benderson, 1983).

Unfortunately, in the decades following the act, national interest in the study of foreign languages declined, and monolingualism hampered our national security efforts.

For example, during the revolution in Iran in 1978 only 6 of the 60 U.S. Foreign Service officers assigned there were Farsi speakers (Kondracke, 1979). As you may remember, anti-U.S. feeling in Iran escalated to monumental proportions that year, culminating in a situation where 53 U.S. embassy personnel were held hostage for nearly a year. According to Simon (1980), only one of the 120 journalists assigned to Iran during the hostage crisis spoke Farsi.

More recently, the demand has surged for speakers of Arabic and other Middle Eastern languages (Dillon, 2003). In a government report (U.S. General Accounting Office, 2002) highlighting the issue, the GAO reviewed four federal agencies, including the U.S. Army, the U.S. Department of State, the Foreign Commercial Service, and the FBI and found shortages of speakers of foreign languages. The report also found deficiencies in the skills of people who hold positions that require abilities in foreign languages. For example, the U.S. Army reported in 2001 that they had only filled 42 of 84 positions authorized for Arabic interpreters and translators (p. 7). And even five years after the events of September 11, 2001, citing the agency's own statistics, the *Washington Post* reported that "only 33 FBI agents have even a limited proficiency in Arabic, and none of them work in sections of the bureau that coordinate investigations of international terrorism" (Eggen, 2006). The FBI has, however, begun an aggressive campaign designed to identify and fast-track recruits who have proficiency in languages essential to national defense (Temple-Raston, 2007).

Americans often assume that everyone speaks English. English is widely used as the language of science and commerce and is the language most used as a second language around the world (Ferguson, 1978). Widespread use of English may facilitate your shopping on a pleasure trip. It is unlikely, however, that you would be able to take the measure of a sensitive political situation in a foreign country using only English.

English speakers in non-English-speaking countries are likely to be members of a country's educated elite and may therefore be incapable of properly assessing the total political climate in which they live. Also, intelligence gathered in English or translated may be inaccurate, lacking in significant cultural and social nuances. The Iranian situation is but one instance where lack of language resources has placed us in a politically dangerous situation.

Recently, there has been renewed interest in foreign language instruction at the elementary level. According to Glod (2006), a significant number of elementary schools in the Washington, DC, area, responding to calls of business and government leaders, have initiated programs in Spanish, French, Arabic, and Mandarin, among other languages. In addition, enrollments in foreign language classes at the university level are increasing. A survey by the Modern Language Association (Welles, 2004) indicates that between 1998 and 2002, the number of college students studying a language increased 17.9 percent, to 1.4 million. After Spanish, French, and German, students favored Italian,

American Sign Language, Japanese, Chinese, Latin, Russian, ancient Greek, biblical Hebrew, Arabic, modern Hebrew, Portuguese, and Korean. In addition, there has been a noticeable growth in student enrollment in languages that the Association identifies as "less commonly taught," including Vietnamese, Hindi, Aramaic, and Swahili.

Finally, early in 2006, the Bush administration launched the National Security Language Initiative (NSLI) to address the need to strengthen national security through foreign language study (U.S. Department of State, January 5, 2006). Although the initiative designated significant funds to support foreign language instruction at every level of education, it was never fully funded (Zehr, 2007). As other countries have known for some time (Pufahl et al., 2000), foreign language instruction takes time and requires a supportive policy infrastructure. NSLI has made modest inroads. With time and full funding, it might enable us to overcome our parochialism and use our language resources effectively for diplomacy and national defense.

LANGUAGE ELITISM

In the United States, bilingualism has often been viewed with disfavor. This is particularly wasteful given that we have large numbers of people within our borders who speak languages other than English and who could serve as language resources to our entire nation.

Yet our attitudes toward bilingualism are ambivalent. We consider it a worthwhile accomplishment for a college graduate from an English-speaking background to master a second language. But we insist that the children of immigrant families relinquish their first languages as part of their "Americanization." Kjolseth (1983) has suggested that we tend to admire individual bilinguals, such as celebrities, scholars, and diplomats, and to disparage group bilinguals, or members of ethnic groups. In the popular view, individual bilingualism is often associated with elevated socioeconomic status; group bilingualism is generally associated with poverty and lack of education. Individual bilinguals acquire their second language through effort and scholarship; group bilinguals acquire their second language at home.

An eighth-grade student from a family of migrant farmworkers in Colorado told me, "I like school better here than in Texas. In Texas they punished me for speaking Spanish in school. The white kids were learning Spanish and tried to practice with us, but when we answered them we got punished." We fail to recognize that bilingualism is valuable regardless of its source.

Hunger of Memory (Rodriguez, 1982), the autobiography of a Mexican American writer and scholar, received much attention when it was published, because the author suggested that giving up Spanish was a first and essential step on his road to "Americanization." Opponents of dual language instruction hailed the book and pointed to the author's experiences as proof positive that English monolingualism leads to successful assimilation. But a persistently apologetic and yearning tone underlies Rodriguez's autobiography, leading the reader to question his assertion that giving up Spanish was necessary and positive in establishing his identity as a North American.

Einar Haugen (1987), a bilingual Norwegian American sociolinguist, observed:

> The loss of the mother tongue in home and church could be a bitter experience. It is well known that a second language learned in later life often fails to convey the cultural, emotional, or religious power of the first language, the mother tongue. Even with my entire schooling in English, my Norwegian background somehow makes a Norwegian poem or quotation warmer and more deeply moving than its English equivalent. (p. 24)

American attitudes toward language study are not shared around the world. Following the European Year of Languages in 2001, in 2003 the European Commission, the executive branch of the European Union, adopted an action plan that promotes language learning and language diversity. The introduction to the action plan states quite simply that "the ability to understand and communicate in other languages is a basic skill for all European citizens" (Commission of the European Communities, 2003, p. 1). And an informal survey in my own classrooms each semester reveals that, unlike students educated in the United States, students educated in Asia, Latin America, and the Middle East almost always were required to study at least one foreign language as a matter of course. (See Chapter 1 for a discussion of dual language instruction in other countries.)

Elitist attitudes about bilingualism cause us to squander our linguistic resources. One can only wonder how many children enter schools in the United States where the use of their first language is discouraged or even punished, only to enroll in high school foreign language classes to try to recapture some of their lost language wealth. Entrenched in English monolingualism, we fail to acknowledge our multilingualism as a national resource, limit our ability to trade on world markets, and endanger our security as a nation.

LANGUAGE RESTRICTIONISM

Language restrictionism is not new in the United States, but it is currently enjoying a renaissance and may have devastating effects both on our education systems and on our political and economic success as a nation. The most visible face of language restrictionism is U.S. English. Founded in 1983 by then Senator S. I. Hayakawa, U.S. English claims 1.8 million members (U.S. English, 2007). Its efforts are directed primarily at making English the official language of the United States. While U.S. English has not been successful at the federal level, it has contributed to the success of official English legislation in 28 states. English First, which claims 150,000 members, intends to "make English America's official language, give every child the chance to learn English, and eliminate costly and ineffective multilingual policies" (English First, 2007).

ℒanguage and Loyalty

Periods of intense immigration often provoke U.S. nativism and with it, language restric-tionism. People who want to restrict language often tie language to political loyalty, even though history bears witness that demeaning or restricting people's use of a particular language is usually a veiled way of demeaning the people themselves. Some prominent U.S. political figures have made the mistake of confusing language and loyalty. In 1751, referring to German immigrants, who were numerous at the time, Benjamin Franklin complained:

Why should the Palatine Boors be suffered to swarm into our settlements and by herding together, establish their language to the exclusion of ours? Why should Pennsylvania, founded by the English, become a colony of aliens, who will shortly be so numerous as to Germanize us instead of our Anglifying them? (Conklin & Lourie, 1983, p. 69)

In 1753, in a letter to a member of the British parliament, Franklin commented:

Those [Germans] who come hither are generally the most ignorant Stupid Sort of their own Nation, and as Ignorance is often attended with Credulity when Knavery would mislead it, and with Suspicion when Honesty would set it right; and as few of the English understand the Ger-man Language, and so cannot address them either from the Press or Pulpit, 'tis almost impos-sible to remove any prejudices they once entertain. (Crawford, 1992b, p. 19)

Two hundred and fifty years later, Newt Gingrich, then Speaker of the House, commented in his book, *To Renew America* (1995, p. 176–78):

if people had wanted to remain immersed in their old culture, they could have done so without coming to America. . . . Bilingualism keeps people actively tied to their old language and habits and maximizes the cost of the transition of becoming an American. . . . America can absorb an amazing number of people from an astonishing range of backgrounds if our goal is assimilation. If people are being encouraged to resist assimilation, the very fabric of American society will eventually break down. . . . The only viable alternative for the American underclass is American civilization. Without English as a common language, there is no such civilization.

Thumbs up to the United States Supreme Court, which declared in 1923 in *Meyer v. Nebraska* (62 U.S. 390, [1923]) that:

the individual has certain fundamental rights that must be respected. The protection of the Constitution extends to all, to those who speak other languages as well as to those born with English on the tongue. Perhaps it would be highly advantageous if all had ready understanding of our ordinary speech, but this cannot be coerced with methods which conflict with the Consti-tution. . . . No emergency has arisen which renders knowledge by a child of some language other than English so clearly harmful as to justify its inhibition with the consequent infringement of rights long freely enjoyed.

And to the New Mexico State Legislature that declared in 1989 in an English Plus Resolu-tion (Crawford, 1992b, p. 154):

Proficiency on the part of our citizens in more than one language is to the economic and cultural benefit of our state and the nation.

English First is currently targeting Executive Order 13166, Improving Access to Services for Persons with Limited English Proficiency. According to a Department of Justice publication, the Order, signed by President Bill Clinton in 2000, requires "federal agencies to take reasonable steps to provide meaningful access for LEP people to federally conducted programs and activities" (2004, p. iii), meaning essentially everything the federal government does. The order also requires the federal government to assist nonfederal agencies that receive federal funds to come into compliance.

Support for the English-only movement is far from unanimous, and language restrictionist laws have not gone unchallenged. Arizona, for example, amended its state constitution in 1988, making English the language of all government actions. In 1994, however, the U.S. Court of Appeals for the Ninth Circuit upheld a federal district court ruling that held the Arizona English-only law in violation of constitutional First Amendment protection of free speech (Contín, 1995). In 1998, Alaska passed an English-only initiative, but in 2002 a Superior Court judge ruled that the initiative violated the free speech provisions of the Alaska Constitution. Figure 12.1 is an amusing but pointed reflection on language restrictionism in the United States.

Chen (1995) has suggested that English-only laws can be challenged on two bases. First, to the extent that language restrictionist laws limit a person's access to government services or ability to communicate with the government, those laws may violate a constitutional right to equal protection under the law. This potential violation is enhanced by the fact that language and national origin tend to overlap, and denial of services based on national origin is clearly illegal. Secondly, English-only laws may restrict government employees from serving the public in languages other than English, which can be seen as a violation of their civil right to free speech.

Voting. Voting is a fundamental right. In 1975 Congress amended the Voting Rights Act to prohibit English-only elections and to require bilingual ballots in jurisdictions where the language minority population exceeds 5 percent and illiteracy rates exceed national norms. English-only advocates have targeted bilingual ballots and voting materials. In 1984, for example, California voters passed an initiative instructing the governor to inform Congress that California wanted to eliminate ballots in languages other than English. Supporters of the proposition no doubt felt that they were voting for assimilation. As legal scholar Kenneth Karst (1986) has observed, however: "Voting is not just an expression of political preferences; it is an assertion of belonging to a political community" (p. 347).

Encouraging people to vote, regardless of their English proficiency, encourages the assimilation process. Where bilingual ballots are used, ethnic minorities' participation in the political system has increased. New Mexico has had bilingual voting since it became a state in 1912, and it is the only state

SOURCE: "Language Police," David Fitzsimmons © *The Arizona Daily Star.* 1988. Reprinted with permission.

where the number of Hispanics in the state legislature is in proportion to their representation in the general population (Trasvina, 1981).

IMPLICATIONS FOR SCHOOLING

As part of their agenda, English-only proponents want to limit the time children spend in bilingual education programs. Del Valle points out (2003, p. 56) that "deciding in which language to educate students is a distinctly different inquiry than whether the parents of these children should be able to vote in a language they can understand. Supporters of English-only, however, can garner greater support by conflating the two issues, especially when there is such national anxiety over bilingual education in particular."

English for the Children, a language restrictionist organization that targets bilingual education, has leveraged the general public's anxiety to great advantage. Formed in 1997 by Ron Unz, a California businessman, the organization promoted laws against bilingual education that were successful in California, Arizona, and Colorado. "English for the children" is misleading, given that bilingual programs for English language learners are meant to facilitate English acquisition. But as we have seen, the rationale for primary language instruction for second language learners is complex and requires an understanding of language, linguistics, and pedagogy. The "English for the Children" message is simple and saleable and does well in referendum votes.

As we saw in Chapters 2 and 6, bilingual programs for limited English proficient children focus largely on English language acquisition, and research shows that primary language instruction is a useful instructional bridge to English. Furthermore, full development of two languages is beneficial to the education of any child. It's difficult to imagine subjecting any other form of pedagogy to a referendum vote, but educational success for second language learners is not the real center of the debate for opponents of bilingual education. Rather bilingual education is one battlefield in a larger political war about American identity.

Dual language instruction will be the subject of ongoing controversy, persisting at best in a transitional and compensatory mode, until the U.S. public begins to understand what privileged classes around the world have always known—that bilingualism is socially, politically, and economically desirable. In discussing U.S. language policy, the sociolinguist Joshua A. Fishman (1981) observed:

> Language policy involves a vision of America. A multilingual enrichment policy envisages a multilingual America as being in the public good. We support a multiparty system. . . . Our anti-trust laws aim to diversify the economic market place. We can similarly diversify the cultural market place. . . . There is a vision of American magnanimity involved, but more than that, a vision of American possibilities, opportunities, appreciations, sensitivities, that we all should savour. (pp. 525–526)

Outcomes. The fears of those who oppose the English-only movement have not been fully realized. In most areas, practical considerations require provisions for non-English speakers in schools, courts, hospitals, and social services. In the private sector, the profit motive promotes multilingual accommodation in businesses, and in many communities advertising and marketing in several languages is the norm. Several major metropolitan areas, for example, support classified telephone directories in languages other than English. Nevertheless, English-only legislation opens the door to restrictions on public service assistance and free speech.

A friend of mine, a physician, voted in favor of an amendment to the California Constitution declaring English as the official language. He explained, "People come into my office every day, and they can't speak a word of English." His reasoning is flawed, because people cannot be legislated into English proficiency.

Language restrictionist legislation often ignores the need for widescale programs to assist newcomers in learning English. It would be far more useful to expand underfunded adult education programs, where waiting lists for English classes are common. In general, limitations on language use threaten to exclude large sectors of our population from the mainstream instead of providing the education and services necessary to enfranchise them.

Summary

In the United States we tend to be linguistically unsophisticated, and our parochial attitudes about multilingualism have hurt us in international trade, national security, and diplomacy. The narrow view we often have about multilingualism, combined with reactions to increased immigration and population changes, provides a growth medium for language restrictionists. Language restrictionism is not new in the United States. Immigration is a constant in American history and has always provoked nativist responses. Currently, increased immigration has turned up the heat on debates about American identity, immigration reform, and language policy. The current movement, like its predecessors, is attempting to limit the use of languages other than English in a variety of areas. The melting pot and salad bowl models may be inadequate in the twenty-first century, with the increased availability of communication and transportation. Language restrictionism is not new in the United States, but the current restrictionist movement has had some success in the arena of public education.

It is difficult to characterize American identity. While assimilationism and pluralism seem to represent polar opposites, in fact "Americanization" is a process that includes both. National language policy is unclear, but multiple languages are part of our American identity and are also socially, politically, and economically valuable. Schools can assist in promoting positive bilingualism for all children, but that will require rethinking our national position on dual language instruction.

Questions to Think About and Discuss

1. Should the United States restrict immigration? Why or why not? If you think immigration should be restricted, what restrictions would you favor?
2. Should the United States have an official language? Why or why not?
3. Is there anything that your school or district does that promotes or represses the use of languages other than English?

Activities

1. Survey colleagues or classmates who have been educated outside the United States. Find out what the requirements were for foreign language learning in their native schools.
2. Survey high schools and colleges in your area. What, if any, are the foreign language requirements for graduation? What languages are offered? Which ones have the highest enrollments?
3. Survey friends, relatives, and colleagues. Ask how many of them would like to know another language. How many would favor foreign or modern language instruction in the schools? How many of them consider bilingual education desirable for limited English proficient children?
4. Is there a local ordinance, a statewide law, or language in the state constitution amendment that makes English the official language in your area? Is such legislation under consideration? What are the potential impacts of such legislation?
5. Create an ethnic profile of the students in your class. How many different backgrounds are represented? To what extent do those having foreign backgrounds feel they have maintained ties with their ethnic heritage(s)? With their language(s)? How do they feel about their relationship to their ethnic and linguistic heritage(s)?

Suggestions for Further Reading

Adams, K. L., and Brink, D. T. (Eds.). (1990). *Perspectives on official English: The campaign for English as the official language of the USA.* Berlin: Mouton de Gruyter.
   This book contains an overview of the general issue of language policy and analyses of language policy around the world. The book then zeroes in on language policy in the United

States with a detailed discussion of California's English-only proposition, as well as discussions of language use and legislation in Florida, New York, and parts of the Southwest. One whole section is devoted to language legislation from the perspective of constitutional law. An appendix contains language legislation from several states, as of 1990.

Baron, D. (1990). *The English-only question: An official language for Americans?* New Haven, CT: Yale University Press.

This book is a detailed history of language policy in the United States. An appendix contains a map overviewing state legislation on English-only as of mid-1990.

Crawford, J. (1992a). *Hold your tongue: Bilingualism and the politics of "English Only."* Reading, MA: Addison-Wesley.

This book is a comprehensive discussion of American reactions to language diversity and an analysis of the English-only movement in the United States.

Crawford, J. (Ed.). (1992b). *Language loyalties: A source book on the official English controversy.* Chicago: The University of Chicago Press.

A collection of articles and legal documents that reflect on language issues in every area of public life, this is an invaluable collection for a serious student of American language policy.

Dicker, S. J. (1996). *Languages in America: A pluralist view.* Clevedon, UK: Multilingual Matters.

At a time when language policy is the subject of constant, and often vituperative, debate, this book makes the case for linguistic diversity, drawing on linguistics, history, sociology, and law.

Kloss, H. (1977). *The American bilingual tradition.* Rowley, MA: Newbury House.

Already recommended in Chapter 1, this book bears another mention as a classic analysis of U.S. language policy.

McCarty, T. L., & Zepeda, O. (1995, Winter). Indigenous Language Education and Literacy. *Bilingual Research Journal, 19*(1).

This special issue of the Bilingual Research Journal *examines the goals and outcomes of bilingual programs in indigenous communities in North America. It merits the attention of those interested in Native American languages and education and contains an article by James Crawford on language endangerment.*

Perea, J. F. (Ed.). (1997). *Immigrants out! The new nativism and the anti-immigrant impulse in the United States.* New York: New York University Press.

This collection of articles reflects on nativism in the United States from both historical and contemporary perspectives. The relationships between newcomers and native-born Americans are analyzed historically, politically, and economically.

Piatt, B. (1990). *¿Only English? Law and language policy in the United States.* Albuquerque: University of New Mexico Press.

A historical and legal analysis of U.S. language policy, this book calls for a balanced formulation of language policy that can meet our political and personal needs in a multicultural and multilingual society.

Simon, P. (1980). *The tongue-tied American.* New York: Continuum.

While not a new publication, this collection of data, anecdotes, and information is still noteworthy. Simon's examples of the outcomes of our national monolingualism in the areas of international trade, national security, and diplomacy call our attention to issues and problems that still exist today.

Skutnabb-Kangas, T., & Phillipson, R. (Eds.). (1994). *Linguistic human rights: Overcoming linguistic discrimination.* Berlin: Mouton de Gruyter.

The editors of this volume are language scholars and well-known proponents of the rights of language minority students. The papers in this book support the idea that "linguistic rights should be considered basic human rights" (p. 1), through an exploration of the issues of language policy in general, and specifically in a number of places around the world.

Tse, L. (2001). *Why don't they learn English? Separating fact from fallacy in the U.S. language debate.* New York: Teachers College Press.

English-only advocates, equating English with political loyalty and personal allegiance, often claim that immigrants don't want to learn English. Tse refutes their arguments and points out that "myths about immigrant language learning skew the public mindset on language-related issues, causing a misdirection of energy . . . toward solving phantom problems while ignoring true crises" (p. 72).

Online Resources

$\mathcal{T}$he following list is far from comprehensive, and given the constantly changing landscape of technology, some resources may have changed by the time this book is published. They are offered just as starting points. Here are some of the possibilities related to dual language instruction that can be found on the Internet:

JAMES CRAWFORD

ourworld.compuserve.com/homepages/jwcrawford/home.htm
James Crawford has published extensively on language policy and bilingual education. His website highlights key issues, describes his books, offers a selection of his recent articles, provides updates on politics and legislation, and links with other sites of related interest.

CENTER FOR APPLIED LINGUISTICS

www.cal.org
The Center for Applied Linguistics is a private, nonprofit organization that disseminates research-based information about language as it relates to educational and societal issues. The site includes publications, databases, and links related to a variety of issues, including immigrant and refugee education, ESL teaching, and foreign language instruction.

THE CENTER FOR RESEARCH ON EDUCATION, DIVERSITY & EXCELLENCE

www.crede.ucsc.edu
CREDE is a federally funded program whose research and development projects are focused on students who are linguistically and culturally diverse. Much of CREDE's current work revolves around its five standards for effective pedagogy. These standards or principles describe best practice in any classroom, and include joint productive activity, language and literacy development across the curriculum, connecting curriculum to students' lived experiences, teaching complex thinking, and teaching through conversation. Professionals who access CREDE's website will find useful research studies as well as publications and multimedia products.

LINGUISTIC MINORITIES RESEARCH INSTITUTE

lmri.ucsb.edu
The website reflects the institute's focus on issues related to language, education, and public policy.

NATIONAL ASSOCIATION FOR BILINGUAL EDUCATION

www.nabe.org
This website provides information about NABE, a professional organization for bilingual educators.

NATIONAL CLEARINGHOUSE FOR ENGLISH LANGUAGE ACQUISITION

www.ncela.gwu.edu
Funded by the U.S. Department of Education and the Office of English Language Acquisition, Language Enhancement, and Academic Achievement for LEP Students (OELA), NCELA offers a large selection of its publications online, all related to the education of linguistically and culturally diverse students. Go to www.ncela.gwu.edu/newsline/subscribe.html to subscribe to a weekly email bulletin published by the U.S. Department of Education Office of English Language Acquisition (OELA). The bulletin provides links to current information about No Child Left Behind, as well as resources, publications, and research related to second language learners.

TERRALINGUA

www.terralingua.org
Terralingua is an international nonprofit organization concerned with the future of the world's cultural and linguistic diversity. Its website is devoted to the issues of preserving linguistic diversity and exploring the linkages between biological and cultural diversity.

TEACHERS OF ENGLISH TO SPEAKERS OF OTHER LANGUAGES

www.tesol.org
TESOL is an international organization that supports professionals who teach English to speakers of other languages. In addition to its online presence, TESOL publishes a scholarly journal, the *TESOL Quarterly*, a magazine, *TESOL Journal*, and a newsletter, *TESOL Matters*. TESOL has developed standards for teaching English and teacher preparation, and advocates for English language learning in a context that respects individual language rights. TESOL has a large membership around the world, and holds a well-attended conference each year.

Bibliography

Adams, K. L., & Brink, D. T. (Eds.). (1990). *Perspectives on official English: The campaign for English as the official language of the USA.* Berlin: Mouton de Gruyter.

Ambert, A. N., & Melendez, S. E. (1985). *Bilingual education: A sourcebook.* New York: Teachers College Press.

American Bible Society. (1995). *De good nyews bout Jedus Christ wa Luke write.* New York: Author.

American Speech-Language-Hearing Association. (1983). Committee on Language Report, *ASHA, 25*(6).

Amoriggi, H. D., & Gefteas, D. J. (1981). *Affective considerations in bilingual education: Problems and solutions.* Rosslyn, VA: National Clearinghouse for Bilingual Education.

Andrews, L. (2001). *Linguistics for L2 teachers.* Mahwah, NJ: Lawrence Erlbaum.

Aratani, L. (1998, January 22). High school leads the way in single-sex classes. *San Jose Mercury News,* pp. 1B, 4B.

Arons, S. (1983). *Compelling belief: The culture of American schooling.* New York: McGraw-Hill.

Artiles, A. J., Rueda R., Salazar, J. J., & Higareda, I. (2002). English-language learner representation in California urban school districts. In D. J. Losen & G. Orfeld (Eds.), *Racial inequity in special education* (pp. 117–136). Cambridge, MA: Harvard University Press.

Arvizu, S. F., Snyder, W. A., & Espinosa, P. T. (1980). *Demystifying the concept of culture: Theoretical and conceptual tools.* Los Angeles: Evaluation, Dissemination and Assessment Center, California State University, Los Angeles.

Asher, J. J. (1982). The total physical response approach. In R. W. Blair (Ed.), *Innovative approaches to language learning* (pp. 54–66). Rowley, MA: Newbury House.

Asher, J. J. (1986). *Learning another language through actions: The complete teacher's guidebook.* Los Gatos, CA: Sky Oaks Productions.

Aspira of New York v. Board of Education of the City of New York, Civ. No. 4002 (S.D. N.Y. consent agreement, August 29, 1974).

Association of Northern California Chinese Schools. (2003). Member schools. Retrieved June 5, 2003, from www.anccs.org.

Au, K. H., & Jordan, C. (1981). Teaching reading to Hawaiian children: Finding a culturally appropriate solution. In H. T. Trueba, C. P. Guthrie, & K. H. Au (Eds.), *Culture and the bilingual classroom: Studies in classroom ethnography* (pp. 139–152). Rowley, MA: Newbury House.

Baca, L. M., & Cervantes, H. T. (1998). *The bilingual special education interface* (3rd ed.). Upper Saddle River, NJ: Merrill.

Baetens, B. H. (1993). *European models of bilingual education.* Clevedon, UK: Multilingual Matters.

Baker, C. (2006). *Foundations of bilingual education and bilingualism* (4th ed.). Clevedon, UK: Multilingual Matters.

Baker, K. A., & de Kanter, A. A. (1981, September 25). *Effectiveness of bilingual education: A review of the literature.* Washington, DC: Office of Planning, Budget and Evaluation, U.S. Department of Education.

Bancroft, W. J. (1978). The Lozanov method and its American adaptations. *Modern Language Journal, 62,* 167–174.

Banks, J. A. (1977). *Multiethnic education: Practices and promises.* Bloomington, IN: Phi Delta Kappa Educational Foundation.

Barinaga, M. (1997, August 1). New insights into how babies learn language. *Science,* 641.

Baron, D. (1990). *The English-only question: An official language for Americans?* New Haven, CT: Yale University Press.

Battle in Spain on teaching in Spanish. (1993, November). *The New York Times*, p. A4.

Beardsley, T. (1995, January). For whom the bell curve really tolls. *Scientific American, 272*(1), 14, 16–17.

Bell, L. A. (1991). Changing our ideas about ourselves: Group consciousness raising with elementary school girls as a means to empowerment. In C. E. Sleeter (Ed.), *Empowerment through multicultural education* (pp. 229–249). Albany: State University of New York Press.

Benderson, A. (1983). *Foreign languages in the schools*. Princeton, NJ: Educational Testing Service (ERIC Document Reproduction Service No. ED 239 516).

Bereiter, C., & Engelmann, S. (1966). *Teaching disadvantaged children in the preschool*. Englewood Cliffs, NJ: Prentice-Hall.

Bialystok, E. (Ed.). (1991). *Language processing in bilingual children*. Cambridge, UK: Cambridge University Press.

Bialystok, E., & Hakuta, K. (1994). *In other words: The science and psychology of second language acquisition*. New York: Basic Books.

Bilingual Education Act, as amended, 20 U.S.C. sec. 3221 et seq.

Bilingual programs in Sweden are truly so. (1985). *The Reading Teacher, 39*, 213.

Blair, R. W. (Ed.). (1982). *Innovative approaches to language teaching*. Rowley, MA: Newbury House.

Block, L. (1992). *A walk among the tombstones*. New York: William Morrow.

Bloom, L., & Lahey, M. (1978). *Language development and language disorders*. New York: John Wiley & Sons.

Bloomfield, L. (1933). *Language*. New York: Holt, Rinehart, and Winston.

Boisson, S. (2006). When America sent her own packing. *American History, 41*, 20–27.

Boyd, S. (1999). Sweden: Immigrant languages. In B. Spolsky (Ed.), *Concise encyclopedia of educational linguis-tics* (pp. 73–74). Oxford, UK: Elsevier Science.

Boykin, A. W. (1984). Reading achievement and the social-cultural frame of reference of Afro-American children. *Journal of Negro Education, 53*, 464–473.

Brecht, R. D., & Rivers, W. P. (2000). Language and national security in the 21st century: The role of Title VI/Fulbright-Hays in supporting national language capacity. Dubuque, IA: Kendall/Hunt.

Brown, H. D. (1980). *Principles of language learning and teaching*. Englewood Cliffs, NJ: Prentice-Hall.

Brown, H. D. (1987). *Principles of language learning and teaching* (2nd ed.). Englewood Cliffs, NJ: Prentice-Hall.

Brown, J. E. (Ed.). (1972). *The North American Indians: A selection of photographs by Edward S. Curtis*. Millerton, NY: Aperture.

Brown, R., Cazden, C., & Bellugi, U. (1973). The child's grammar from I to III. In C. Ferguson & D. Slobin (Eds.), *Studies of child language development* (pp. 295–333). New York: Holt, Rinehart, & Winston.

Brown v. Board of Education of Topeka, 347 U.S. 483 (1954).

Bryson, B. (1994). *Made in America: An informal history of the English language in the United States*. New York: William Morrow.

Butler-Pascoe, M. E., & Wiburg, K. M. (2003). *Technology and teaching English language learners*. New York: Pearson.

Butterfield, F. (1986, August 3). Why Asians are going to the head of the class. *The New York Times*, Sec. XII, pp. 18–19.

Butterfield, F. (1994, December 30). Programs seek to stop trouble before it starts. *The New York Times*, p. A11.

California Department of Education. (2003). *Number of English learners in California public schools by language and grade*. Retrieved 2003 from Dataquest: www.cde.ca.gov/dataquest.

California Department of Education (Ed.). (2007). Number of English Learners by

Language, 2006–2007. Retrieved January 7, 2008 from dq.cde.ca.gov/dataquest.

California State Department of Education (Ed.). (1984). *Studies on immersion education: A collection for United States educators.* Sacramento, CA: Office of Bilingual Bicultural Education.

California State Department of Education (Ed.). (1986). *Beyond language: Social and cultural factors in schooling language minority students.* Los Angeles: Evaluation, Dissemination and Assessment Center, California State University, Los Angeles.

California State Department of Education (Ed.). (1994). *Schooling and language minority students: A theoretical framework* (2nd ed.). Sacramento, CA: Bilingual Education Office.

Campbell-Jones, S. (Producer). (1985). *Baby talk* [video]. San Diego, CA: Media Guild.

Canale, M., & Swain, M. (1980). Theoretical bases of communicative approaches to second language teaching and testing. *Applied Linguistics, 1,* 1–47.

Capps, R., Fix, M. E., & Passel, J. S. (2002). The dispersal of immigrants in the 1990's. Washington, DC: The Urban Institute. Retrieved January 7, 2008, from www.urban.org/publications/410589.html.

Carle, E. (1969). *The very hungry caterpillar.* New York: World Publishing.

Carter, T. P. (1970). *Mexican Americans in school: A history of educational neglect.* New York: College Entrance Examination Board.

Castañeda v. Pickard, 648 F.2d 989 (5th Cir. 1981).

Castellanos, D. (1983). *The best of two worlds: Bilingual-bicultural education in the U.S.* Trenton, NJ: New Jersey State Department of Education.

Center for Applied Linguistics. (2007). *Directory of two-way immersion programs in the U.S.* Retrieved September 4, 2007, from www.cal.org/twi/directory.

Chaika, E. (1989). *Language: The social mirror* (2nd ed.). Rowley, MA: Newbury House.

Chamot, A. U., & O'Malley, J. M. (1987). The cognitive academic language learning approach: A bridge to the mainstream. *TESOL Quarterly, 21,* 227–249.

Chamot, A. U., & O'Malley, J. M. (1994). *The CALLA handbook: Implementing the cognitive academic language learning approach.* New York: Addison-Wesley.

Chavez, L. (1987, January 29). Struggling to keep Spanish in the U.S. pure. *The New York Times,* Section II, p. 1.

Chen, E. (1995). Implications of "Official English" Legislation. http://archive.aclu.org/congress/chen.html.

Cheng, L. L. (1987). *Assessing Asian language performance: Guidelines for evaluating limited-English-proficient students.* Rockville, MD: Aspen Publishers.

Chomsky, N. (1968). *Language and mind.* New York: Harcourt, Brace & World.

Civil Rights Act of 1964, 42 U.S.C. sec. 2000(d).

Cohen, A. D. (1980). *Testing language ability in the classroom.* Rowley, MA: Newbury House.

Cohen, E. G. (1986). *Designing groupwork: Strategies for the heterogeneous classroom.* New York: Teachers College Press.

Collier, V. P. (1987). The effect of age on acquisition of a second language for school. *New Focus, 1*(2).

Commission of the European Communities. (2003). *Promoting language learning and linguistic diversity: An action plan 2004–2006.* Brussels: Author.

Conklin, N., & Lourie, M. (1983). *A host of tongues: Language communities in the United States.* New York: The Free Press.

Consentino de Cohen, C., & Chu Clewell, B. (2007). *Putting English language learners on the map.* Washington, DC: Urban Institute.

Contín, M. (1995, February 1). U.S. Ninth Circuit Court reverses Arizona English-only. *NABE News,* p. 1.

Corballis, M. C. (2002). *From hand to mouth: The origins of language.* Princeton, NJ: Princeton University Press.

Corson, D. (1995). The learning and use of academic English words. *Language Learning, 47*, 671–718.

Cortés, C. E. (1986). The education of language minority students: A contextual interaction model. In California State Department of Education (Ed.), *Beyond language: Social and cultural factors in schooling language minority students* (pp. 3–33). Los Angeles: Evaluation, Dissemination and Assessment Center, California State University, Los Angeles.

Cortés, C. E. (1990, March/April). Multicultural education: A curricular basic for our multiethnic future. *Doubts and Certainties, 4*(78), 1–5.

Council of Chief State School Officers. (1990). *School success for limited English proficient students: The challenge and state response.* Washington, DC: Author.

Crawford, J. (1986, April 23). Immersion method is faring poorly in bilingual study. *Education Week*, pp. 1, 10.

Crawford, J. (1989). *Bilingual education: History, politics, theory, and practice.* Trenton, NJ: Crane.

Crawford, J. (1992a). *Hold your tongue: Bilingualism and the politics of "English only."* Reading, MA: Addison-Wesley.

Crawford, J. (1992b). *Language loyalties: A source book on the official English controversy.* Chicago: University of Chicago Press.

Crawford, J. (1997). *Best evidence: Research foundations of the Bilingual Education Act.* Washington, DC: NCBE.

Crawford, J. (2007, June 6). A diminished vision of civil rights: No Child Left Behind and the growing divide in how educational equity is understood. Retrieved January 6, 2008 from ourworld.compuserve.com/homepages/JWCrawford/home.htm.

CREDE. (2003). *Research brief #10: A national study of school effectiveness for language minority students' long-term academic achievement.* Berkeley, CA: Center for Research on Education, Diversity and Excellence.

Crystal, D. (1987). *The Cambridge encyclopedia of language.* Cambridge, UK: Cambridge University Press.

Crystal, D. (1997). *The Cambridge encyclopedia of language* (2nd ed.). Cambridge, UK: Cambridge University Press.

Crystal, D. (2000). *Language death.* Cambridge, UK: Cambridge University Press.

Crystal, D. (2001). *Language and the internet.* Cambridge, UK: Cambridge University Press.

Cummins, J. (1981). The role of primary language development in promoting educational success for language minority students. In California State Department of Education (Ed.), *Schooling and language minority students: A theoretical framework* (pp. 3–49). Los Angeles: Evaluation, Dissemination and Assessment Center, California State University, Los Angeles.

Cummins, J. (1984). Linguistic minorities and multicultural policy in Canada. In J. Edwards (Ed.), *Linguistic minorities, policies and pluralism* (pp. 81–105). London: Academic Press.

Cummins, J. (1989). *Empowering minority students.* Sacramento, CA: California Association of Bilingual Education.

Cummins, J. (1994). Primary language instruction and the education of language minority students. In California State Department of Education (Ed.), *Schooling and language minority students: A theoretical framework* (2nd ed.) (pp. 3–46). Los Angeles: Evaluation, Dissemination and Assessment Center, California State University, Los Angeles.

Cummins, J. (1996). *Negotiating identities: Education for empowerment in a diverse society.* Ontario, CA: California Association for Bilingual Education.

Cummins, J., & Swain, M. (1986). *Bilingualism in education.* White Plains, NY: Longman.

Curran, C. A. (1982). Community language learning. In R. W. Blair (Ed.), *Innovative approaches to language teach-*

ing (pp. 118–133). Rowley, MA: Newbury House.

Dalby, A. (2003). *Language in danger: The loss of linguistic diversity and the threat to our future.* New York: Columbia University Press.

Danoff, M. N., Coles, G. J., McLaughlin, D. H., & Reynolds, D. J. (1977a). *Evaluation of the impact of ESEA Title VII Spanish/English bilingual education programs, Volume I: Study design and interim findings.* Palo Alto, CA: American Institutes for Research.

Danoff, M. N., Coles, G. J., McLaughlin, D. H., & Reynolds, D. J. (1977b). *Evaluation of the impact of ESEA Title VII Spanish/English bilingual education programs, Volume II: Project descriptions.* Palo Alto, CA: American Institutes for Research.

Danoff, M. N., Coles, G. J., McLaughlin, D. H., & Reynolds, D. J. (1978). *Evaluation of the impact of ESEA Title VII Spanish/English bilingual education programs, Volume III: Year two impact data, educational process, and in-depth analysis.* Palo Alto, CA: American Institutes for Research.

Day, E. C. (1981). Assessing communicative competence: Integrative testing of second language learners. In J. U. Erickson & D. R. Omark (Eds.), *Communication assessment of the bilingual bicultural child: Issues and guidelines* (pp. 179–197). Baltimore, MD: University Park Press.

Day, E. C., McCollum, P. A., Cieslak, V. A., & Erickson, J. G. (1981). Discrete point language tests of bilinguals: A review of selected tests. In J. G. Erickson & D. R. Omark (Eds.), *Communication assessment of the bilingual bicultural child: Issues and guidelines* (pp. 129–161). Baltimore, MD: University Park Press.

DeAvila, E., Duncan, S., & Navarrete, C. (1987). *Finding Out/Descubrimiento.* Northvale, NJ: Santillana.

de la Luz Reyes, M. (2001). Unleashing possibilities: Biliteracy in the primary grades. In M. de la Luz Reyes & J. J. Halcón (Eds.), *The best for our children: Critical Perspectives on literacy for Latino students* (pp. 96–121). New York: Teachers College Press.

de la Luz Reyes, M., & Halcón, J. J. (Eds.). (2001). *The best for our children: Critical perspectives on literacy for Latino students.* New York: Teachers College Press.

Del Valle, S. (2003). *Language rights and the law in the United States: Finding our voices.* Clevedon, UK: Multilingual Matters.

de Villiers, P. A., & de Villiers, J. G. (1979). *Early language.* Cambridge, MA: Harvard University Press.

Diana v. State Board of Education, C-70-37 RFP, N. D. Cal, Jan. 7, 1970, and June 18, 1972.

Dicker, S. J. (1996). *Languages in America: A pluralist view.* Clevedon, UK: Multilingual Matters.

Diller, K. C. (1978). *The language teaching controversy.* Rowley, MA: Newbury House.

Dillon, S. (2003, March 19). Suddenly, a seller's market in Arabic studies. *The New York Times,* p. A24.

Doerner, W. R. (1987, September 14). Troubles of a tongue en crise. *Newsweek,* p. 49.

Dunbar, R. (1996). *Grooming, gossip, and the evolution of language.* Cambridge, MA: Harvard University Press.

Echevarria, J. & Graves, A. (2007). *Sheltered content instruction: Teaching English language learners with diverse abilities* (3rd ed.). Boston: Pearson.

Education Trust. (2003). *ESEA: Myths versus realities: Answers to common questions about the new No Child Left Behind Act.* Washington, DC: Author.

Education Week. Retrieved August 24, 2007, from www.edweek.org.

Edwards, J. (1998). *Language in Canada.* Cambridge, UK: Cambridge University Press.

Eggen, D. (2006, October 11). FBI agents still lacking Arabic skills. *Washington Post,* p. A01.

Elford, G., & Woodford, P. (1982). *A study of bilingual instructional practices in nonpublic schools: Final report.* Princeton, NJ: Educational Testing Service. (ERIC Document Reproduction Service No. ED 240 855).

Ellis, R. (1988). Theories of second language acquisition. In P. A. Richard-Amato (Ed.), *Making it happen: Interaction in the second language classroom, from theory to practice* (pp. 319–329). White Plains, NY: Longman.

English First. (2007). Retrieved July 19, 2007, from www.English-first.org.

Equal Educational Opportunities Act of 1974, 20 U.S.C. 1703(f).

Erickson, J. G., & Omark, D. R. (Eds.). (1981). *Communication assessment of the bilingual bicultural child: Issues and guidelines.* Baltimore, MD: University Park Press.

Ervin-Tripp, S. M. (1976). Language development. *Psychological Documents, 6,* 4. (Ms. No. 1336).

Escamilla, K. (1980). German-English bilingual schools 1870–1917: Cultural and linguistic survival in St. Louis. *Bilingual Journal, 5*(2), 16–20.

Escamilla, K. (1993). Promoting biliteracy: Issues in promoting English literacy in students acquiring English. In J. V. Tinajero & A. Flor Ada (Eds.), *The power of two languages* (pp. 220–233). New York: Macmillan/McGraw-Hill.

Ferguson, C. A. (1978). Language and global interdependence. In E. M. Gerli, J. E. Alatis, & R. I. Brod (Eds.), *Language in American life: Proceedings of the Georgetown University Modern Language Association Conference October 6–8, 1977, Washington, DC* (pp. 23–31). Washington, DC: Georgetown University Press.

Ferguson, C. A., & Heath, S. B. (Eds.). (1981). *Language in the USA.* New York: Cambridge University Press.

Feuerstein, R. (1978). The dynamic assessment of retarded performers: The learning potential assessment device, theory, instruments, and techniques. Baltimore, MD: University Park Press.

Fincher, B. H. (1978). Bilingualism in contemporary China: The coexistence of oral diversity and written uniformity.

In B. Spolsky & R. L. Cooper (Eds.), *Case studies in bilingual education* (pp. 72–87). Rowley, MA: Newbury House.

Fishman, J. A. (1981). Language policy: Past, present and future. In C. A. Ferguson & S. B. Heath (Eds.), *Language in the USA* (pp. 516–526). New York: Cambridge University Press.

Fishman, J. A. (1985). *Ethnicity in action: The community resources of ethnic languages in the United States.* Binghamton, NY: Bilingual Press/Editorial Bilingüe.

Fishman, J. A. (Ed.). (2001). *Can threatened languages be saved? Reversing language shift revisited: A 21st century perspective.* Clevedon, UK: Multilingual Matters.

Fishman, J. A., Gertner, M. H., Lowy, E. G., & Milan, W. G. (Eds.). (1985). *The rise and fall of the ethnic revival: Perspectives on language and ethnicity.* Berlin: Mouton de Gruyter.

Fishman, J. A., & Keller, G. D. (Eds.). (1982). *Bilingual education for Hispanic students in the United States.* New York: Teachers College Press.

Fleischman, H. L., & Staples-Said, M. (1994). *Descriptive study of services to limited English proficient students.* Arlington, VA: Development Associates.

Flor Ada, A. (1988). The Pajaro Valley experience: Working with Spanish-speaking parents to develop children's reading and writing skills through the use of children's literature. In T. Skutnabb-Kangas & J. Cummins (Eds.), *Minority Education: From Shame to Struggle.* Clevedon, UK: Multilingual Matters.

Foley, D. E. (1994). Reconsidering anthropological explanations of minority school failure. In F. Schultz (Ed.), *Multicultural Education 94/95.* Guilford, CT: Dushkin.

Fordham, S. (1991). Peer-proofing academic competition among black adolescents: "Acting White" black American style. In C. E. Sleeter (Ed.), *Empowerment through multicultural education* (pp. 69–93). Albany: State University of New York Press.

Foreman, G. (1938). *Sequoyah*. Norman, OK: University of Oklahoma Press.

Frederickson, J. (1995). *Reclaiming our voices: Bilingual education, critical pedagogy & praxis*. Los Angeles: California Association for Bilingual Education.

Freeman, D. E., & Freeman, Y. S. (2001). *Between worlds: Access to second language acquisition* (2nd ed.). Portsmouth, NH: Heinemann.

Freeman, D. E., & Freeman, Y. S. (2004). *Essential linguistics: What you need to know to teach reading, ESL, spelling, phonics, grammar*. Portsmouth, NH: Heinemann.

Freire, P. (1970). *Pedagogy of the oppressed*. New York: The Seabury Press.

Garcia, E., & Figueroa, R. A. (Fall, 1994). Issues in testing students from culturally and linguistically diverse backgrounds. *Multicultural Education, 2*(1), 10–19.

Gargan, E. A. (1997, December 24). Move to Cantonese in schools shakes up Hong Kong. *The Mercury News*, p. 11A.

Garnica, O. K. (1977). Some prosodic and paralinguistic features of speech to young children. In C. E. Snow & C. A. Ferguson (Eds.), *Talking to children* (pp. 63–88). New York: Cambridge University Press.

Gass, S. M., & Selinker, L. (1994). *Second language acquisition: An introductory course*. Hillsdale, NJ: Lawrence Erlbaum.

Genesee, F. (1987). *Learning through two languages: Studies of immersion and bilingual education*. Cambridge, MA: Newbury House.

Genesee, F. (Ed.). (1994). *Educating second language children: The whole child, the whole curriculum, the whole community*. Cambridge, UK: Cambridge University Press.

Genesee, F., & Hamayan, E. V. (1994). Classroom-based assessment. In F. Genesee (Ed.), *Educating second language children: The whole child, the whole curriculum, the whole community*. Cambridge, UK: Cambridge University Press.

Gingrich, N. (1995). *To Renew America*. New York: HarperPaperbacks.

Giroux, H. (1988, March). *Teacher empowerment and the struggle for public life*. Paper presented at San Jose State University, San Jose, CA.

Givón, T. (1985). Function, structure, and language acquisition. In D. I. Slobin (Ed.), *The crosslinguistic study of language acquisition: Vol. 2. Theoretical issues* (pp. 1005–1027). Hillsdale, NJ: Lawrence Erlbaum.

Gleason, J. B. (1973). Code switching in children's language. In T. E. Moore (Ed.), *Cognitive development and the acquisition of language* (pp. 159–167). New York: Academic Press.

Gleason, J. B. (1985). Studying language development. In J. B. Gleason (Ed.), *The development of language* (pp. 1–35). Columbus, OH: Merrill.

Gleason, P. (1984). Pluralism and assimilation: A conceptual history. In J. Edwards (Ed.), *Linguistic minorities, policies and pluralism* (pp. 221–257). London: Academic Press.

Glod, M. (2006, August 8). Schools Try Elementary Approach to Teaching Foreign Languages. *Washington Post*.

Goldhor Lerner, H. (September, 1993). Good advice. *New Woman*, p. 40.

Gomez v. Illinois State Board of Education, 811 F.2d 1030 (7th Cir. 1987).

Gonzalez, A., & Guerrero, M. (1983). *A cooperative/interdependent approach to bilingual education*. Hollister, CA: Hollister School District.

Gonzalez, G., & Maez, L. F. (1980). To switch or not to switch: The role of code-switching in the elementary bilingual classroom. In R. V. Padilla (Ed.), *Ethnoperspectives in bilingual education research: Theory in bilingual education* (pp. 125–135). Ypsilanti, MI: Eastern Michigan University.

Gonzalez, V., Brusca-Vega, R., & Yawkey, T. (1997). *Assessment and instruction of culturally and linguistically diverse students with or at-risk of learning problems: From research to practice*. Boston: Allyn & Bacon.

Goodenough, W. (1971). *Culture, language, and society.* Reading, MA: Addison-Wesley.

Gray, P. (Fall, 1993). Teach your children well [Special Issue]. *Time,* pp. 69–71.

Grittner, F. M. (1969). *Teaching foreign languages.* New York: Harper & Row.

Grosjean, F. (1982). *Life with two languages.* Cambridge, MA: Harvard University Press.

Growth of a nation. (1985, July 8). *Newsweek,* pp. 34–35.

Guido, M. (1995, March 16). Model escuela: Two-way language immersion program to be emulated by schools in other regions. *San Jose Mercury News,* pp. 1A, 22A.

Gumperz, J. J. (1981). Conversational inference and classroom learning. In J. L. Green & C. Wallat (Eds.), *Ethnography and language in educational settings* (pp. 3–23). Norwood, NJ: Ablex.

Hadaway, N. L., Vardell, S. M., & Young, T. A. (2002). *Literature-based instruction with English language learners.* Boston: Allyn and Bacon.

Hakuta, K. (1985, December). Bilingualism and its potential impact on the nation's schools. *CABE Newsletter,* pp. 1, 5, 13.

Hakuta, K. (1986). *Mirror of language: The debate on bilingualism.* New York: Basic Books.

Hakuta, K., & Gould, L. J. (1987). Synthesis of research on bilingual education. *Educational Leadership, 44*(6), 38–45.

Hall, E. T. (1959). *The silent language.* Garden City, NY: Doubleday.

Hall, E. T. (1966). *The hidden dimension.* Garden City, NY: Doubleday.

Hamayan, E., & Damico, J. (Eds.). (1991). *Limiting bias in the assessment of bilingual students.* Austin, TX: Pro-ed.

Hamayan, E. V., & Perlman, R. (1990, Spring). *Helping language minority students after they exit from bilingual/ESL programs: A handbook for teachers.* Rosslyn, VA: National Clearinghouse for Bilingual Education.

Harman, S. (1991). One more critique of testing—with two differences. In C. Edelsky (Ed.), *With literacy and justice for all: Rethinking the social in language and education.* London: The Falmer Press.

Haugen, E. (1987). *Blessings of Babel: Bilingualism and language planning.* Berlin: Mouton de Gruyter.

Hayes, C. W., Ornstein, J., & Gage, W. W. (1977). *ABC's of language and linguistics: A practical primer to language science in today's world.* Silver Spring, MD: Institute of Modern Languages.

Heath, S. B. (1983). Language policies. *Society, 20*(4), 57–63.

Here they come, ready or not. (1986, May 14). *Education Week,* pp. 14–39.

Hernandez-Chavez, E., Burt, M., & Dulay, H. (1978). Language dominance and proficiency testing: Some general considerations. *NABE Journal, 3*(1), 41–54.

Higgs, T. V. (1991). Research on the role of grammar and accuracy in classroom-based foreign language acquisition. In B. F. Freed (Ed.), *Foreign language acquisition research and the classroom* (pp. 46–53). Lexington, MA: D. C. Heath and Company.

Hudelson, S. (1994). Literacy development of second language children. In F. Genesee (Ed.), *Educating second language children: The whole child, the whole curriculum, the whole community* (pp. 129–158). Cambridge, UK: Cambridge University Press.

Idaho Migrant Council v. Board of Education, 647 F.2d 69 (9th Cir. 1981).

Igoa, C. (1995). *The inner world of the immigrant child.* New York: St. Martin's Press.

Immigration Project of the National Lawyers Guild. (1981). *Immigration law and defense* (2nd ed.). New York: Clark Boardman.

International School of the Peninsula. Mission and accreditations. Palo Alto, CA: International School of the Peninsula. Retrieved June 5, 2003, from www.istp.org.

Iowa State University. (2006, December 12). The national K–12 Foreign Language Resource Center receives $1.3 million grant. Press release. Retrieved September 4, 2007, from www.hs.iastate.edu/news/release/view.php?article=63.

Jacobson, R. (1987). *Allocating two languages as a key feature of a bilingual methodology.* Paper presented at the meeting of the National Association for Bilingual Education, Denver, CO.

Jensen, A. R. (1969). How much can we boost IQ and scholastic achievement? *Harvard Educational Review, 39,* 1–123.

Jernudd, B. H. (1999). Language education policy—Asia. In B. Spolsky (Ed.), *Concise encyclopedia of educational linguistics* (pp. 116–122). Oxford, UK: Elsevier Science.

Jespersen, O. (1922). *Language: Its nature, development and origin.* London: George Allen & Unwin.

Kagan, S. (1986). Cooperative learning and sociocultural factors in schooling. In California State Department of Education (Ed.), *Beyond language: Social and cultural factors in schooling language minority students* (pp. 231–298). Los Angeles: Evaluation, Dissemination and Assessment Center, California State University, Los Angeles.

Kamin, L. J. (1995, February). Behind the curve. *Scientific American,* pp. 99–103.

Karst, K. L. (1986). Paths to belonging: The Constitution and cultural identity. *North Carolina Law Review, 64,* 303–377.

Kaufman, D. (2003, April). Letters for the people. *Language Magazine, 7,* 24–26.

Keller, G. D., & Van Hooft, K. S. (1982). A chronology of bilingualism and bilingual education in the United States. In J. A. Fishman & G. D. Keller (Eds.), *Bilingual education for Hispanic students in the United States* (pp. 3–19). New York: Teachers College Press.

Kelley, T. (1998, April 30). It is for you defective day of hats, no? *The New York Times,* pp. D1, D7.

Kester, E. S., & Pena, E. D. (2002). Limitations of current language testing practices for bilinguals. (ERIC Document Reproduction Service No. ED 470 203).

Keyes v. School District No. 1, Denver, 380 F. Supp. 673 (D. Colo. 1974).

Khubchandani, L. M. (1978). Multilingual education in India. In B. Spolsky & R. L. Cooper (Eds.), *Case studies in bilingual education* (pp. 88–125). Rowley, MA: Newbury House.

Kilpatrick, J. F. (1965). *Sequoyah of earth & intellect.* Austin, TX: The Encino Press.

Kim, K. H. S., Relkin, N. R., Lee, K., & Hirsch, J. (1997). Distinct cortical areas associated with native and second languages. *Nature, 388,* 171–174.

Kindler, A. L. (2002, October). *Survey of the states' limited English proficient students and available educational programs and services: 2000–2001 summary report.* Washington, DC: NCELA.

Kinzer, S. (1998, January 26). Nehru spoke it, but it's still 'foreign.' *The New York Times,* p. A4.

Kirkland, R. I., Jr. (1988, March 14). Entering a new age of boundless competition. *Fortune,* pp. 40–42, 46, 48.

Kjolseth, R. (1976). Bilingual education programs in the United States: For assimilation or pluralism? In F. Cordasco (Ed.), *Bilingual schooling in the United States: A sourcebook for educational personnel* (pp. 122–140). New York: McGraw-Hill.

Kjolseth, R. (1983). Cultural politics and bilingualism. *Society, 20*(4), 40–48.

Kloss, H. (1977). *The American bilingual tradition.* Rowley, MA: Newbury House.

Kondracke, M. (1979, March 31). The ugly American redux. *The New Republic,* pp. 55–62.

Kotlowitz, A. (2007, August 5). Our Town. *New York Times,* Section 6, pp. 30–37, 52, 57.

Krashen, S. D. (1981). Bilingual education and second language acquisition theory. In California State Department of Education (Ed.), *Schooling and language minority students: A theoretical framework* (pp. 51–79). Los Angeles: Evaluation, Dissemination and Assessment Center, California State University, Los Angeles.

Krashen, S. D. (1996). *Under attack: The case against bilingual education.* Culver City, CA: Language Education Associates.

Krashen, S. D. (December 1997/January 1998). Bridging inequity with books. *Educational Leadership, 55*(4), 18–22.

Krashen, S. D. (2003). *Explorations in language acquisition and use: The Taipei lectures*. Portsmouth, NH: Heinemann.

Krashen, S. D., & Biber, D. (1988). *On course: Bilingual education's success in California*. Sacramento, CA: California Association for Bilingual Education.

Krashen, S. D., & Terrell, T. D. (1983). *The natural approach: Language acquisition in the classroom*. San Francisco: Alemany.

Krauss, C. (2003, April 13). Quebec seeking to end its old cultural divide: Getting along in English and en Francais. *The New York Times*, p. A6.

Krauss, M. (1992). The world's languages in crisis. *Language, 68,* 6–10.

Labov, W. (1970). *The study of nonstandard English*. Champaign, IL: National Council of the Teachers of English.

Labov, W. (1995). The logic of nonstandard English. In D. Benett Durkin (Ed.), *Language issues: Readings for teachers.* New York: Longman. [Reprinted from *Report of the twentieth annual round table meeting on linguistics and language studies,* Monograph Series on Language and Linguistics, Alatis, J. P. (Ed.), 1979].

Lambert, W. E., & Taylor, D. M. (1987). Language minorities in the United States: Conflicts around assimilation and proposed modes of accommodation. In W. A. Van Horne & T. V. Tonnesen (Eds.), *Ethnicity and language* (pp. 58–89). Milwaukee: The University of Wisconsin System Institute on Race and Ethnicity.

Langer, J. A. (1991). Literacy and schooling: A sociocognitive perspective. In E. H. Hiebert (Ed.), *Literacy for a diverse society: Perspectives, practices, and policies* (pp. 9–27). New York: Teachers College Press.

Larsen-Freeman, D., & Long, M. H. (1991). *An introduction to second language research*. White Plains, NY: Longman.

Lau v. Nichols, 414 U.S. 563 (1974).

Legarreta-Marcaida, D. (1981). Effective use of the primary language in the classroom. In California State Department of Education (Ed.), *Schooling and language minority students: A theoretical framework* (pp. 83–116). Los Angeles: Evaluation, Dissemination and Assessment Center, California State University, Los Angeles.

Lemberger, N. (1997). *Bilingual education: Teachers' narratives*. Mahwah, NJ: Lawrence Erlbaum Associates.

Lenneberg, E. (1967). *Biological foundations of language*. New York: John Wiley & Sons.

Lessow-Hurley, J. (1977). *Como ellos lo ven: Migrant children look at life in Longmont*. Boulder, CO: Western Interstate Commission on Higher Education.

Levine, R. (1997). *A geography of time: The temporal misadventures of a social psychologist, or how every culture keeps time just a little bit differently*. New York: Basic Books.

Lewis, E. G. (1976). Bilingualism and bilingual education: The ancient world to the Renaissance. In J. A. Fishman (Ed.), *Bilingual education: An international sociological perspective* (pp. 150–200). Rowley, MA: Newbury House.

Lewis, M. (1972). Parents and children: Sex-role development. *School Review, 80,* 229–240.

Lieberman, P. (1998). *Eve Spoke.* New York: W. W. Norton.

Liebowitz, A. H. (1971). *Educational policy and political acceptance: The imposition of English as the language of instruction in American schools*. Washington, DC: Center for Applied Linguistics. (ERIC Document Reproduction Service No. ED 047 321).

Liebowitz, A. H. (1978). Language policy in the United States. In H. LaFontaine, B. Persky, & L. H. Golubehick (Eds.), *Bilingual Education* (pp. 3–15). Wayne, NJ: Avery.

Lightbown, P., & Spada N. (1993). *How languages are learned.* Oxford, UK: Oxford University Press.

Lindholm, K. J. (1994). Promoting positive cross-cultural attitudes and perceived competence in culturally and linguistically diverse classrooms. In R. A. DeVillar, C. J. Flatis, & J. P. Cummins (Eds.), *Cultural diversity in schools: From rhetoric to practice* (pp. 189–206). Albany: State University of New York Press.

Lindholm, K. J., & Molina, R. (1998). Learning in dual language education classrooms in the U.S.: Implementation and evaluation outcomes. *Proceedings of the III European Conference on Immersion Programmes.*

Lippi-Green, R. (1997). *English with an accent.* London and New York: Routledge.

Long, M. H., & Porter, P. A. (1985). Group work, interlanguage talk, and second language acquisition. *TESOL Quarterly, 18,* 207–227.

Losen, D. J., & Orfield, G. (Eds.). (2002). *Racial inequity in special education.* Cambridge, MA: Harvard University Press.

Lozanov, G. (1982). Suggestology and Suggestopedia. In R. W. Blair (Ed.), *Innovative approaches to language teaching* (pp. 146–159). Rowley, MA: Newbury House.

Macaulay, R. (1980). *Generally speaking: How children learn language.* Rowley, MA: Newbury House.

Macías, R. F., & Kelly, C. (1996). *Summary report of the survey of the states' limited English proficient students and available educational programs and services 1994–1995.* Washington, DC: National Clearinghouse for Bilingual Education.

Mackey, W. F. (1972). *Bilingual education in a binational school.* Rowley, MA: Newbury House.

Mackey, W. F. (1978). The importation of bilingual education models. In J. E. Alatis (Ed.), *Georgetown University round table on languages and linguistics 1978* (pp. 1–18). Washington, DC: Georgetown University Press.

Marin, C., & Macgregor-Scott, P. (Producers). (1987). *Born in East L. A.* [Film]. Universal City, CA: Universal Pictures.

Mayer, J. (May/June 2002). The promise of ESEA, Title III. *Multilingual News, 25*(6), 1, 6–7, 9.

McCarty, T. L., & Zepeda, O. (1995, Winter). Indigenous Language Education and Literacy. *Bilingual Research Journal, 19*(1).

McCollum, P. A., & Day, E. C. (1981). Quasi-integrative approaches: Discrete point scoring of expressive language samples. In J. G. Erickson & D. R. Omark (Eds.), *Communication assessment of the bilingual bicultural child: Issues and guidelines* (pp. 163–177). Baltimore, MD: University Park Press.

McCrum, R., Cran, W., & MacNeil, R. (1986). *The story of English.* New York: Elizabeth Sifton Books (Viking).

McDermott, R. P. (1997). Achieving school failure (1972–1997). In G. D. Spindler (Ed.), *Education and cultural process: Anthropological approaches* (3rd ed., pp. 110–135). Prospect Heights, IL: Waveland Press.

McDermott, R. P., & Gospodinoff, K. (1981). Social contexts for ethnic borders and school failure. In H. T. Trueba, G. P. Guthrie, & K. H. Au (Eds.), *Culture and the bilingual classroom: Studies in classroom ethnography* (pp. 212–230). Rowley, MA: Newbury House.

McFadden, B. J. (1983). Bilingual education and the law. *Journal of Law and Education, 12,* 1-27.

McMurrer, J. (2007). *Choices, changes, and challenges: Curriculum and instruction in the NCLB era.* Washington, DC: Center on Education Policy.

McWhorter, J. (2001). *The power of Babel: A natural history of language.* New York: W. H. Freeman.

Menendez, R., Musca, T., & Olmos, E. J. (Producers). (1988). *Stand and deliver* [Film]. Burbank, CA: Warner Bros.

Menken, K. (2008). *English learners left behind: Standardized testing as language policy.* Clevedon, UK: Multilingual Matters.

Mercer, J., & Lewis, J. F. (1979). *System of multicultural pluralistic assessment.* New York: The Psychological Corporation.

Met, M. (1994). Teaching content through a second language. In F. Genesee (Ed.), *Educating second language children: The whole child, the whole curriculum, the whole community.* Cambridge, UK: Cambridge University Press.

Meyer v. Nebraska, 262 U.S. 390 (1923).

Miller, H., & Miller, K. (1996). Language policy and identity: The case of Catalonia. *International Studies in Sociology of Education, 6,* 113–128.

Miller, J. (1983). *Many voices: Bilingualism, culture and education.* London: Routledge & Kegan Paul.

Miller, T. (2007). *How I learned English.* Washington, DC: National Geographic.

Mohatt, G. V., & Erickson, F. (1981). Cultural differences in teaching styles in an Odawa school: A sociolinguistic approach. In H. T. Trueba, G. P. Guthrie, & K. H. Au (Eds.), *Culture and the bilingual classroom: Studies in classroom ethnography* (pp. 105–119). Rowley, MA: Newbury House.

Morris, D. (1977). *Manwatching: A field guide to human behavior.* New York: Harry N. Abrams.

Murray, C., & Herrnstein, R. (1994). *The bell curve: The reshaping of American life by differences in intelligence.* New York: The Free Press.

National Clearinghouse for English Language Acquisition. (2007). NCELA FAQ: Which states offer certification or endorsement in Bilingual Education or ESL? Retrieved January 5, 2008, from www.ncela.gwu.edu/expert/faq/09certif.htm.

National Defense Education Act. (1958). 20 U.S.C. sec. 401 et seq., P.L. 85-864, 72 Stat. 1580.

National Public Radio. (March 7, 1995). *Morning Edition.* Washington, DC.

NCELA. (2003). Poster. The growing numbers of LEP students 2001–2002. Retrieved 2003 from www.ncela.gwu.edu/states/stateposter.pdf.

New York Times Magazine (1997, July 20), advertisement on p. 31.

Nieto, S. (1992). *Affirming diversity: The sociopolitical context of multicultural education.* White Plains, NY: Longman.

Nunberg, G. (2001). *The way we talk now: Commentaries on language and culture.* Boston: Houghton Mifflin.

Office of Bilingual Bicultural Education, California State Department of Education. (1984). *Studies on immersion education: A collection for United States educators.* Sacramento: California State Department of Education.

Ogbu, J. U. (1978). *Minority education and caste: The American system in cross-cultural perspective.* New York: Academic Press.

Ogbu, J. U. (1992). Understanding cultural diversity and learning. *Educational Researcher, 21*(8), 5–14.

Ogbu, J. U. (1994). Racial stratification and education in the United States: Why inequality persists. *Teachers College Record, 96,* 264–298.

Ogbu, J. U., & Matute-Bianchi, M. E. (1986). Understanding sociocultural factors: Knowledge, identity, and school adjustment. In California State Department of Education (Ed.), *Beyond language: Social and cultural factors in schooling language minority students* (pp. 73–142). Los Angeles: Evaluation, Dissemination and Assessment Center, California State University, Los Angeles.

Okazaki, S. (Director). (1987). *Living on Tokyo time* [Film]. Los Angeles: Skouras Pictures.

Olsen, L. (1997). *Made in America: Immigrant students in our public schools.* New York: The New Press.

Olsen, L. et al. (1994). *The unfinished journey: Restructuring schools in a diverse society.* San Francisco: California Tomorrow.

O'Malley, J. M., & Valdez Pierce, L. (1991, November). Portfolio assessment: Using portfolio and alternative assessment with LEP students. *Forum, 15*(1), pp. 1–2.

O'Malley, J. M., & Valdez Pierce, L. (1992, Spring). *Performance and portfolio assessment for language minority students.* Washington, DC: National Clearinghouse for Bilingual Education.

O'Riagain, P. (1997). *Language policy and social reproduction: Ireland 1893–1993.* New York: Oxford University Press.

O'Riagain, P. (2001). Irish language production and reproduction 1981–1996.

In J. Fishman (Ed.), *Can threatened languages be saved? Reversing language shift, revisited: A 21st century perspective* (pp. 195–214). Clevedon, UK: Multilingual Matters.

Ovando, C. J., & Collier, V. P. (1985). *Bilingual and ESL classrooms.* New York: McGraw-Hill.

Owens, R. E. (1984). *Language development: An introduction.* Columbus, OH: Merrill.

Patinkin, M. (1998). *Mamaloshen* [CD]. New York: Nonesuch. 1998.

Perea, J. F. (Ed.). (1997). *Immigrants out! The new nativism and the anti-immigrant impulse in the United States.* New York: New York University Press.

Peregoy, S. F., & Boyle, O. F. (2005). *Reading, writing, & learning in ESL: A resource book for K–8 teachers* (4th ed.). White Plains, NY: Longman.

Pérez, B. (Ed.). (1998). *Sociocultural contexts of language and literacy.* Mahwah, NJ: Lawrence Erlbaum.

Pérez, B., & Torres-Guzmán, M. (1992). *Learning in two worlds: An integrated Spanish/English biliteracy approach.* White Plains, NY: Longman.

Perssons, L. (1993). *Parent handbook: Kokopelli's flute.* (Unpublished classroom materials).

Peske, H. G., & Haycock, K. (2006). *Teaching inequality: How poor and minority students are shortchanged on teacher quality.* Washington, DC: Education Trust.

Peters, A. M. (1985). Language segmentation: Operating principles for the perception and analysis of language. In D. I. Slobin (Ed.), *The crosslinguistic study of language acquisition: Vol. 2. Theoretical issues* (pp. 1029–1067). Hillsdale, NJ: Lawrence Erlbaum.

Pfeiffer, J. (1988, January). How not to lose the trade wars by cultural gaffes. *Smithsonian,* pp. 145–146, 148, 150–152, 154–155.

Philips, S. U. (1983). *The invisible culture: Communication in classroom and community on the Warm Springs Indian Reservation.* White Plains, NY: Longman.

Piatt, B. (1986). Toward domestic recognition of a human right to language. *Houston Law Review, 23,* 885–906.

Piatt, B. (1990). *¿Only English? Law and language policy in the United States.* Albuquerque: University of New Mexico Press.

Pinker, S. (1994). *The language instinct.* New York: William Morrow.

Plessy v. Ferguson, 163 U.S. 537 (1896).

Portes, A., and Rumbaut, R. G. (2006). *Immigrant America: A portrait* (3rd ed.). Berkeley: University of California Press.

Postman, N. (1995). *The end of education: Redefining the value of school.* New York: Alfred A. Knopf.

Pringle, I. (1999). Canadian Language Policy. In B. Spolsky (Ed.), *Concise encyclopedia of educational linguistics* (pp. 81–83). Oxford, UK: Elsevier Science.

Pufahl, I., Rhodes, N. C., & Christian, D. (2000). *Foreign language teaching: What the United States can learn from other countries.* Washington, DC: Center for Applied Linguistics.

Quebec seeking to end its old cultural divide. (2003, April 13). *The New York Times,* p. A6.

Ramírez, A. G. (1995). *Creating contexts for second language acquisition: Theory and methods.* White Plains, NY: Longman.

Ramírez, D., Yuen, S. D., & Ramey, D. R. (1991). *Final report: Longitudinal study of English immersion strategy, early-exit and late-exit transitional bilingual education programs for language-minority children.* (Department of Education Contract No. 300-87-0156.) San Mateo, CA: Aguirre International.

Ramírez, M., & Castañeda, A. (1974). *Cultural democracy, bicognitive development, and education.* New York: Academic Press.

Reacting to *The Bell Curve.* (1995, January 11). *Education Week,* pp. 29–32.

Rheingold, J. (1988). *They have a word for it.* Los Angeles: Jeremy P. Tarcher.

Richard-Amato, P. A. (1988). *Making it happen: Interaction in the second language classroom from theory to practice* (2nd ed.). White Plains, NY: Longman.

Richard-Amato, P. A., & Snow, M. A. (1995). *The multicultural classroom: Readings for content-area teachers* (2nd ed.). White Plains, NY: Longman.

Riches, C., & Genesee, F. (2006). Literacy: Crosslinguistic and crossmodal issues. In F. Genesee, K. Lindholm-Leary, W. M. Saunders, & D. Christian (Eds.), *Educating English language learners: A synthesis of research evidence* (pp. 64–108). Cambridge, UK: Cambridge University Press.

Riggs, P. (1991). Whole language in TESOL. *TESOL Quarterly, 25,* 521–542.

Rodriguez, R. (1982). *Hunger of memory: The education of Richard Rodriguez.* Boston: David R. Godine.

Rossell, C., & Baker, K. (1996). The educational effectiveness of bilingual education. *Research in the Teaching of English, 30,* 7–74.

Roth Pierpont, C. (1997, February 17). A society of one. *The New Yorker,* 80–86.

Rubin, J. (1972). Bilingual usage in Paraguay. In J. A. Fishman (Ed.), *Readings in the sociology of language* (pp. 512–530). The Hague, Neth.: Mouton.

Sachs, J. (1985). Prelinguistic development. In J. B. Gleason (Ed.), *The development of language* (pp. 37–60). Columbus, OH: Merrill.

Saravia-Shore, M., & Arvizu, S. F. (1992). *Cross-cultural literacy: Ethnographies of communication in multiethnic classrooms.* New York: Garland.

Saville-Troike, M. (1976). Bilingual children: A resource document. In F. Cordasco (Ed.), *Bilingual schooling in the United States: A sourcebook for educational personnel* (pp. 165–188). New York: McGraw-Hill.

Saville-Troike, M. (1982). *The ethnography of communication: An introduction.* Oxford, UK: Basil Blackwell.

Schieffelin, B. B. (1985). The acquisition of Kaluli. In D. I. Slobin (Ed.), *The crosslinguistic study of language acquisition: Vol. 1. The data* (pp. 525–593). Hillsdale, NJ: Lawrence Erlbaum.

Schmemann, S. (1996, January 31). A word handed down, but not set in stone. *The New York Times,* pp. A1, A4.

Schmidley, A. D., & Robinson, J. G. (October 2003). Measuring the foreign-born population in the United States with the current population survey: 1994–2002. *Population Division Working Paper No. 73.* Washington, DC: Population Division, U.S. Bureau of the Census.

Sedaris, D. (1997, May). The ashtray is on the table today . . . and other misadventures of a would-be French speaker. *Travel & Leisure,* 70–73.

Seliger, H. (1977). Does practice make perfect? A study of interaction patterns and L2 competence. *Language Learning, 27*(2), 263–278.

Serna v. Portales Municipal Schools, 499 F.2d 1147 (10th Cir. 1974).

Short, D. J. (Spring, 2002). Language learning in sheltered social studies classes. *TESOL Journal, 11*(1), 18–24.

Siguan, M. (1991). The Catalan language in the educational system of Catalonia. *International Review of Education, 37,* 87–98.

Simon, P. (1980). *The tongue-tied American.* New York: Continuum.

Skutnabb-Kangas, T. (1981). *Bilingualism or not: The education of minorities.* Clevedon, UK: Multilingual Matters.

Skutnabb-Kangas, T. (1998, March). *Linguistic education: A national perspective.* Paper presented at the San Jose Unified School District, San Jose, CA.

Skutnabb-Kangas, T., & Phillipson, R. (Eds.). (1994). *Linguistic human rights: Overcoming linguistic discrimination.* Berlin: Mouton de Gruyter.

Snow, C. (1977). The development of conversation between mothers and babies. *Journal of Child Language, 4,* 1–22.

Snow, M. A., Met, M., & Genesee, F. (1989). A conceptual framework for the integration of language and content in second/foreign language instruction. *TESOL Quarterly, 23*(2), 201–217.

Solano-Flores, G. , & Trumbull, E. (2003). Examining language in context: The need for new research and practice in the testing of English-language learners. *Educational Researcher 32*(2), 1–13.

Speech therapist who gives and takes accents. (1993, August 11). *The New York Times,* p. A10.

Spolsky, B. (1986). *Language and education in multilingual settings.* San Diego, CA: College-Hill Press.

Spolsky, B. (1995). *Measured words: The development of objective language testing.* Oxford, UK: Oxford University Press.

Spolksy, B. (2004). *Language policy.* Cambridge, UK: Cambridge University Press.

Spradley, J. P. (Ed.). (1972). *Culture and cognition: Rules, maps, and plans.* San Francisco: Chandler.

Sridhar, K. K. (1993). Meaning, means, and maintenance. In J. E. Alatis (Ed.), *Georgetown University round table on languages and linguistics 1992: Language, communication, and social meaning* (pp. 56–65). Washington, DC: Georgetown University Press.

Stockwell, P. (2002). *Sociolinguistics: A resource book for students.* London: Routledge.

Strength through wisdom: A critique of U.S. capability. (1980). *Modern Language Journal, 64,* 9–57.

Study reveals teachers' superstitious beliefs. (1988, September 11). *San Jose Mercury News,* p. 20A.

Suárez-Orozco, M. M. (2005). Everything you ever wanted to know about assimilation but were afraid to ask. In M. M. Suárez-Orozco, C. Suárez-Orozco, & D. Baolian Qin (Eds.), *The new immigration: An interdisciplinary reader* (pp. 67–83). New York: Routledge.

Suarez-Orozco, M. M., & Suarez-Orozco, C. E. (1993). Hispanic cultural psychology: Implications for teacher education and research. In P. Phelan & A. Locke Davidson (Eds.), *Renegotiating cultural diversity in American schools.* New York: Teachers College Press.

Sue, S., & Padilla, A. (1986). Ethnic minority issues in the United States: Challenges for the educational system. In California State Department of Education (Ed.), *Beyond language: Social and cultural factors in schooling language minority students* (pp. 36–72). Los Angeles: Evaluation, Dissemination and Assessment Center, California State University, Los Angeles.

Swain, M. (1985). Communicative competence: Some roles of comprehensible input and comprehensible output in its development. In S. Gass & C. Madden (Eds.), *Input in second language acquisition* (pp. 235–253). Rowley, MA: Newbury House.

Swain, M. (1991). French immersion and its offshoots: Getting two for one. In B. F. Freed (Ed.), *Foreign language acquisition research and the classroom* (pp. 91–103). Lexington, MA: D. C. Heath and Company.

Tannen, D. (1990). *You just don't understand: Women and men in conversation.* New York: Morrow.

Temple-Raston, D. (2007, July 30). FBI recruiting class shows language diversity. San Francisco: KQED.

Terrell, T. D. (1981). The natural approach in bilingual education. In California State Department of Education (Ed.), *Schooling and language minority students: A theoretical framework* (pp. 117–146). Los Angeles: Evaluation, Dissemination and Assessment Center, California State University, Los Angeles.

Thiong'o, N. (2004). Recovering the original. In W. Lesser (Ed.), *The genius of language* (pp. 102–110). New York: Pantheon.

Thomas, R. M., Jr. (1998, February 1). Carl Gorman, code talker in World War II, dies at 90. *The New York Times,* p. A31.

Thomas, W., & Collier, V. (1997). Two languages are better than one. *Educational Leadership, 55*(4), 23–26.

Thonis, E. (1983). *The English-Spanish connection.* Northvale, NJ: Santillana.

Todd, L. (2001). Pidgins and creoles: An overview. In R. Mesthrie (Ed.), *Concise encyclopedia of sociolinguistics,* (pp. 534–530). Oxford, UK: Elsevier Science.

Tollefson, J. W. (2002). *Language policies in education.* Mahwah, NJ: Lawrence Erlbaum.

Tomlinson, E. H., & Eastwick, J. F. (1980). Allons enfants. *Independent School, 40*(1), 23–31.

Trasvina, J. (1981, August 7). Bilingual elections safeguard rights of linguistic minorities. *The Denver Post.*

Trueba, H. T., Guthrie, G. P., & Au, K. H. (Eds.). (1981). *Culture and the bilingual classroom: Studies in classroom ethnography.* Rowley, MA: Newbury House.

Tse, L. (2001). *Why don't they learn English? Separating fact from fallacy in the U.S. language debate.* New York: Teachers College Press.

Tyack, D. B. (1974). *The one best system: A history of American urban education.* Cambridge, MA: Harvard University Press.

U.S. Bureau of the Census (1997). Statistical Abstract of the United States: 1997 (117th ed.) Washington, DC: U.S. Bureau of the Census.

U.S. Department of Education, Office of the Secretary. (1992). *The condition of bilingual education in the nation: A report to congress and the president, June 30, 1992.* Washington, DC: Government Printing Office.

U.S. Department of Education, Office of Educational Research and Improvement. (1997). *Digest of Education Statistics.* Washington, DC: U.S. Government Printing Office.

U.S. Department of Justice, Civil Rights Division. (2004, September 21). Executive order 13166, Limited English proficient resource document: Tips and tools from the field. Washington, DC: Author.

U.S. Department of State. (2006, January 5). *National Security Language Initiative fact sheet.* Retrieved January 5, 2008, from www.state.gov/r/pa/prs/ps/2006/58733.htm.

U.S. English. (2007). Retrieved July 19, 2007, from www.us-english.org/inc/about.

U.S. General Accounting Office. (1987a). *Bilingual education: A new look at the research evidence* (GAO/PEMD-87-12BR). Washington, DC: Government Printing Office.

U.S. General Accounting Office. (1987b). *Bilingual education: Information on limited English proficient students* (GAO/HRD-87-85BR). Washington, DC: Government Printing Office.

U.S. General Accounting Office. (January, 2002). *Foreign languages: Human capital approach needed to correct staffing and proficiency shortfalls.* (GAO-02-375). Washington, DC: Author.

Valdés, G. (2001). *Learning and not learning English.* New York: Teachers College Press.

Valdés, G., & Figueroa, R. A. (1994). *Bilingualism and testing: A special case of bias.* Norwood, NJ: Ablex Publishing.

Valdes, J. M. (Ed.). (1986). *Culture bound: Bridging the cultural gap in language teaching.* New York: Cambridge University Press.

Van Horne, W. A., & Tonnesen, T. V. (Eds.). (1987). *Ethnicity and language.* Milwaukee: The University of Wisconsin System Institute on Race and Ethnicity.

Ventriglia, L. (1982). *Conversations with Miguel and Maria: How children learn English as a second language: Implications for classroom teaching.* Reading, MA: Addison-Wesley.

Viadero, D. (1997, July 9). Two different worlds, *Education Week,* pp. 31–35.

Villarreal, A. (1999). Rethinking the education of English language learners: Transitional bilingual education programs. *Bilingual Research Journal 23*(1). Washington DC: National Association for Bilingual Education.

Voting Rights Act of 1965, as amended, 42 U.S.C. sec. 1973 et seq.

Wang, P. C. (1986). A bilingual education lesson from China. *Thrust, 16*(1), 38–39.

Wardhaugh, R. (1993). *Investigating language: Central problems in linguistics.* Oxford, UK: Blackwell.

Warren-Leubecker, A., & Bohannon J. N. III. (1985). Language in society: Variation and adaptation. In J. B. Gleason (Ed.), *The development of language* (pp. 331–367). Columbus, OH: Merrill.

Wasserman, J. (1973). Immigration law and practice. Philadelphia: American Law Institute.

Weinberg, M. (1977). *A chance to learn: A history of race and education in the United States.* New York: Cambridge University Press.

Weiner, R., and Pristoop, E. (2006). *How states shortchange the districts that need the most help.* Washington, DC: Education Trust.

Welles, E. (2004). Foreign language enrollments in United States institutions of higher education, Fall 2002, *ADFL Bulletin 35*(2–3): 7–26.

Wells, S. (1986, July 28). Bilingualism: The accent is on youth. *U.S. News & World Report,* p. 60.

Wesman, A. G. (1969). Intelligent testing. *American Psychologist, 23,* 267–274.

When a snow day is more than just play. (2003, April 17). *The New York Times.* p. A14.

Wilbur, R. (1980). The linguistic description of American sign language. In H. Lane & F. Grosjean (Eds.), *Recent perspectives on American sign language* (pp. 7–31). Hillsdale, NJ: Lawrence Erlbaum Associates.

Williams, J. D., & Capizzi Snipper, G. (1990). *Literacy and bilingualism.* White Plains, NY: Longman.

Williams, S. W. (1991). Classroom use of African American language: Educational tool or social weapon? In C. E. Sleeter (Ed.), *Empowerment through multicultural education* (pp. 199–215). Albany: State University of New York Press.

Willig, A. C. (1985). A meta-analysis of selected studies on the effectiveness of bilingual education. *Review of Educational Research, 55,* 269–317.

Wineburg, S. S. (1987). When good intentions aren't enough. *Phi Delta Kappan, 68,* 544–545.

Wolcott, H. F. (1997). The teacher as an enemy. In G. D. Spindler (Ed.), *Education and cultural process: Anthropological approaches* (3rd ed.) (pp. 77–92). Prospect Heights, IL: Waveland Press.

Wolfram, W., & Ward, B. (Eds.). (2006). *American voices: How dialects differ from coast to coast.* Oxford, UK: Blackwell.

Wolfson, N., & Manes, J. (Eds.). (1985). *Language of inequality.* Berlin: Mouton de Gruyter.

Wong Fillmore, L. (1979). Individual differences in second language acquisition. In C. J. Fillmore, D. Kempler, & Wang, S. Y. William (Eds.), *Individual differences in language ability and language behavior.* New York: Academic Press.

Wong Fillmore, L. (1985). Second language learning in children: A proposed model. In National Clearinghouse for Bilingual Education (Ed.), *Issues in English language development* (pp. 33–42). Rosslyn, VA: National Clearinghouse for Bilingual Education.

Wong Fillmore, L. (1991). Second-language learning in children: A model of language learning in social context. In E. Bialystok (Ed.), *Language processing in bilingual children* (pp. 49–69). Cambridge, UK: Cambridge University Press.

Woolard, K. A. (1985). Catalonia: The dilemma of language rights. In N. Wolfson & J. Manes (Eds.), *Language of inequality* (pp. 91–107). Berlin: Mouton de Gruyter.

Wurm, S. A. (Ed.). (1996). *Atlas of the world's languages in danger of disappearing.* Paris/Canberra: UNESCO Publishing/Pacific Linguistics.

Zehr, M. A. (2007, August 1). Students get taste of "national security languages." *Education Week,* pp. 5, 12.

Index